Poems: Song and *The*

Brigit Pegeen Kelly teaches in the creative writing program at the University of Illinois in Urbana-Champaign. Her first volume of poetry, *To the Place of Trumpets*, was awarded the Yale Series of Younger Poets Prize in 1987 and published by Yale University Press the following year. Her second book, *Song*, published by BOA Editions, Ltd., was the 1994 Lamont Poetry Selection from the Academy of American Poets. Her third book, *The Orchard*, published by BOA Editions, Ltd. in 2004, was a finalist for the Pulitzer Prize, the National Book Critics Circle Award and the *Los Angeles Times* Book Award. Her work has appeared widely in journals and anthologies and she has been awarded many prizes and fellowships, including a Whiting Award, two fellowships from the National Endowment for the Arts, The Witter Bynner Prize from the Academy of Arts and Letters, and grants from the Illinois Arts Council and the New Jersey State Council on the Arts.

Brigit Pegeen Kelly

Poems

Song and *The Orchard*

CARCANET

First published in Great Britain in 2008 by
Carcanet Press Limited
Alliance House
Cross Street
Manchester M2 7AQ

Song first published in the United States in 1995 by BOA Editions, Ltd., 250
North Goodman Street, Suite 306, Rochester, New York 14607; *The Orchard* first
published in the United States in 2004 by BOA Editions, Ltd.

A CIP catalogue record for this book is available from the British Library

ISBN 978 1 85754 979 9

The publisher acknowledges financial assistance from Arts Council England

Printed and bound in England by SRP Ltd, Exeter

Contents

Song

I

II

The Orchard

II

III

IV

Song

for Huck, Maria, and Macklin
and for Michael

Song by Brigit Pegeen Kelly is the 1994 Lamont Poetry
Selection of The Academy of American Poets.

From 1954 through 1974 the Lamont Poetry Selection
supported the publication and distribution of a first
collection of poems.
Since 1975 this distinguished award has been given for an
American poet's second book.

Judges for 1994:
Jorie Graham, Richard Kenney, David St. John

The Column of Mercury
Recording the Temperature of Night

No sleep in the night. No Sleep prowling like a caged animal.
And the smell of hyacinth heady in the air. Seductive.
Flirtatious. A mummery of scent. A museum of scent:

The wax figure house of things better forgotten. There
Are carved lions on the lawn but they offer small protection.
The lions hold up the stone table, the thick slate table

Like the tablets of the law engraved on the heart. *Each*
Man who eats sour grapes, his teeth shall be set on edge.
Or the tablets we take to sleep, whose carved words

Are about the erasure of other words. A kind of forgiveness.
The baby bleats. All night. No Sleep in his wolf suit
Shuttling back and forth, back and forth, a dark habitant,

Like the train crossing the landscape. The landscape is flat
But still the melancholy grows steeper. And the train
Slows in the night. There is no station here, but the train

Takes a long slowing. It makes a flutelike sound: a sound
Like held breath escaping, or the last drops falling
From a cloth wrung so tightly that it can be wrung no more.

Beside the hospital the giant flag blows out in soft decorum.
And then folds down like a bush or an abashed bird
As the train crosses before it. Blots it out. The train

Like a shovel in the garden. The train like a suited cadaver
In a coffin. All proper and on schedule. Though
There is no station here. Though the sound of the train slowing

Is like the sound of a flute played not by lips but by wind.
The hospital is a white dream, an unfathomable chalk cliff
With dark caves in it. A garden of sleeplessness. A garden

Full of sleep eaters and the audience they have captured:
The ones they hurt as they eat the heart's carved tablets.
And then eat the memory of them. A kind of forgiveness.

No sleep and the body shudders. The body's heat diminishes.
The unsocked feet grow cold. The child bleats. Is it hate
Does this? Oh, yes, probably. But how can we guess at it?

The depths of it? The train passes. The flag pours out
Again in slow motion.... White fleece of moonlight.
No, the moonlight is dirty lamb's wool. Something a child

Sucked on and then dropped behind her on the tracks.
Paired tracks. Twinned. Locked, like the carved lions
On the lawn, in the small posture of their destiny.

I

Song

Listen: there was a goat's head hanging by ropes in a tree.
All night it hung there and sang. And those who heard it
Felt a hurt in their hearts and thought they were hearing
The song of a night bird. They sat up in their beds, and then
They lay back down again. In the night wind, the goat's head
Swayed back and forth, and from far off it shone faintly
The way the moonlight shone on the train track miles away
Beside which the goat's headless body lay. Some boys
Had hacked its head off. It was harder work than they had
      imagined.
The goat cried like a man and struggled hard. But they
Finished the job. They hung the bleeding head by the school
And then ran off into the darkness that seems to hide everything.
The head hung in the tree. The body lay by the tracks.
The head called to the body. The body to the head.
They missed each other. The missing grew large between them,
Until it pulled the heart right out of the body, until
The drawn heart flew toward the head, flew as a bird flies
Back to its cage and the familiar perch from which it trills.
Then the heart sang in the head, softly at first and then louder,
Sang long and low until the morning light came up over
The school and over the tree, and then the singing stopped....
The goat had belonged to a small girl. She named
The goat Broken Thorn Sweet Blackberry, named it after
The night's bush of stars, because the goat's silky hair
Was dark as well water, because it had eyes like wild fruit.
The girl lived near a high railroad track. At night
She heard the trains passing, the sweet sound of the train's horn
Pouring softly over her bed, and each morning she woke
To give the bleating goat his pail of warm milk. She sang
Him songs about girls with ropes and cooks in boats.
She brushed him with a stiff brush. She dreamed daily
That he grew bigger, and he did. She thought her dreaming
Made it so. But one night the girl didn't hear the train's horn,
And the next morning she woke to an empty yard. The goat

Was gone. Everything looked strange. It was as if a storm
Had passed through while she slept, wind and stones, rain
Stripping the branches of fruit. She knew that someone
Had stolen the goat and that he had come to harm. She called
To him. All morning and into the afternoon, she called
And called. She walked and walked. In her chest a bad feeling
Like the feeling of the stones gouging the soft undersides
Of her bare feet. Then somebody found the goat's body
By the high tracks, the flies already filling their soft bottles
At the goat's torn neck. Then somebody found the head
Hanging in a tree by the school. They hurried to take
These things away so that the girl would not see them.
They hurried to raise money to buy the girl another goat.
They hurried to find the boys who had done this, to hear
Them say it was a joke, a joke, it was nothing but a joke....
But listen: here is the point. The boys thought to have
Their fun and be done with it. It was harder work than they
Had imagined, this silly sacrifice, but they finished the job,
Whistling as they washed their large hands in the dark.
What they didn't know was that the goat's head was already
Singing behind them in the tree. What they didn't know
Was that the goat's head would go on singing, just for them,
Long after the ropes were down, and that they would learn to
        listen,
Pail after pail, stroke after patient stroke. They would
Wake in the night thinking they heard the wind in the trees
Or a night bird, but their hearts beating harder. There
Would be a whistle, a hum, a high murmur, and, at last, a song,
The low song a lost boy sings remembering his mother's call.
Not a cruel song, no, no, not cruel at all. This song
Is sweet. It is sweet. The heart dies of this sweetness.

Of Royal Issue

The sun only a small bird flitting, a wren
    in the stripped forsythia, of little
note. A boy stands and watches it for a moment
    but then he loses interest and cuts
across the dull winter grass to play a game
    with a stick and a rock and soft repeated
shouts, and the bird is nothing again
    but a brown thing, within a fabric of brown
branches, mind and heart, the cages of.
    Days and days from now, each a web
of small branches, in the weeks of high wet
    winds that bring out low patches
of wild onion along the swollen creek
    and call up countless red-bellied birds
to dibble the grass with their blunt beaks,
    the bush's royal bloodline will briefly show,
a tide of gold, a small inland sea, and the wren
    will speak for it, words of royal issue,
tongue after tongue, worthy of note.
    But now the bush is mute. Our common blood
slows but will not sleep, a kind of footpath
    the mind trudges over, back and forth,
back and forth, packing the cold dirt down.... O little bird,
    how small you are, small enough to fit in a palm,
no contender, a featherweight. Perhaps
    we can pay the boy to trick you out of the bush,
and trap you, and bring you in to this spot
    by the window where your little song may
amount to more than a tablespoon's worth of salt.
    The glass will quicken your call, multiply it,
multiply your nervous figure and your habit
    of play, until you are not one bird but a hundred,
not one tongue but a thousand, sweet prophesy
    of the wind lighting the white strips
of the bed sheets the boy will tear and tie

to the black branches of all the garden's
trees, for no reason, because his hands
    will not stop, *bird in the mind, bird in the bush,*
the bird of the blood brightening
    as it calls and calls for its mate.

A Live Dog Being Better Than a Dead Lion

Rain. Rain from Baltimore. The ballroom floor
Is lit. See the gold sheen on the over-
Whelmed grasses? See the starched ruff of the hedgerow?
And the dancers are dressing. They tease
Their toes into shoes. Tease their breath into stays:
Stay the moment. Stay the luck. Stay, stay, the fields
Are full of rain and baby's breath. These will
Fashion the heart, and the heart fastened to the sleeve
Will break fire as the redbird did this morning
Bursting his small buttons against the glass. The glass
Was not black-hearted. It was an innocent pretender.
It took to itself the idea of sky and the bird bought
It, played his brave swan dive into our palms.
So let us wear it. Let us wear the bird like
A boutonniere to remind us that caution snares
Nothing. O the cautious are caught in the net
Of their cares: *Stop, No Turn, Leave Your Shoes*
At the Door. Please Don't Spit on the Statue and
Tokens Go Here. But the bird rode his cheer up.
Rode the high wire of his cheer up. Left
Without counting the cost his spittle-bright snail
Trail for the rain to erase, for the wind to wash
Out. Booted his small body beyond the Beyond.
Now the wrecked grace of the morning trails
Its tattered clouds. But they are flowers.
The pink flowers of Maryland turn softly above us.

Courting the Famous Figures
at the Grotto of Improbable Thought

A jester or a buffoon might play with demons and not pay.
A jester might see these vines as bell ropes
And drag a sound from them. A commiserating sound. Rain
Or bird fall through wet air. The fall of angels.

God watched the angels fall. It was something like
A thunderstorm: out of keeping with the season: spectacular
In the way it dressed the sky: a surge of romantic music
Overplayed: and then that feeling of famous entry.

A jester might deliver a benediction but who would believe him?
Would God? Would God in his sad figure here? Would you?
The statue is very cold. It is lodged in the cave
Like a pocket mirror reflecting our distress. The boy

Lies dead on his mother's legs: his arm dropped:
Like the head of a flower dropped: the stalk snapped:
The head trailing: the mother's face afflicted
With the indecency of it all: the undressed moment:

The exposure of the broken motion. The statue might have been
A lamp if the stage had been managed properly. But
The double figure is only a shrunken reproduction: one
Of a thousand rabbit-like offspring of a more solemn notion.

The original that the madman leapt over the velvet ropes
To disfigure with his busy hammer keeps lurking
Behind it and laughing. Or is that the madman laughing?
There are no ropes here. The boy is lost to the wet shades.

He sleeps a child's sleep: his face bearded by the milk
He drank before bed: the milk beard: the beard before the man
Beard that these walls have grown. They have grown a face.
Not like the face of Moses who broke the tablets of the law.

Not like splendid Moses who came down from the mountain
And burned the golden calf to powder. And made the sons
Of Israel drink it. A magnificent rebuke. A meal
Of such extravagance it had to be concocted from phantoms.

But more like the face of a bearded lady: vaguely indecent:
Sexual in its longing. Water braids down the swollen vines.
And the moss is thick and singular: frosted with pale
Fluorescence. The story seems to be about overblown failure.

A passion for the morose. For perpetual rains. A heavy
Foot on the pedal prolonging the melancholic denouement.
The candles quaver in the long shadows the pines lay down.
And the saints assume their assigned postures: Posture

Of swallowing the ribald joke whole. Posture of turning
The quiet cheek for yet another slung tomato or stone.
One saint pulls his plaster cassock up with a coy motion,
His perfect lips pouted, exposing for us the leg wound

That was healed: a figure of the sweet lyric. Tra la la la.
Because it worked out wisely. Because it worked out well.
At his naked feet the sparrows scatter seed on the wet
Pavement. The child who sells holy trinkets feeds them....

Now, see. We came for a revelation. A thick-headed
Generation: needing a miracle. We came for a show of Mercy.
Something as tangible as the trees' dropped cones: full
Of like kind: of like seed. Something we could juggle

Or plant against the coming need. We came with our orders
In hand. We came with our costumes. We had practiced
Our roles for a long time: the songs of suffering heroically
Endured, the parables and puns, conundrums and complaints,

The pantomimed fables and two-headed jokes, limericks and jigs,
The whole bag of tricks designed to catch God off guard
And relieve him of one or two of his multitudinous gifts.
We followed the rules. Though your ankles are weak

We climbed the steep cliff to the main attraction. The Goliath
The grotto is named for: The Lady of Improbable Thought.
The Lady of Prolonged Silence. The Lady of Strange Shape
That the hand of Anonymous hammered from the stone.

High-wrought hand. Awkward but unique. Possessing the power
Of Origins. How many years did it contend with the Lady?
How many hammer blows to uncover the brow? The neck?
The giant cloaked breasts that paraded above us?

The Lady is a ship stalled and willing for the wait.
The gulls cut from her skirts cross over. She is a ship
And figurehead in one: a blind form: having no pupils.
(Unless we are her pupils? The sight she has forsaken?)

We followed the rules. *We followed them all.* We moved
About her skirts: the blank tablets of her nomenclature:
We skirted the main issue. We did our tricks
And waited for applause. Was that it in the bird flurry?

Was that it in the yellow rag trussed to the tree?
Water dripped down the stone. There was the smell of dirt
And the smell of small illegal fires. There was
Expectancy and need: the clearing they made in the trees

Through which something might have moved. But
There was a deficit in the faculty of the Imagination.
We were no lions of Judah. We had no slingshot.
Not one smooth stone with which to reach her monstrous

Forehead. Wherever we stood the Lady looked away:
As if she were listening to something that made no sound:
Her sideward habit shouldered by the art we've lost:
The assumption of the scene behind the scene: that pulls

The action forward: that gives it meaning. Couple
Vengeance with those things we cannot subtract. Coins
In the saints' cups. Smiles like weak flowers. Solace
Sliding as we did back down to this plaster strong-

Hold of saints.... *O Lady. O Lady. Around us an ocean.*
A field of disinterest. But still we push forward.
We bow, we bend. We keep moving. *Though we feel nothing.*
We keep moving. Here in the theater of public longing.

The Music Lesson

Collect of white dusk. And
The first epistolary drops
Strike sparks from the leaves,

Send up the sweet fragrance
Of the Far Gone. Where
The maple fell in another rain

Red and white umbrellas
Hold back the weather: sun
And moon and the seasonal

Displays the four hands
Keep time to: the telling
And the told. Back and forth:

Back and forth: the lesson's
Passion is patience. Through
The domino tumble and clutter

Of the pupil's untutored touch
The metronome keeps
A stiff upper lip, pays out

Its narrow train of thought,
While above, God,
Gold carrion in a lit frame,

Rehearses His reproach, one-
Noted. Final. The unnegotiable
Real estate of absolute loss:

Discipleship's cost. O hands,
Hands, doing their work:
The steeple hat of the dunce

Is stiff with recalcitrant
Notes, but still the ghost hammers
Leap. And luck makes an entrance

In this: See: lightning
Partitions the dusk—illuminating
Our brief lease—and with

A cocksure infusion of heat
Luck lays hands on
The boy's hands and prefigures

The pleasure that will one day
Possess this picture for good.
This is the stone the builders

Rejected. Pleasure. *Pleasure.*
The liquid tool, the golden
Fossil that will come to fuel

In lavish and unspeakable ways
All the dry passages
The boy does not now comprehend

Or care for. And then his
Stricken hands will blossom
Fat with brag. And play.

Of Ancient Origins and War

And briefly stay, the junketing sparrows, briefly,
Briefly, their flurries like small wine spills,

While the one divides into two: the heart and its shadow,
The world and its threat, the crow back of the sparrow.

Near the surface, beneath the soft penetrable mask—
The paste of white blossoms slurring the broken ground—
Alarm begins its troubled shoot: *the fruit tree*

Beareth its fruit: a load of old fruit tricked out
By the scattershot light, figured gold by the furious light.

The will given early to the dream of pleasure falters,
In a slurry of scent, in a posture of doubled-over gold,
And then there is the rift, the sound of cloth tearing

As the crow shoots up—fast with apparent purpose—
Splitting wide the leaves of a tree we cannot name,
Growing by a gate made from another tree, a gate

That cries as it swings, the cry of the broken safety.
The world and its haste, the world and its threat,
The here where we will die coming closer. All the sorrow

Of it, sparrow trouble, sparrow blow, our hands
These sparrows, quick and quick, but tippling now,

Toppling, bellies full of the bad seed the hair spilled
When it broke from the last comb it was locked into.
The will given early to the dream of pleasure falters.

And now, in the dark, listen, in the dark
The tulip poplar is singing, the leaves are singing,
The clear high green of a boy's imperilled soprano.

The moon is rising, the sound like wine spilling.
The boy will grow a beard, the boy will be bearded.
The bird will dive back down in perfect execution.

The damaged will can only watch and wonder
Through a surface alarmed with dust.... And so now.
And so that now. We are in the trouble of a sleep

We did not dream of. And the shadows of the trees
Are breaking. The shadows of the world's broken vessels.

Garden of Flesh, Garden of Stone

The little white throat has his head in the boy's ear.
      Maybe he has found some seed in it. Or maybe
he is telling the boy a secret, some sweet nothing.
      Or maybe he has mistaken the rimmed flesh,
taut and sweet as the skin of a fig, for his bathing dish,
      and is about to dive through the pale sky
reflected in it, lengths of blue, lengths of gray,
      yards and yards of quarried white. And the boy,
who is made of stone, who has stood still for a long time,
      pissing in the stone basin, seems this morning
in the peculiar light to be leaning his large head,
      barely balanced on a narrow neck, toward the sparrow,
as if he likes the soft sewing motion of the beak
      within his ear, the delicate morse of the white throat,
a bird as plain as dust, but swift-witted and winged,
      and the possessor of the saddest of all calls,
five slow notes that bring to mind a whole garden
      of fruit trees in winter, trunk after scarred trunk,
the mist stiff in the branches, and the sound
      of single drops of water striking the charred ground
as desolate as the sound of the boy's fountain
      dripping and dripping into the drained basin
long after the water has been shut off. Today the basin
      is full. The boy stands above it, one hand on his hip,
as if he were a gunslinger, the other in front,
      guiding the narrow stream of water up and out
in a spinning arc that changes color in the light
      and tosses when it hits the flat surface of the water
a handful of silver seed up. This seems to be
      the source of the boy's smile, this and some
teasing riddle the bird has dropped in the boy's ear
      that the boy turns over and over. Now the bird
hops to the boy's shoulder. When he whistles,
      as he will in a moment, his chest will puff out,
and the patch of feathers at his throat will echo

the pouched whiteness of the boy's belly,
a purse of stone crossed by roses, tall roses, long overgrown,
     the dark blooms lapping and lapping at the boy's flesh,
and then, one by one, diving slowly sideways,
     distracted by their own swooning reflections
in the water. The boy is roughly fashioned,
     the chisel marks still visible, but this belly
the flowers fall for is impossibly beautiful.
     The sun has bleached it, and the wind has buffed it,
until it is a perfect rind of fruit, or the perfect curve
     of the moon on nights when it is full and hangs
over the neglected trees behind the boy,
     the pocked stone matching the pallor of the boy's skin,
white gone dusky, shallow water in a shallow basin,
     and the pale hands, too, that move over and under
as they wash themselves in it, the water sighing
     as it falls.... Five notes. Five slow notes.
This is the song of the white throat. Five notes
     so high and sad, and so like a boy's whistle,
they press on a spot deep in the throat, deep
     where the cords band the bone and the breath,
and the boy made of stone shivers. The boy looks up.
     Why has he never heard this song before?
He likes the strangeness of it. He likes the ghostly trees
     that rise up around him like the remnant
of a garden he once stood in but has forgotten—
     a garden in which there was no fountain.
He likes the charred smell of wet dirt and the mist
     that slides across the blackened branches
in strands as slow and milky as the horned snails
     that come out at dusk and drag their silver trails
down the walk. He likes his shaking body
     and the taste of old fruit on his tongue....
But abruptly the song stops. The trees step back.
     Now the bird is all business. The bird snaps
his beak as he moves brusquely up and down
     the boy's long arm, measuring it as if it were
a length of cloth, smoothed and ready for cutting.

The bird snaps. And the boy, who is made of stone,
who is crudely fashioned but still lovely,
        slowly, slowly shifts his weight from his back foot
to his front, which unbalances his narrow shoulders,
        and makes the stream of water, arced like a bow,
arrowless, but ready, thin to a thread,
        and the water in the basin go slack. The boy
wants the bird to stop. He wants the bird
        to come back and croon in his ear, like the lover
he has never had, or he wants the white throat
        to go for good. He will not stand for this cutting.
Why should he? Doesn't the bird know of the pact?
        The privilege the boy was granted when the one
with somewhat clumsy hands chose to make him
        not of wood or of gold or of pale washed flesh
but of stone? No cloth would ever darken
        his body with shadow. No shadow would grow
from his feet and loop its noose around him,
        the way it does those other boys, the ones
behind the wall, who with rocks and shrill shouts
        bring down bird after singing bird. He traded
that pleasure for this. To stand harmless
        and never move. To never move and never be dressed,
as even this white throat is, in his own shroud.
        Why did he listen to the bird's song? What is this
weight of stone in his belly? Where is the one
        with heavy hands? How will he call him?
And what, when he raises his small voice
        for the first time, will that voice sound like?

                        ⌒

II

Field Song

What stands? The walnut:
    the tower of story
        dark with crows,

The leafy way station
    for doomsayers:
        Say nay, say no,

Say the morning comes in
    with a silver spoon
        and the spoon rattles

In a cup because
    the child is gone.
        But still the child

Stands, the way a statue
    does in the mind:
        or in a field: a fawn

Figure with a filigreed
    grin: there beside
        the walnut and the way

Of passing things:
    the wide road down
        the middle of it all.

The middle ground
    gives way and we
        are on either side,

As in a game:
    You're it. You're not.
        You're out. Arms up

You stand,
    with those taken
        for all they're worth:

The lace of Anne,
    the rods of gold,
        the stalks made from iron:

Their color drains away,
    but still they hold
        on: a dry feast:

The way things fast
    toward their absent
        forms: go in hunger.

Go in grace.

Dead Doe

for Huck

The doe lay dead on her back in a field of asters: no.

The doe lay dead on her back beside the school bus stop: yes.

Where we waited.
Her belly white as a cut pear. Where we waited: no: off

from where we waited: yes

at a distance: making a distance
we kept,
as we kept her dead run in sight, that we might see if she chose
to go skyward;
that we might run, too, turn tail
if she came near
and troubled our fear with presence: with ghostly blossoming:
    with the fountain's

                            unstoppable blossoming
        and the black stain the algae makes when the water
                                stays near.

We can take the gilt-edged strolling of the clouds: yes.
But the risen from the dead: no!

The haloey trouble-shooting of the goldfinches in the bush:
                    yes: but *in season:*

kept within bounds,

not in the pirated rows of corn,
not above winter's pittance of river.

The doe lay dead: she lent

her deadness to the morning, that the morning might have weight, that
　　our waiting might matter: be upheld by significance: by light
　　　　on the rhododendron, by the ribbons the sucked mint
　　　　　　loosed on the air,

by the treasonous gold-leaved passage of season, and you

from me / child / from me /

from . . . not mother: no:
but the weather that would hold you: yes:

hothouse you to fattest blooms: keep you in mild unceasing rain,
　　and the fixed
　　　　　　　　stations of heat: like a pedaled note: or the held
　　　　　　　　　　breath sucked in, and stay: yes:
stay

but: no: not done: can't be:

the doe lay dead: she could
do nothing:

the dead can mother nothing . . . nothing
but our sight: they mother that, whether they will or no:

they mother our looking, the gap the tongue prods when the
　　tooth is missing, when
　　　　　　　　　　fancy seeks the space.

The doe lay dead: yes: and at a distance, with her legs up and
　　frozen, she tricked
　　　　　　　　　　our vision: at a distance she was
　　　　　　　　　　　for a moment no deer
at all

but two swans: we saw two swans
　　　　　　　　and they were fighting

or they were coupling
or they were stabbing the ground for some prize
worth nothing, but fought over, so worth *that,* worth
the fought-over glossiness: the morning's fragile-tubed glory.

And this is the soul: like it or not. Yes: the soul comes down: yes: comes
into the deer: yes: who dies: yes: and in her death twins herself into swans:
fools us with mist and accident into believing her newfound finery

and we are not afraid
though we should be

and we are not afraid as we watch her soul fly on: paired
as the soul always is: with itself:
  with others.
                Two swans....

Child. We are done for
in the most remarkable ways.

Arguments of Everlasting

My mother
gathers gladiolas: the little tubes
shout and clamor: a poppling
of unstoppled laughter: the guileless leaps
and quiet plosives
of the fountain when it is working: when
mechanics and meaning are flush
and untroubled. Not like
my brother's stammer: speech and its edicts
broken by that intruder
between tongue and tooth: something
winged: of insect color.
    My mother
gathers gladiolas. The gladness
is fractured. As when
the globe with its thousand mirrors
cracked the light. How
it hoarded sight: all the stolen perspectives
and the show of light
they shot around us: so that
down the dark hall the ghosts danced
with us: down the dark hall
the broken angels.
    What keeps
the grass from slipping? The steep
grass? Like my brother
it imitates the stone's arrest: *this done*
this done and nothing
doing. In the face of the wind
it plants its foot
and fights its own going:
a travelling line
of adamance.
    My mother,
the doves are in full cry

this morning.
The leaves are heavy
with silken grieving: soft packages
of sorrow: cacophonies
of sighing. It is a pretty
thing, a pretty thing,
the light lathered like feathers,
and the day's spendage
beginning. The flag unspools its furl
above the school,
pulsing out and out: a wake
of color on the air:
blue: red: blue:

and how white the sky is. How white.

Wild Turkeys:
The Dignity of the Damned

Because they are shame, and cannot flee from it,
And cannot hide it, they go slow,
One great variegated male and his harem of four wild hens

Halting our truck as they labor
To cross the road into the low fields they are indentured to.
They go slow, their hearts hardened to this;

Those laughingstock, shriveled, lipstick red hearts—
Swinging on throat and foreneck
Beneath the narrow heads that are the blue

Not of the sky but of convicts' shaved skulls—
Have been long indurated by rains and winds and filth
And the merciless exposures of the sun.

They do not look up, they do not fly—
Except at night when dark descends like shame,
When shame is lost to dark, and then,

Weak-winged, they heave themselves
Into the low tree roosts they drop from in the morning,
Crashing like swag-bellied bombers

Into the bare fields and stingy stands of trees
They peck their stones and seeds from.
Yesterday they were targets, but now they go slow,

As if this lacuna between winter and spring, still gray,
But full of the furred sumacs' pubescent probings,
And the faint oily scent of wild onion vials crushed open,

Gave hope to even them, or as if they knew
All seasons to be one, the going back,
The crossing over, the standing still, all the same,

When the state you defend is a lost state,
When lurching into an ungainly run
Only reminds you that there is nowhere to run to.

And this movement, this jerking
Of these heavy goffered carapaces forward,
This dumb parading that looks at first glance furtive,

Like skulking, the hunkered shoulders, the lowered heads,
Reveals, as we watch, the dignity that lines
Of pilgrim-sick possess as they halt toward some dark grotto—

A faith beyond the last desire to possess faith,
The soldier's resolve to march humpbacked straight into death
Until it breaks like oil over him

And over all that is lost.

Divining the Field

Through the body of the crow the finch flies:
Small yellow-green patch of flower springing
Up in the weedy field: of briefest flight.
The flower will be shot dead by the coming cold
Or by the woman's disregard. Her forgetfulness
Arrows him the way Saint Sebastian was arrowed:
Poor man stuck with a hundred bony wings, laddered,
The stripped shafts trembling, as if Sebastian
Had been instructed to climb his own flesh
Up into the high regard his skewered sight
Was planting there: Crow's Nest: House of the Spy.
Regards grow up like trees. The thing Sebastian
Was thinking when he died: a leafy assemblage
With a driven core: swift monument of oak or stone
The heart passes through, the way the finch
Passes through the body of the crow: the lord
Of highness. From his post the crow shouts
The other hawkers down: sells tickets to
Sebastian's fledging: devours in one gesture
The finch like a piece of fruit: like a roasted morsel.
It is too much to bear sometimes: a tree
Of flame-flung arrows, a bird selling portions,
Our endless lust for spectacle to rouse
The stupored sight. As if the body of Sebastian's
Death were not always with us: This high
White garment of grasses the birds fly through,
Opening with their sharp gold wings
The purple and crimson wounds of the flowers.

Pipistrelles

i.

In the damp dusk
The bats playing spies and counterspies by the river's
Bankrupt water station

Look like the flung hands of deaf boys, restlessly
Signing the dark. Deaf boys
Who all night and into the half-lit hours

When the trees step from their shadows
And the shadows go to grass
Whistle those high-pitched tunes that, though unheard, hurt

Our thoughts. Pipistrelles, little pipes, little
Night pipes, the peculiar
Lost fluting of the outcast heart. Poor heart.

The river's slate waters slide
Silt and grief, the whole destroyed mountain of winter
Over the weir. Never stopping,

Sometimes slowing, but never stopping. And
Along the banks the skinflint trees
Clasp their weak heat. Well, they are a touchy choir,

A confused congregation, breathing
The thin air of our unteneted world. The sun pales,
The leafy dogma goes, and we are left

To our freedom. But do we see now
The world as it actually is? Or merely another world?
A world within a world? Perhaps

In spring, when the dogwood
Slowly discloses its hoard of pale mothlike blossoms
It is the mind that mulls

The sap—perhaps it is the mind
That makes its worlds
And the miracles therein.

ii.

The bats resemble the deaf.
But they are not deaf. They live by echoes, as we do.
Negotiate by echoes. Send signals out

And field the reflections on the wing. And only
Great fear will hang them
On the piano wires we string to test them,

Dead certain of our right to know
At any cost the mechanism of another's flight.
Even blindfolded, even painted

All over with nail polish, the bats will manage
Those wires pulled free
From their instrument, from their sound, will play

Around them a makeshift music
So lovely the pianist's fingers will falter in envy,
And only great fear will hang them.

But it is different with us. Fear in us
Is central. Of the bone. It is our inheritance.
Our error. What flies back at us

From rocks and trees, from the emptiness
We cannot resist casting into,
Is colored by the distortions of our hearts,

And what we hear almost always blinds us.
We stumble against phantoms, throw
Ourselves from imaginary cliffs, and at dusk, like children, we

Run the long shadows down. Because the heart, friend,
Is a shadow, a domed dark
Hung with remembered doings. A night feeder—moths,

Fur over the tongue and the wet jewel of blood,
The cracked shells of insects
Split on the wing. And elsewhere, by connection,

Blood draining from the perfect cut
That brings the rabbit down, a slow singing out,
As in a dream, the blood sliding,

As the water of the overflowing creek does, sideways
In its brief bid for freedom,
While above, something wings away.

iii.

We are not birds. Despite our walls covered
With winged men, we are not birds.
And all that is birdlike in the bats

Is also deception. They have
No feathers, no beak, no high-pitched heart.
Their wings are skin. Skin! Stretched

From shoulder to foot like the cloth
We nailed to wood to build
Our doomed medieval contraptions for flight,

Or like our taut sheets, the high-strung skin,
The great single wing of sex we lean on
But we are not birds. All that is birdlike

In us, in the bats, is illusion.
There is nothing at all of the bird in us....
Except for flight. Except for flight.

Cry of the Jay

An admiral
riposte: the blue dress of the jay
on the high fence: his high way
of regarding down the otherness:
the blank looks
that would defeat.
The sky is not so blue
or so contained:
bird breast a cobalt pistol: shot:
the small heart exploding
into raucous cry: the whole
packed-in warmth of June focused
and set free.
Free borne this fiery
fracas of bird and flesh and
smoldering air:
free freight
the light that slides like struck sand
down: though still the light
stands above: as light will do:
behaving in lustrous banks
of unseamed richness.
Unlimited
gratitude might take such
a shape: *We are within. It is the only*
place: Sanctuary of sameness
made strange by hard-hit
sight: gathering place
of the wayward protocols
dressing now for dinner
after their dressed-down
state.....

The jay is above

           it all. As the seed
                   of the self will be:
               If that other
larger call
       comes in.

The White Pilgrim: Old Christian Cemetery

The cicadas were loud and what looked like a child's
Bracelet was coiled at the base of the Pilgrim.
It was a snake.   Red and black.   The cemetery
Is haunted.   Perhaps by the Pilgrim.   Perhaps
By another.   We were looking for names
For the baby.   My daughter liked Achsa and Luke
And John Jacob.   She was dragging her rope
Through the grass.   It was hot.   The insect
Racket was loud and there was that snake.
It made me nervous.   I almost picked it up
Because it was so pretty.   Just like a bracelet.
And I thought, Oh, the child will be a girl,
But it was not.   This was around the time
Of the dream.   Dreams come from somewhere.
There is this argument about nowhere,
But it is not true.   I dreamed that some boys
Knocked down all the stones in the cemetery
And then it happened.   It was six months later
In early December.   Dead cold.   Just before
Dawn.   We live a long way off so I slept
Right through it.   But I read about it the next
Day in the Johnsonburg paper.   There is
This argument about the dead, but that is not
Right either.   The dead keep working.   If
You listen you can hear them.   It was hot
When we walked in the cemetery.   And my daughter
Told me the story of the White Pilgrim.
She likes the story.   Yes, it is a good one.
A man left his home in Ohio and came East,
Dreaming he could be the dreamed-of Rider
In St. John's Revelation.   He was called
The White Pilgrim because he dressed all
In white like a rodeo cowboy and rode a white
Horse.   He preached that the end was coming soon.
And it was.   He died a month later of the fever.

The ground here is unhealthy.   And the insects
Grind on and on.   Now the Pilgrim is a legend.
I know your works, God said, and that is what
I am afraid of.   It was very hot that summer.
Even the birds were quiet.   *God's eyes are like*
A flame of fire, St. John said, *and the armies*
Of heaven.... But these I cannot imagine.
Many dreams come true.   But mostly it isn't
The good ones.   That night in December
The boys were bored.   They were pained to the teeth
With boredom.   You can hardly blame them.
They had been out all night breaking trashcans
And mailboxes with their baseball bats.   They
Hang from their pickups by the knees and
Pound the boxes as they drive by.   The ground
Here is unhealthy, but that is not it.
Their satisfaction just ends too quickly.
They need something better to break.   They
Need something holy.   But there is not much left,
So that night they went to the cemetery.
It was cold, but they were drunk and perhaps
They did not feel it.   The cemetery is close
To town, but no one heard them.   The boys are part
Of a larger destruction, but this is beyond
What they can imagine.   War in heaven
And the damage is ours.   The birds come to feed
On what is left.   You can see them always
Around Old Christian.   As if the bodies of the dead
Were lying out exposed.   But of course they are
Not.   St. John the Evangelist dreamed of birds
And of the White Rider.   That is the one
The Ohio preacher wanted to be.   He dressed
All in white and rode a white horse.
His own life in the Midwest was not enough,
And who can blame him?   My daughter thinks
That all cemeteries have a White Pilgrim.
She said that her teacher told her this.   I said
This makes no sense but she would not listen.

There was a pack of dogs loose in my dream
Or it could have been dark angels.   They were
Taking the names off the stones.   St. John said
An angel will be the one who invites the birds
To God's Last Supper, when he eats the flesh
Of all the kings and princes.   Perhaps God
Is a bird.   Sometimes I think this.   The thought
Is as good as another.   The boys shouldered
Over the big stones first, save for the Pilgrim.
And then worked their way down to the child-
Sized markers.   These they punted like footballs.
The cemetery is close to town but no one
Heard them.   They left the Pilgrim for last
Because he is a legend, although only local.
My daughter thinks that all cemeteries
Have a White Pilgrim, ghost and stone, and that
The stone is always placed dead in the center
Of the cemetery ground.   In Old Christian
This is true.   The Ohio Pilgrim was a rich man
And when he died the faithful sunk his wealth into
The marble obelisk called by his name.   We saw
The snake curled around it.   Pretty as a bracelet.
But the child was not a girl.   The boys left
The Pilgrim till last, and then took it down,
Too.   The Preacher had a dream but it was not
Of a larger order so it led to little.   Just
A stone broken like a tooth, and a ghost story
For children.   God says the damage will be
Restored.   Among other things.   At least
They repaired Old Christian.   The historical
Society took up a collection and the town's
Big men came out to hoist the stones.   The boys
Got probation, but they won't keep it.... I
Don't go to the cemetery anymore.   But once
I drove past and my babysitter's family
Was out working.   Her father and mother were
Cutting back the rose of Sharon and my red-haired
Sitter, who is plain and good-hearted, was

Pushing a lawn mower.   Her beautiful younger
Sister sat on the grass beside the Pilgrim
Pretending to clip some weeds.   She never works.
She has asthma and everybody loves her.
I imagined that the stones must have fine seams
Where they had been broken.   But otherwise
Everything looked the same.   Maybe better....
The summer we walked in the cemetery it was hot.
We were looking for names for the baby
And my daughter told me the story of the White
Pilgrim.   This was before the stones fell
And before the worked-for restoration.
I know your works, says God, and talks of
The armies of heaven.   They are not very friendly.
Some dreams hold and I am afraid that this
May be one of them.   The White Rider may come
With his secret name inscribed on his thigh,
King of Kings, Lord of Lords, and the child
Is large now . . . but who will be left standing?

Percival

Percival comes. If I pretend he is not here
He grows larger in the barn, filling all the shadows,
And then I cannot go in to feed the cows

And I hear those who give milk crying for milk
And I see their hearts, like children's palms,
Opening and closing in the garden. Even in winter

I keep the garden. And Percival, who never looks
At flowers, taps his fingers on the water
That has frozen in buckets in the barn.

I hear that tapping. Even as I heard him coming,
Last night through my sleep, through the snow,
His heavy black coat dropping like wings.

III

Past the Stations

A washed corpse, the body of rain-drenched trees
That below my window darkens further. In
Remembrance. Grave blanket of dusk over it.
Cold sheet of mist over it. Death a bird shadow
On the sill. This is the plot of my consideration.
The copse below my window, the small wood
Without an oracle, with no significant episode.
It is a hand's breadth. It is a small ache.
The hand knocks at the window. The window opens.
The smell of wetted dirt and wild fruit steps
Up. Blood fruit: Blood apples. Bitter to the taste
And good. The hand reaches out and the sheet
Slips down. Sigh of silence and a cat passing,
Pale as a ghost, pale as peeled fruit, pale as
Its own pale claws looking for another find....
Like caskets, trees can be counted, together
Or apart. If you stand above the woods, the tree
Is one. It is many, if you walk below. Many,
If you step past the stations of your thought
And number your steps. Smaller and smaller.
The faculty of expansion decreasing. The faculty
Of breath decreasing. The rain withdrawing
With a whistling hush.... Somebody thinks
Or somebody turns. Into what? Into what?

Silver Lake

Fast-locked the land for weeks. Of ice we dream.
Of ice and the low fires the fishermen feed on Silver Lake.
All the lakes are called silver here, though none are that.
And this one now is white and shot through with fishing holes.
It looks like the blasted back of one of those huge turtles
That summer drags out of the weeds with the lure of sweeter bogs.
They lumber with the ponderous slowness of some interminable
        sermon
And they are easy game for the long-legged boys in pickups
Who hack their backs with axes to make thick soup. Years
In that soup. Unseen years and depth to mull the blond meat
That my great great Uncle Lusty in England made his fortune from.
But that is another story. Now the lake—with its toppled shrine
And the memory of its lone heron, seasonal and proud—is sealed;
And on these frigid fog-bound days the sun comes late,
If at all, comes like a slow yellow age stain on linen,
Or like the muted blare of the fluorescent lights you can see
Through the smeared windows of the Gulf Station garage.
Sometimes it has the iridescence of spilled oil, and always
In the fog you can look straight at it, as you can look
At the sun in Medjugorje, and it will not burn your eyes,
Though here we are not changed much by such sights.
Once you were alone on the ice. Too cold for the rest.
All day the wind was rank with the metallic smell of old snow,
Blowing over and over itself, tangling like lost laundry,
And even the hungry packs of snowmobiles—that sound
As they cross the cornfields with their shrill chain-saw whine
As if they are felling whole forests—were silent.
Dusk was coming on. And I watched you for a long time.
I was in the open, though you did not see me, did not turn
To where I stood in the high grasses the weather had stained black.
You sat on your three-legged stool by a numb fire, your boot
Cocked on the coughed-up collar of ice the awl leaves,
And waited for the fish to spring your trap, spring
The pink plastic flag that made me think of the lawn flamingos

In the yard of the Kinkel's Corner antique shop. Few stop there
Because the highway's hairpin curves are deadly and blind,
But one morning I stood among the flocks of those plastic birds
And the statues posturing in the yard. Virgins and trolls.
Saints and satyrs and naked women with no arms. "Things
That keep and do not change," as the proprietor told me.
And he pointed to the painted figure of a shirtless slave
Up the narrow walk to his house. "See that colored boy," he said.
"I've had him sixty years, and all he needs is a little varnish."
The lower rims of the man's eyes belled forward and were very red
And it was impossible not to look at that soreness....
You sat for so long on the ice my tongue went numb in my mouth
And I woke to see you paying your line out slow as a delicious
        thought
Into the circled dark. There was a pause before whatever contract
You made with the darkness was complete, the wind repeated
Its wolf whistle in the reeds, and then the prisoner was released—
The orange-winged, green-and-black striped perch flew up, flew fast,
Iced by the fire's light, scattering bright hot pellets as it flew,
The way the priest scatters holy water during the Asperges
At Easter Vigil. And when you put your hand on the fish
I felt how it burned your flesh, burned for the two worlds to meet....
I don't lie to myself. This is what men love the best.
The thoughts they deal from the dark. Better than any woman's
        flesh.

Distraction of Fish and Flowers in the Kill

People fish the kills here. Black, the kills, with shade,
Moist with shade, and the graveyard odors, the graveyard hush,

The hush of weedy distracted flowers, grass flowers, bush flowers,
Flowers of savor, and those of ill repute.

And beyond, there is always the Island beckoning, to destroy or save,
The lure of the Island, though there is nothing on it

But fireweed and gravel, and between here and there the water
Is deep, the water is deep between.

Fireweed grows where things have burned. The day
Squats with its magnifying glass. The boy in blue shorts squats

On the stones burning ants with his glass, and fireweed, which is not
The color of fire, grows in profusion. Fireweed is purple,

As in shrouds, as in *to destroy or put an end to.*
This we understand. This thing on our hands we would be free of,

One crime or another, the plotted errors, all the dumb-show
    passages
We play over and over. The unrhymed passages

That call up the chief complaints: Chiefly the wind's fault. Chiefly
That of the Boy Actor....

The water's lights go off and on and the Island beckons.
There seem to be many hands waving. There seem to be many voices
    saying,

Jump now, before the fire gets you, the heart fire, the brain fire.
We are holding the sheets, holding the bedclothes.

And, yes, the air is full of white stuff: feathers or grave wrappings:
Something broadcast wholesale to the wind. But the warm water

Shackles our ankles, and the wrong ideas are firm
In the body: the idea that harm can hasten

The coming of good. That rain can make a lasting forgetfulness. The
        non-
Swimmer's reckonings that weaken the ankle. Poor

Lily-white ankle, dreaming it will step forward
As if for the first time.

The Witnesses

The Witnesses come again. They come to my mind
Before they come to the door. The young man wears a red scarf.
And the old woman is soft in the head. We sit on the porch
And she fans the waves painted on the *Watchtower*'s cover.

The waves are blue as rebellion. "The ocean," she says,
"See here . . . the ocean . . . the ocean is full of dirt . . .
And it is going...." And she is gone. Stares blindly
At the spot where two drab deer made the baby laugh

By eating dead bushes. He thought they were cows. "Moo,"
He said. "Moooo." He names things by their sounds.
The young Witness picks up the dropped conversation.
He plies a soft black book. Is pledged to persuasion.

Once he was a Papist, but now is not. He frowns
At the statue of Mary covered with bird lime. "The signs
Will come," he says. "The signs, and then the End.
Only the chosen will stand." My mind lies quiet.

I hear the crows barking. The ocean is going.
And the trees in good faith are drinking our poison.
How dark the night is and high up. Starless
With ignorance. There through the low branches

The turning river shines gold as a prize ribbon,
Gold and proud as a seal of approval. But the water
Has no fish in it. And the watchtower has no beacon.
Or the beacon is broken. The beacon limps over the ocean

Like the mind of an old person coming to thought
And receding.... Or like the flight of a damaged bird....
My sister had a bird once and my cousin got it. He
Pulled its feathers out. He stood under the street lamp

And pulled its feathers out. Then he pitched it
Into the air again and again, whistling as it plummeted
Like a falling star.... *O kill the bird! Kill it!*
Be done with it!... O do . . . not kill . . . the bird....

"Don't let the Witnesses in," says my husband. "They
Pollute the place. Talk to them on the porch," he says.
"Or better, at the bottom of the hill." Posted with signs
The fence row there guards the game preserve the hunters

Flush deer from. They shoot the deer dead on the road
And then strap the bodies upside down to the tailgates
Of their trucks, so that the deer's necks arch back as ours do
In sex, but soft, soft.... *The Witnesses come again.*

Guest Place

Hospice of wanting. Hindmost of the day. Back
Of the cedar bush. The guest place in the shadow

Where I lay down my longing, little cat, little bird.
Of split leaves the scratched dirt smells, of mice,

And of the blue shade that salvages the forehead, milk
Shadow, sweet liquid brimming the flesh's shallow basin.

But there is the other shadow. The hostile shadow
Outside that spills blackly over the face: shadow

Of the wind's rebuke dashing a paper down the street:
Flint shadow striking the bushes so that laughter

Sprays out: atomized: a shrill gaudiness: our words
Coming back to us as cheap thrill: cheap perfume....

The nursling cries for milk. For milkiness.
The crow cries for his own poor behavior.

The fledged effort stumbles on the air. The air
Is thin and powdered with the leaves' exhalations:

A series of soft blows: the soft finery pumped
Out like dispensations. But hard to catch: hard

To catch the breath.... Under the bush of dogged
Mildness we lie. And think of the busyness all around.

The unthinking cruelty. Our own genius for harm.

The Pear Tree

The jewel called citrine is yellow. And so are my pears.
And so is the eye of the crow. No, that is not right.
Now I remember. The crow's eye is black, like his feathers.
Not red or yellow or gold. And the pears this year

Are green and misshapen. But you can see this for yourself,
Pears like the organs of chickens, plucked for cooking.
The rains did them in. The rains came in early, bringing
The cold, and the crows came soon after, squalling and fretting,

A hundred crows, a thousand, day after day, too many
To count. They set up house in the elms by the bog
And now the yard smells of dogs. They bring the dusk
In early. The little pears can't hold it off. Their lamps

Are low on oil. They shed no light on the dirt I dig....
I wanted the ring for my wedding. The *citrine*. But the man
Said it was too expensive. It was an old ring,
Lying on black cloth, locked under glass. I wish you

Could have seen it. The color of my pears in good years
When they steep, fat and sweet, in their own hot grease,
Or of the sun when it comes in behind the falling rain,
A blurred gold, an amber spill that turns the dark rain

Into a coat of many colors, a hundred colors, a thousand,
As many as the colors in the songs of God. Or in
The finch's feathers.... *Bird like a jewel*.... Do you know
The kind I mean? Yellow and green. The bird I bury is one—

The man's pet. *The plaything of the man's heart*. The pretty one
In the silver cage with the silver bell and the rope
Plaited from strips of silk. I held him this morning
Folded on his back like a piece of fine linen. I stroked

And I sang. His wings dusky as the leaves of the pear tree,
The rings of his feet bright as the pears when the pears
Are gold.... Now his song will be forgotten.... *Poor little pears*
The rain has bullied.... Poor little finch I killed

And bury.... Poor little heart with its ruined gardens....
Do you want to see them? Five are the gardens. Daily
I count them. Here are the sunflowers, bagged of their boast.
The rains did them in, stole their seeds and their size. And this

Is where the tulips stood, red tulips, yellow tulips, white.
Their heads were all topped by the deer and the rabbits.
I put out poison from my little pail to stop the moles
But it did nothing. One garden, two, and garden three—

Drowning now in rust—is the small patch of strawberries
That the man first bedded in the middle of the grass
Where the little plants looked like something spilled,
So I dug them up, but they have not taken to their place

By the gate—the only berries were snagged by the crows.
And the fourth garden is the garden of the graves of pets:
One-armed monkey, a voiceless cat, a rat called Goliath,
Toads, snails . . . and now in the shoebox that darkens in the rain,

The finch of many colors, a hundred colors, a thousand,
Too many to count. This garden thrives in any weather,
Here beneath the pear tree, the last of my gardens,
Fast by the bog. But now the pears I count on are green

And misshapen. They have no breasts or feathers, nothing
Soft to stick your fingers in. Even the crows don't want them....
Filthy birds. *Look at them.* Black as the waters of the bog
They brood over. Liars' tongues are black like that.

And so are the songs of Darkness. And so is the skirt
I smothered the bird with. Shrouding the cage,
Bringing the dusk in early.... How loud the rain is.
How loud the sound. Listen to it falling. It falls

On the shovel. It sounds like stones hitting tin cans
Lined up on a wall. Ping, ping, ping. Or like bullets.
And the sound gets louder.... *It was the rain....* No . . . no...
It was . . . *the cries* . . . the vocables morning and evening....

I could not hear myself think.... My thoughts were all broken.
The bird's cries were so sharp . . . sharp as the saw grass....
Or the pronged sumacs that spring up everywhere and threaten
The gardens.... I have to yank them out by the roots

Or they eat up all the ground.... *What else is there to do?*
Count the gardens, count the graves, count the fallen jewels.
But it all . . . seems . . . *uncountable* . . . the varying hues.
This little bird alone had a thousand colors. And now

Its mate will die. That is what the man told me.
As one finch goes, so goes the other. As one garden,
The others follow. One crow, then a thousand.
A thousand days to the heart's desire. A thousand

Hands to its ruin. And the sounds I make, they, too,
Are a thousand. I flap my arms and call in the dark
To the bird I hated. While the rain falls faster
And the moon comes up like a pail of poison. And the voice

Of the bog grows louder and louder. Do you hear
The singing?... *O foolish woman. O foolish woman,*
What were you thinking? Which of your thoughts
Was so important? Put down your spade. Leave off

Your weeping. The rain will keep falling. The crows
Will keep flying. Sit on the ground and wait. Sit
On the ground and wait. Perhaps the bird you planted
Beneath the pear tree . . . will become . . . another pear tree.

Petition

These are the long weeks. The weeks
Of waiting. Let them be
Longer. Let the days smolder
Like the peat slung
In plastic sacks by the greenhouse
And let the seedlings not rush
Into growth but climb the air slowly
As if it were a ladder,
One small foot at a time.
Let the fetid smell of bone meal
Be the body unlocking
As the river does, slowing to a hazy laze
That pulls the boaters in
And makes the fish rise up. And
As the wide-wheeled yellow tractors
Roll along the highway,
Stalling traffic in their wakes,
And the dust from the playing fields
Settles over us like pollen,
Like the balls dropping softly
Into our mitts, let
The willow's love of water—
Its dark and beaded rain—
Be the only storm we long for.

Botticelli's St. Sebastian

I have seen a robin cock his head so,
Listening for the change in weather,
Feeling in the field's pale grass turning paler
The moment of his own departure.
I have seen the bird throw his whole body
In the air, and go, the small bird go,
And the bared ground at once lose heart,
As if taken by a sudden grippe.

And I have seen blond wood, fine-grained
As this stripped flesh, seen the long
Boards of strong wood—when bound fast
And bitten by the drill—spew up phrases
As curled and extravagant as Sebastian's gaze,
The way the lover does at consummation,
Lost to himself and to the world, but still
Safely shaded by the tree he rose from.

I have seen, I have seen the lake's heart
When the rain comes through, when the water's
Dark flesh is driven, *I have seen* the heart
Move like a doe through the woods, move
Like a stunned doe, deeper and deeper,
Through trees that turn and close behind her,
The way water closes over a dropped stone,
Or a torn limb, or a lasting wound....

O, the forgotten traveller!

All Wild Animals Were Once Called Deer

Some truck was gunning the night before up Pippin Hill's steep
    grade
And the doe was thrown wide. This happened five years ago now,
Or six. She must have come out of the woods by Simpson's red
    trailer—

The one that looks like a faded train car—and the driver
Did not see her. His brakes no good. Or perhaps she hit the truck.
That happens, too. A figure swims up from nowhere, a flying figure

That seems to be made of nothing more than moonlight, or vapor,
Until it slams its face, solid as stone, against the glass.
And maybe when this happens the driver gets out. Maybe not.

Strange about the kills we get without intending them.
Because we are pointed in the direction of something.
Because we are distracted at just the right moment, or the wrong.

We were waiting for the school bus. It was early, but not yet light.
We watched the darkness draining off like the last residue
Of water from a tub. And we didn't speak, because that was our way.

High up a plane droned, drone of the cold, and behind us the flag
In front of the Bank of Hope's branch trailer snapped and
    popped in the wind.
It sounded like a boy whipping a wet towel against a thigh

Or like the stiff beating of a swan's wings as it takes off
From the lake, a flat drumming sound, the sound of something
Being pounded until it softens, and then—as the wind lowered

And the flag ran out wide—a second sound, the sound of
    running fire.
And there was the scraping, too, the sad knife-against-skin scraping
Of the acres of field corn strung out in straggling rows

Around the branch trailer that had been, the winter before, our
    town's claim to fame
When, in the space of two weeks, it was successfully robbed twice.
The same man did it both times, in the same manner.

He had a black hood and a gun, and he was so polite
That the embarrassed teller couldn't hide her smile when he
    showed up again.
They didn't think it could happen twice. But sometimes it does.

Strange about that. Lightning strikes and strikes again.
My piano teacher watched her husband, who had been struck as
    a boy,
Fall for good, years later, when he was hit again.

He was walking across a cut cornfield toward her, stepping over
The dead stalks, holding the bag of nails he'd picked up at the
    hardware store
Out like a bouquet. It was drizzling so he had his umbrella up.

There was no thunder, nothing to be afraid of.
And then a single bolt from nowhere, and for a moment the man
Was doing a little dance in a movie, a jig, three steps or four,

Before he dropped like a cloth, or a felled bird.
This happened twenty years ago now, but my teacher keeps
Telling me the story. She hums while she plays. And we were
    humming

That morning by the bus stop. A song about boys and war.
And the thing about the doe was this. She looked alive.
As anything will in the half light. As even lawn statues will.

I was going to say as even children playing a game of statues will,
But of course they *are* alive. Though sometimes
A person pretending to be a statue seems farther gone in death

Than a statue does. Or to put it another way,
Death seems to be the living thing, the thing
That looks out through the eyes. Strange about that....

We stared at the doe for a long time and I thought about the way
A hunter slits a deer's belly. I've watched this many times.
And the motion is a deft one. It is the same motion the swan uses

When he knifes the children down by his pond on Wasigan road.
They put out a hand. And quick as lit grease, the swan's
Boneless neck snakes around in a sideways circle, driving

The bill hard toward the softest spot.... All those songs
We sing about swans, but they are mean. And up close, often ugly.
That old Wasigan bird is a smelly, moth-eaten thing,

His wings stained yellow as if he chewed tobacco,
His upper bill broken from his foul-tempered strikes.
And he is awkward, too, out of the water. Broken-billed and gaited.

When he grapples down the steep slope, wheezing and spitting,
He looks like some old man recovering from hip surgery,
Slowly slapping down one cursed flat foot, then the next.

But the thing about the swan is this. The swan is made for the
        water.
You can't judge him out of it. He's made for the chapter
In the rushes. He's like one of those small planes my brother flies.

Ridiculous things. Something a boy dreams up late at night
While he stares at the stars. Something a child draws.
I've watched my brother take off a thousand times, and it's always

The same. The engine spits and dies, spits and catches—
A spurting match—and the machine shakes and shakes as if it
        were
Stuck together with glue and wound up with a rubber band.

It shimmies the whole way down the strip, past the pond,
Past the wind bagging the goosenecked wind sock, past the banks
Of bright red and blue planes. And as it climbs slowly

Into the air, wobbling from side to side, cautious as a rock climber,
Putting one hand forward then the next, not even looking
At the high spot above the tree line that is the question,

It seems that nothing will keep it up, not a wish, not a dare,
Not the proffered flowers of our held breath. It seems
As if the plane is a prey the hunter has lined up in his sights,

His finger pressing against the cold metal, the taste of blood
On his tongue . . . but then, just before the sky
Goes black, at the dizzying height of our dismay,

The climber's frail hand reaches up and grasps the highest rock,
Hauling with a last shudder, the body over,
The gun lowers, and perfectly poised now, high above

The dark pines, the plane is home free. It owns it all, *all*.
My brother looks down and counts his possessions,
Strip and grass, the child's cemetery the black tombstones

Of the cedars make on the grassy hill, the wind-scrubbed
Face of the pond, the swan's white stone....
In thirty years, roughly, we will all be dead.... That is one thing...

And you can't judge the swan out of the water.... That is another.
The swan is mean and ugly, stupid as stone,
But when it finally makes its way down the slope, over rocks

And weeds, through the razory grasses of the muddy shallows,
The water fanning out in loose circles around it
And then stilling, when it finally reaches the deepest spot

And raises in slow motion its perfectly articulated wings,
Wings of smoke, wings of air, then everything changes.
Out of the shallows the lovers emerge, sword and flame,

And over the pond's lone island the willow spills its canopy,
A shifting feast of gold and green, a spell of lethal beauty.
O bird of moonlight. O bird of wish. O sound rising

Like an echo from the water. Grief sound. Sound of the horn.
The same ghostly sound the deer makes when it runs
Through the woods at night, white lightning through the trees,

Through the coldest moments, when it feels as if the earth
Will never again grow warm, lover running toward lover,
The branches tearing back, the mouth and eyes wide,

The heart flying into the arms of the one that will kill her.

IV

Three Cows and the Moon

We were playing baseball on the hill by the cow field.
It was late March. The trees were getting dark.
The moon was coming up. We couldn't see it yet.

It came up almost like a sound behind the stand
Of scrub trees to the South. And it would be full.
I knew this because I hadn't slept for two nights.

The bull and the two heifers had their heads stuck
Between the fence slats so they could watch us. We were
Throwing a tennis ball and hitting it with a stick.

My son was wearing one of those flimsy plastic jackets.
It had a broken zipper and it was yellow,
The color the moon would be later. The color

Also of my daughter's hair, which was uncombed.
Uncombed or not she is always beautiful.
It's the funny laugh and those long legs.

But she can't catch. She is awkward. She kept
Dropping the ball and she couldn't do anything
With the stick that my son swung like a soldier.

It was an old branch with the bark peeled off.
I picked it up from the poplar that was felled
During the hurricane. For two years the tree bloomed

Where it lay, flat out on the ground. It didn't
Know it was dead. It was like a garden
Someone planted and then abandoned. A pitiful thing,

The trunk split clean in two and the fallen branches
Still blooming.... It gets cold fast in March
And dark. The three of us were playing ball. And dusk

Was coming out of the ground. I heard a poet say this.
That darkness doesn't come down but rises up.
And he was right. It gets the ankles first. It circles

The ankles like flood water gradually filling
The basement of a house. Dark water full
Of unnameable things. It circles the thin trunks

Of the trees, a black current, soft as the current
Of fear that almost always runs through me,
Or the scent of a bruised flower eddying outward....

Our old cocker was playing, too, yapping in his god-awful
Way, running back and forth and stealing the ball.
We don't shave him so his mane was flying.

We'd chase him and tackle him to get the ball back,
Smearing our faces with dirt and grass,
And we didn't notice when the cows started playing

Their own game. It might have been when the moon
First came up behind the trees: it was huge
And close, a blurred ruddy color. The color of a body

Just stepping from a bath. Or a body pulled
From icy water. When I was a child we used to swim
In the Little Pigeon River at just this time

Of year when the ice was still floating in it.
We could stay in the water for only a minute.
We'd hold our breath and jump and when

We were hauled out seconds later our skin was red,
Our skin was hot, even in the cold air.
The moon was like that. Or like a child's cheek

Struck by a parent—no, because it didn't hurt—
And the cows were playing their game. They'd come
Together with their flat noses touching, and then

Very slowly they'd start turning like a wheel.
The cow field is pitched steeply to the East
And to the West. The runoff from both directions

Leaves a black stain down the middle of the field
And even in hot times a trickle of water.
The cows drink from it, though it's probably not clean

Because the septic bleeds into it. The turning
Was difficult because of the field's steep pitch
But the wheel kept moving. It moved faster and faster

In ragged circles. Always clockwise. Three
Thick-legged bodies, matted with dung and grass,
Held together as if by invisible ropes. Up and down

The field, snorting and thumping, the laboring
Wheel would move. As if to cover all the ground,
As if to break up the hard ground for planting,

And then all at once the wheel would shatter,
The way a wooden wheel shatters when it strikes rock,
Spokes flying off in all directions. The cows

Would stagger to their corners, shaking their heads.
And then after awhile they'd make another circle.
Sometimes our hearts are stone. Sometimes not.

When the moon came up ruddy, the sky around it
Was blue, though the field was very dark.
And the top of the sky was dark. The sky

On the opposite hill to the North was white,
It was white, but also very dark. It gets
Dark faster on the hill because of the trees.

The trees get bigger at night and shut out the light.
The darkness seems to leak out of them. It leaks
Out of the ground and out of the trees, and it

Is as beautiful and sharp-edged as the leaves
Of the mandrake flooding the swale at the hill's base.
The dark was cold. Our shoulders were warm.

But the dark was cold. And it was getting harder to see.
But still the cows kept turning. There was the low
Cry of winter birds left back like dumb children

Kept behind in school. And the bats were whistling
Around us, whistling and shuttling, as the moon
Came up over the trees, smaller and clearer now.

It looked like a pale bird moving through the air
That smelled of old batteries, a ghost bird
Beating its wings above the ghost light of the bull's horns

Rising and falling through the field's dark rooms.
My son would swing the peeled stick back and forth,
Back and forth, as if he were swinging a scythe,

The rhythmic flash of the yellow wood writing and erasing
Faint messages on the dark in answer to those
Sent out by the slow dance of the bull's horns.

Once there was a sacrifice for sin. And it
Was a bull like this one. A first born.
Once there was a garden of god. And we were in it.

I raised the bull and he had a man's face.
His mother died right after he was born in the field
Back of the house in the town of Harmony

Where we used to live. She dropped him by the creek,
And then walked off and lay down to die.
Maybe she didn't want him to see her. She made

A terrible sound. Like a ship that was going down.
A foghorn sound. It was late morning and I was sleeping.
I didn't want to get up. I didn't know what

The sound was. It kept breaking into my dream,
Which was about a window that had been shattered
By rocks. The window was black and large, and as it

Opened wider and wider it became the mouth of a lion,
Out of which something issued, something small,
Maybe some bees, or maybe the song of a child.

By the time I went to find the sound it was too late.
The heifer died of milk fever. The other
Cows stood off staring. They have stupid eyes.

And I took the bull so he wouldn't be made into veal.
I bought the bull who had never seen his mother
And tied him to a stick and fed him with buckets

Of a watery white solution. And he grew bigger.
And his face was human. You can take my word for it.
There are four angels standing at the four corners of the earth.

The sky turns light all over just before it blacks out,
And the moon gets clearer and clearer as it
Gets smaller. The dark comes up and then it comes down

All at once in a black rain. We were losing
Our faces. There was no color now to the sky
And the cows kept moving. The bull had a human face.

And there was a hum starting up. Not the moon,
Though that might have been making a sound.
Not the bats nor the softening ground

The cows were working. But there was something.
Maybe the high whine of the cold working in.
Or maybe there were wings. We were watching now

And not playing. Watching the heavy circles
We could barely see move over the wet field
And we were listening. Maybe there were wings.

Maybe the cows had wings under their legs.
Or arms. Maybe they had arms with hands
Under their wings. Maybe the dark was winged.

The bull had no mother and so I raised him.
He had a human face. And the wheels moved
Over the field. The spirit was in the wheels

And we were watching though we were going blind.
We were watching as if the wheels were a cart
And we'd ride it through to its destination.

And then we started moving again. Throwing the ball
That we could no longer see. The yellow
Of the ball, the yellow of the horns, the yellow

Of the dog tearing back and forth between us
All blacked out now. Our skin was alive
And we were getting hot while the sky got colder

And the moon turned to salt, turned bright and fine
As salt or oil, a river of oil sliding by.
There was one poplar in the field and sometimes

We'd grope for it, as if for safety. We'd
Put our arms around the rough bark and press our faces
Close. The poplar held itself perfectly still

Like a seer, the top leaves visible against the sky.
But then the game would pull us back. We fell
Toward the sounds of each other. The shapes

Of each other. Whatever we were without bodies.
We were playing blind and the moon was rising.
The spirit was in the wheels. And there were eyes

All around. No movement in the poplar. The sound
Of flesh being punched. Of fur being torn.
The air all dizzy and kicked-up. A holy insect

Buzz in the air. The high whining buzz of the cold
Catching fire. The smell of frozen manure
And dead flies. Of old grass and new grass. The sound

Of something small crying. There were wheels
All around. And the spirit was in the wheels.
And the children's skin pricked by cold

Smelled of bleeding. And blood tastes of cooked
Flowers. And the ball dropped as if into water.
And the last sound was the sound of the cows stopping

In the final circle. And it was quiet then.
And we were looking up. Light flooding a room.
The four corners of the night all staked out.

The moon high up and small. High up and small.
Perfect like a flower. Or an oracle. Something
Completely understood. But unspeakable.

The Orchard

for Maria

I

Black Swan

I told the boy I found him under a bush.
What was the harm? I told him he was sleeping
And that a black swan slept beside him,
The swan's feathers hot, the scent of the hot feathers
And of the bush's hot white flowers
As rank and sweet as the stewed milk of a goat.
The bush was in a strange garden, a place
So old it seemed to exist outside of time.
In one spot, great stone steps leading nowhere.
In another, statues of horsemen posting giant stone horses
Along a high wall. And here, were triangular beds
Of flowers flush with red flowers. And there,
Circular beds flush with white. And in every bush
And bed flew small birds and the cries of small birds.
I told the boy I looked for him a long time
And when I found him I watched him sleeping,
His arm around the swan's moist neck,
The swan's head tucked fast behind the boy's back,
The feathered breast and the bare breast breathing as one,
And then very swiftly and without making a sound,
So that I would not wake the sleeping bird,
I picked the boy up and slipped him into my belly,
The way one might slip something stolen
Into a purse. And brought him here....
And so it was. And so it was. A child with skin
So white it was not like the skin of a boy at all,
But like the skin of a newborn rabbit, or like the skin
Of a lily, pulseless and thin. And a giant bird
With burning feathers. And beyond them both
A pond of incredible blackness, overarched
With ancient trees and patterned with shifting shades,
The small wind in the branches making a sound
Like the knocking of a thousand wooden bells....
Things of such beauty. But still I might
Have forgotten, had not the boy, who stands now

To my waist, his hair a cap of shining feathers,
Come to me today weeping because some older boys
Had taunted him and torn his new coat,
Had he not, when I bent my head to his head,
Said softly, but with great anger, "I wish I had never
Been born. I wish I were back under the bush,"
Which made the old garden rise up again,
Shadowed and more strange. Small birds
Running fast and the grapple of chill coming on.
There was the pond, half-circled with trees. And there
The flowerless bush. But there was no swan.
There was no black swan. And beneath
The sound of the wind, I could hear, dark and low,
The giant stone hooves of the horses,
Striking and striking the hardening ground.

Blessed Is the Field

In the late heat the snakeroot and goldenrod run high,
White and gold, the steaming flowers, green and gold,
The acid-bitten leaves....It is good to say first

An invocation. Though the words do not always
Seem to work. Still, one must try. Bow your head.
Cross your arms. Say: *Blessed is the day. And the one*

Who destroys the day. Blessed is this ring of fire
*In which we live....*How bitter the burning leaves.
How bitter and sweet. How bitter and sweet the sound

Of the single gold and black insect repeating
Its two lonely notes. The insect's song both magnifies
The field and casts a shadow over it, the way

A doorbell ringing through an abandoned house
Makes the falling rooms, papered with lilies and roses
And two-headed goats, seem larger and more ghostly.

The high grasses spill their seed. It is hard to know
The right way in or out. But here, you can have
Which flower you like, though there are not many left,

Lady's thumb in the gravel by the wood's fringe
And on the shale spit beneath the black walnut that houses
The crow, the peculiar cat's-paw, sweet everlasting,

Unbearably soft. Do not mind the crow's bark.
He is fierce and solitary, but he will let us pass,
Patron of the lost and broken-spirited. Behind him

In the quarter ring of sumacs, flagged like circus tents,
The deer I follow, and that even now are watching us,
Sleep at night their restless sleep. I find their droppings

In the morning. And here at my feet is the self-heal,
Humblest of flowers, bloomless but still intact. I ate
Some whole once and did not get well but it may strike

Your fancy. The smell of burning rubber is from
A rabbit carcass the dog dragged into the ravine.
And the smell of lemon is the snakeroot I am crushing

Between my thumb and forefinger....There could be
Beneath this field an underground river full
Of sweet liquid. A dowser might find it with his witching

Wand and his prayers. Some prayers can move
Even the stubborn dirt....Do you hear? The bird
I have never seen is back. Each day at this time

He takes up his ominous clucking, fretting like a baby,
Lonely sweetling. It is hard to know the right way
In or out. But look, the goldenrod is the color

Of beaten skin. Say: *Blessed are those who stand still
In their confusion. Blessed is the field as it burns.*

The Garden of the Trumpet Tree

Someone stuck an apple in the stone head's open mouth. A grave insult. But I did not take it out. Maybe a boy did it, running through the gardens at night, his pockets full of fruit. Or maybe it was a ghost bored with its lot. It does not matter. Today I stood for the first time before the bodiless head and the strange flowering tree it guards. I tried not to laugh. The head on its post stood no taller than I. The head that had bullied me for so long, the great stone head that only the darkness had been able to silence, bagging it each night with a soft cloth sack, the way the heads of those to be hanged are bagged, made no sound. I tried not to think: This is your just dessert: Pillar of pride, pilloried. I touched with both hands the eyes of the head the way a blind person might. They were huge and swollen like the eyes of the deaf composer, or the eyes of the mad poet who left his wife alone while he spent his days in paradise. I touched with one finger the warm fruit. Against the pale cast of the stone the apple shone uncommonly bright, and behind it the thousand and thousand blossoms of the trumpet tree shone uncommonly bright. The fruit and the blossoms were the same scarlet color, and I could see for the first time in the yellow morning light the curious tree for what it was. Not a tree in flower, as I had so long thought, but a flowerless tree coupled with a blossoming trumpet vine. The vine had grown snakelike up and around the trunk, and it had grown so large it had half-strangled the small tree, crawling over every branch and shoot, until the vine and the tree were almost indistinguishable, green flesh and charred wood, flowers and rot, a new creation, a trumpet tree, tree out of time, the smoldering center of some medieval dream. The flowers swam forward in the light, each scarlet bloom so intricate and unlikely—downswung, fluted, narrower than the narrowest piping, forked with yellow silk—it looked as if it had been sewn by hand, the whole improbable tree looked as if it had been worked with impossible patience by a woman's pale hands. Bees stumbled in and out, shaking the flowers. From nowhere a hummingbird appeared, iridescent, green, flipping its shining tail, a creature more fish than bird, more insect than fish, spinning and sipping. To nowhere it returned. The garden stood perfectly still.

And for a moment in that garden it seemed as if sound and silence were the same thing, for a moment it seemed as if the thousand and thousand tiny trumpets were blowing a thousand and thousand shining notes, blown glass notes, the liquid substance of the air itself, glass and fire, the morning flushed to perfect fullness. I stood for a long time, breathing in the strange perfume of those scentless flowers. I thought of how the crow would come in an hour or two and plant his dusty feet on the carved head and pluck the fruit apart, piece by sweetened piece. I looked at the blossoming tree. I looked at the stone head. I touched the warm fruit. And I took the apple out. There was no sound. It was like closing the eyes of the dead.

Blacklegs

The sheep has nipples, the boy said,
And fur all around. The sheep
Has black legs, his name is Blacklegs,
And a cry like breaking glass.
The glass is broken. The glass
Is broken, and the milk falls down.

The bee has a suffering softness,
The boy said, a ring of fur,
Like a ring of fire. He burns
The flowers he enters, the way
The rain burns the grass. The bee
Has six legs, six strong legs,
And when he flies, the legs
Whistle like a blade of grass
Brought to the lips and blown.

The boy said, The horse runs hard
As sorrow, or a storm, or a man
With a stolen purse in his shirt.
The horse's legs are a hundred
Or more, too many to count,
And he holds a moon white as fleece
In his mouth, cups it like water
So it will not spill out.

And the boy said this. I am a boy
And a man. My legs are two,
And they shine black as the arrows
That drop down on my throat
And my chest to draw out the blood
The bright animals feed on,
Those with wings, those without,

The ghosts of the heart—whose
Hunger is a dress for my song.

The Wolf

The diseased dog lowered her head as I came close, as if to make
Of her head a shadow, something the next few hours
Would erase, swiftly, something of no account. And what came
To mind was the she-wolf, beneath the wild fig, nursing
The boys who would build what amounted to a lasting city
On this earth. And it was as if, on that hot afternoon, I was standing
Not in the empty aisle between the gardens, that have been
Reduced to nothing except the most rudimentary plants
And the eroding outlines of brick walls and barren terraces,
But in the white light of a studio, in which a sculptor,
Working from the only model he has, a poor dog, is carving
Out of the blackest of black stones a female wolf with two rows
Of triangular tits, which look like the twin rows of cedars the dog
Swam through and from which two boys are suspended,
Fat-thighed and fated. And the truth is both dog and wolf
Are ancient, for the sick dog comes not from the garden
But from another time, in another city, a sabbath day, foreign,
The street completely empty, the day shapely around me,
The houses, the walks, all ordered and white; and then
Out of the ordered whiteness proceeds a thing of great disorder,
A shape from the world of shadows, something to drive
Away. But I did not drive her away, though I could do
Nothing for her. And now I would make of her something
Better than she could make of herself—though the wolf
Is only remembered in her prime, and not as she must
Have been years later, after all that would pass had passed.

Brightness from the North

Bright shapes in the dark garden, the gardenless stretch
Of old yard, sweetened now by the half-light
As if by burning flowers. Overture. First gesture.
But not even that, the pause before the gesture,
The window frame composing the space, so it
Seems as if time has stopped, as if this half-dark,
This winter grass, plated with frost, these unseen
Silent birds might stay forever. It seems as if
This might be what forever is, the presence of time
Overriding the body of time, the fullness of time
Not a moment but a being, watchful and unguarded,
Unguarded and gravely watched this garden—
The black fir with its long aristocratic broken branches,
The cluster of three tiny tipped arborvitae
Damp as sea sponges, the ghostly sycamore shedding
Its skin, and the sweet row of yews along the walk
Into which people throw their glittering trash....
And who, when the light rises, will come up the walk?
We can say no one will come—the day will be empty
Because you are no longer in it. We can say
The things of the day do not fill it. We can say
The eye is not filled by seeing. Nor silenced
By blinding. We can say, we can say your body
Appeared on the table, and swiftly disappeared—
Do not let the sun go down on the dead figure,
Do not fix the dead figure in mind, the false face,
Remember as you should remember, by heart,
In the garden's dark chamber—and the ground
Took the body, and the ground was pleased.
And oh, now, the busy light comes too quickly,
The gray grass unrolling, birds mewling in the trees,
Dawn raising the walls of day, the rooms we live in,
All our murals, pictures of gardens and presiding deities,
Things painted on plaster to keep the dying company,
A toppled jar, a narrow bird, an ornamental tree

With no name, and crouched beneath the stone table,
The lion with four heads, who looks this morning
As he rises from the shadows, like the creature
Who carries on his back the flat and shining earth.

Sheep Child

I wanted a child. What then, this? The sheep
Stands dumb behind the fence. Stands dumb.
Demanding what? Pity? Affection? A breast full
Of milk? He's up to his neck in his filthy fur.
Honey to the flies. Rancid honey. Each coarse
Curl dipped in it. The flies reeling. A sullen
Moment....Oh, Sheep, Sheep, this is my undoing,
That you have a thought and I would read it. I would
Put my head up to your smelly head and watch
The pretty pictures sliding past: Look! there goes
The flowerless larch, lurching over the ground
Like a skiff. And that black thing spinning in the dung
Is a truck tire stuffed with hay. And here, now,
Down from the elm, comes the crow, bully bird
Beating and beating the air with his wide wings,
As if calling the field to order....There is no order.
What day of the week is this? Wash day?
Bake day? What hour of what day?....Behind you,
Flanked by steely thistle, stands the old goat,
Contemptuous, uninterested, gnawing on the last
Of a Sunday dress; and "I had a goat once,"
The thought that comes to me, "I had a small
Black goat, who pounded his head against a tree
Until he was dead. His name was Bumblebee...."
Well, night is coming on. No, it is dead afternoon.
But there is something about night in this cloud-
Shadowed field. Perhaps the stars are shifting
Behind the veil of day? Perhaps. Perhaps....Oh,
I would turn this pretty. You see the cowbirds
Riding the boney heifer by the overturned bathtub?
The birds are dung-colored, yes, but when
They rise and swim together they change color,
Brown to red, the way the light changes color
At dusk. And, yes, the swans by the back fence
Are foul-tempered and mean as sin, but look

How their necks wave about now like the stems
Of lilies in the wind....lilies blowing in the wind....
The goat snorts and turns his back. He has
Swallowed the last of the dress....Oh, Sheep, Sheep,
This is my undoing, that you have a thought
And I *can* read it. Dear Monstrous Child, I would
Nurse you if I could. But you are far too large,
And I am far too old for such foolishness.

⁓

The South Gate

Light cups the breasts of the lion. Who remains
Unbothered. Stone lion. Stained breasts suddenly
Full of milk. And no one to feed on them. No one
To catch the warm liquid as it falls, sweet and fast,
To the ground. Moss on the lion's legs. Moss
Bloodying her small feet. Moss darkening the fruit trees
Dressed now in the snow that raises the ghosts
Of dead flowers: a visible shadow: a touchable shadow:
Flesh of water and ash. Like the sun, the lion
Is a two-faced creature. One face looks forward.
The other back. One grins. The other grimaces.
Her four eyes are old. *Oh, it is a far, far country*
The lion comes from. A place almost unimaginable,
So dull are we. The lion herself almost unimaginable,
Even with her curious form stationed above us.
Wide the arms of the roses nailed to the wall below her.
Dry the weeds. White the snow dressing the ground
And then dressing it no more. Low the sound
Where no sound should be. Deep in the heart of the ground.
The lion will bear a child. How can a stone lion
Bear a living child? Because still in the corner
Of her deformed head a dream lodges. Her breasts
Produce milk. The sweet milk falls to the ground.
The ground is a flock of dead birds. The wind
Rises. The fed offspring stirs. Soon he will stagger
From burial. Terrible. Wrapped in soiled cloth.
Stinking. Lion flesh and bird flesh and man flesh.
We would prefer this were a trick. Strings
And ropes. But it is not. The lion will grow large.
The greenness is his hunger. His hunger will overtake
The ground and soon devour even the mother.
She will sleep in his belly. He will rock her softly.

Sheet Music

If you cannot trust the dog, the faithful one?
And is this anyway a dog? The shadows move,
Dog and dog, two lanky figures, three, sniffing
The garden's charred terrain, the darkening grass

The bleeding beds of flowers, sniffing the stones
And lunging at the rabbits that spring from the beds,
Wet creatures, mad with haste, mad and wet
And white as the half-hearted moon that stepped

Behind the clouds and has not come back....The rain
Fell hard, and now the mist rises, consolidates, disperses,
That thought, this, your face, mine, the shapes
Complicating the air around the abandoned birdhouse,

Big as a summer hotel, thirty rooms
For thirty birds, thirty perches from which to sing.
Such is the moon when it is full. A giant birdhouse
Tilted high on a steel pole, a pale blue box

Full of the shredded sheet music of long-dead birds....
The dogs move fast. How will I follow? And which one?
They are not in agreement. If the dog cannot be trusted,
Then what? The foot? But the foot is blind, the grass

Cold through the thin socks, the instep bared like a neck.
And now the flowers rise. The mums and asters,
The tall gladioli knocked back as the rain creeps up
In the mist, and the mist thickens and moves about me

Like a band of low-bred mummers, dripping scent,
Pulling my hair, my arms, trying to distract me,
But still I hear it, the dark sound that begins at the edge
Of the mind, at the far edge of the uncut field

Beyond the garden—a low braying, donkey
Or wolf, a low insistent moan. If I whistle
Will the dogs come? Can I gather their trailing leashes
And hold them in my hand? They cannot be held.

How pale the paint of the birdhouse. How ghastly pale
The sound of the cry coming closer....If I forsake
The dogs?....If I forsake the mummers?....If I step
Like a fool into the glassy outer darkness?....*O self*....

II

The Satyr's Heart

Now I rest my head on the satyr's carved chest,
The hollow where the heart would have been, if sandstone
Had a heart, if a headless goat man could have a heart.
His neck rises to a dull point, points upward
To something long gone, elusive, and at his feet
The small flowers swarm, earnest and sweet, a clamor
Of white, a clamor of blue, and black the sweating soil
They breed in....If I sit without moving, how quickly
Things change, birds turning tricks in the trees,
Colorless birds and those with color, the wind fingering
The twigs, and the furred creatures doing whatever
Furred creatures do. So, and so. There is the smell of fruit
And the smell of wet coins. There is the sound of a bird
Crying, and the sound of water that does not move....
If I pick the dead iris? If I wave it above me
Like a flag, a blazoned flag? My fanfare? Little fare
With which I buy my way, making things brave?
No, that is not it. Uncovering what is brave. The way
Now I bend over and with my foot turn up a stone,
And there they are: the armies of pale creatures who
Without cease or doubt sew the sweet sad earth.

Two Boys

The boy drowned in the bog. Not a pretty sight.
Not a pretty end. And it no accident. And him
A stranger in town. Rank the berries in the bushes.
And mute the birds. Not like birds at all.
And afternoon come too soon, and then
Come no longer....*What is the life of a man?*
Or one not even a man? Has it the shape of a bird?
Or a dog? Or an insect dressed in robes of white
And robes of green? And if a life takes its own life?
If a man takes from himself a man? Or a bird
From a bird? Or a dog from a dog? What is
That like? Birds may fall faster than thought,
But a dog is no lamb, it will not easily strangle—
Greenness like fire will not swiftly stamp out....
The boy drowned in the bog. He came from
A long way off to lie down in such sickly water.
Not like water at all. Poor and brown. Not one
Fish in it, not one blind fish. There would
Have been a better time. Or place. Better.
But fate, what is it? Who met the boy
By daylight? And how did he know him? By
What seal on the forehead? Talon or star?
Who said, *Thus far shall you come and no
Farther?* This circle of beaten trees. This ring
Of dark water. Who raised the curtain?
Who prompted the action? Who conceived
It in the first place? What prophet in what
Dark room? Did he weep when he wrote
Down the words? Did he watch till the end,
Or did he leave that for others? And what
Did the flesh smell like when the prophecy
Was sealed? A burned flower? Or ripened fruit?
What sang in the trees before the boy
Lay down or after? A child? Or the light?
Or nothing. Just a bird. Nothing. And then

Night coming on. And morning coming after....
And so we have a story. But still the story
Does not end. Green the cress by the water.
Green the insect's wing. Now the living boy
Finds the dead one. A gift for early rising.
A worm for the bird. The boy did not know
What he saw. He thought the dead boy
Must be something other. Flesh of a lily.
Or a fallen hat. He thought what he thought.
And then he thought no longer. The wind
At once loud in the trees. The birds loud.
The boy had wanted a brother. But this
Was not what he meant. Had he said
The wrong words? *Did words have such power?*
And then he saw what he saw, and he knew
From this day forward, for better or worse,
For worse or better, he would carry this shadow
Of no certain shape—now a lamb, now a bird,
Now a boy dressed as a woman—from here
To there, and there to here. Back to this bog
Or another. This wood or another. Berries
Bright or rank. Water foul or pure. Birds loud
In the trees. Or still. And softer than fleece,
Softer than grass, it already raining.

Rose of Sharon

I loved the rose of Sharon. I would have loved it
For its name alone. I loved its fleshy blossoms.
How fat they were. How fast they fell. How the doves,
Mean as spit, fought the finches and the sparrows
For the golden seed I spilled beneath the bush.
How I threw seed just to watch the birds fight.
And the blossoms fallen were like watered silk
Loosely bound. And the blossoms budding
Were like the dog's bright penis first emerging
From its hairy sheath. And the blossoms opened wide
Were like the warm air above the pool of Siloam.
Tree of breath. Pink flowers floating on water.
The flushed blossoms themselves like water.
Rising. Falling. The wind kicking up skeins
Of scented foam. High-kicking waves. Or laughing
Dancers. O silly thoughts. But a great sweetness....
And then it was over. An ice storm felled the tree.
With a clean cut, as if with a hatchet. One year
A whole flock of birds. One year a crop of fruit
That melted on the tongue, a kind of manna, light
As honey, just enough to sustain one. And then nothing.
The breasts gone dry. The window opening onto
Bare grass. The small birds on the wire waiting
For the seed I do not throw. *Pride of my heart,*
Rose of Sharon. *Pool of scented breath.* Rose
Of Sharon. How inflated my sorrow. But the tree
Itself was inflated. A perpetual feast. A perpetual
Snowfall of warm confetti....And now I worry.
Did the bush fear the ice? Did it know of the ice's
Black designs? Did its featherweight nature darken
Just before it was felled? Was it capable of darkening?

⤚

Windfall

There is a wretched pond in the woods. It lies at the north end of a piece of land owned by a man who was taken to an institution years ago. He was a strange man. I only spoke to him once. You can still find statues of women and stone gods he set up in dark corners of the woods, and sometimes you can find flowers that have survived the collapse of the hidden gardens he planted. Once I found a flower that looked like a human brain growing near a fence, and it took my breath away. And once I found, among some weeds, a lily white as snow....No one tends the land now. The fences have fallen and the deer grown thick, and the pond lies black, the water slowly thickening, the banks tangled with weeds and grasses. But the pond was very old even when I first came upon it. Through the trees I saw the dark water steaming, and smelled something sweet rotting, and then as I got closer, I saw in the dark water shapes, and the shapes were golden, and I thought, without really thinking, that I was looking at the reflections of leaves or of fallen fruit, though there were no fruit trees near the pond and it was not the season for fruit. And then I saw that the shapes were moving, and I thought they moved because I was moving, but when I stood still, still they moved. And still I had trouble seeing. Though the shapes took on weight and muscle and definite form, it took my mind a long time to accept what I saw. The pond was full of ornamental carp, and they were large, larger than the carp I have seen in museum pools, large as trumpets, and so gold they were almost yellow. In circles, wide and small, the plated fish moved, and there were so many of them they could not be counted, though for a long time I tried to count them. And I thought of the man who owned the land standing where I stood. I thought of how years ago in a fit of madness or high faith he must have planted the fish in the pond, and then forgotten them, or been taken from them, but still the fish had grown and still they thrived, until they were many, and their bodies were fast and bright as brass knuckles or cockscombs. I tore pieces of my bread and threw them at the carp, and the carp leaped, as I have not seen carp do before, and they fought each other for the bread, and they were not like fish but like gulls or wolves, biting and leaping. Again and again, I threw the bread. Again and again, the fish leaped and wrestled. And below them, below the leaping fish, near the bottom of the pond, something slowly circled, a giant form that never rose to the bait and never came fully into view, but moved patiently in and out of the murky shadows, out and in. I watched that form, and after the bread was gone and after the golden fish had again grown quiet, my mind at last constructed a shape for it, and I saw for the space of one moment or two with perfect clarity, as if I held the heavy creature in my hands, the tarnished body of an ancient carp. A thing both fragrant and foul. A lily and a man's brain bound together in one body. And then the fish was gone. He turned and the shadows closed around him. The water grew blacker, and the steam rose from it, and the golden carp held still, still uncountable. And softly they burned, themselves like flowers, or like fruit blown down in an abandoned garden.

Midwinter

And again, at dusk, I find the madwoman,
Crouched on the stone bridge by the cornfields,
Feeding corn to the fish. Though there are no fish

In the river. The river is dead or nearly so,
The water gray as stolen sleep or spoiled sheets.
The woman looks sheepish. But not like a sheep.

Her skin is sallow. Her hair uncombed. Her coat
Unravelling at wrist and hem. The coat's woven cloth
Has faded from overwashing and it is the same color

As the haze the fields exude in the morning or sometimes
At dusk, a foggy lavender mist that smells of tin
And fresh blood and of the slender green sticks we burn

When we strip back the garden in the first warm weather....
Not like a sheep. More like a child who has gotten
The sum wrong, but stubbornly knows the sum

Doesn't matter as much as one thinks....Corn cobs
Drop into the poisoned water. The ghostly cobs
Float and turn like boats made from paper. And the day

Grows colder....When the woman speaks she does not
Look up. She does not take her eyes from the sliding water.
"Feed the fish?" she asks. And then she shudders.

Frightened, perhaps, as I am by the flat sound of her voice.
Or by the sudden thinning of the air. Or by the way
The narrow rim of light over the blackened tree line

Comes and is gone before one has time to see it....
If I say, "We can go home now," if I kneel down
And say, "We can go home, the fish are sleeping,"

To *whom* do I speak? And out of *what* knowledge?...
The water moves like ash. And like ash it makes
No sound. The woman crouched on the stone bridge

Picks from the corn heaped at her feet one pale cob,
And without looking up, she holds it out toward me.

⁓

Elegy

Wind buffs the waterstained stone cupids and shakes
Old rain from the pines' low branches, small change
Spilling over the graves the years have smashed
With a hammer—*forget this, forget that, leave no
Stone unturned.* The grass grows high, sweet-smelling,
Many-footed, ever-running. No one tends it. No
One comes....*And where am I now?*....Is this a beginning,
A middle, or an end?....Before I knew you I stood
In this place. Now I forsake the past as I knew it
To feed you into it. But that is not right. You *step*
Into it. I *find* you here, in the shifting grass,
In the late light, as if you had always been here.
Behind you two torn black cedars flame white
Against the darkening fields....If you turn to me,
Quiet man? If you turn? If I speak softly?
If I say, *Take off, take off your glasses....Let me see
Your sightless eyes?....I will be beautiful then....*
Look, the heart moves as the moths do, scuttering
Like a child's thoughts above this broken stone
And that. And I lie down. I lie down in the long grass,
Something I am not given to doing, and I feel
The weight of your hand on my belly, and the wind
Parts the grasses, and the distance spills through—
The glassy fields, the black black earth, the pale air
Streaming headlong toward the abbey's far stones
And streaming back again....The drowned scent of lilacs
By the abbey, it is a drug. It drives one senseless.
It drives one blind. You can cup the enormous lilac cones
In your hands—ripened, weightless, and taut—
And it is like holding someone's heart in your hands,
Or holding a cloud of moths. I lift them up, my hands.
Grave man, bend toward me. Lay your face....here....
Rest....I took the stalks of the dead wisteria
From the glass jar propped against the open grave
And put in the shell-shaped yellow wildflowers

I picked along the road. I cannot name them.
Bread and butter, perhaps. I am not good
With names. But nameless you walked toward me
And I knew you, a swelling in the heart,
A silence in the heart, the wild wind-blown grass
Burning—as the sun falls below the earth—
Brighter than a bed of lilies struck by snow.

~

Pale Rider

I found her beneath the fruiting honeysuckle,
The fallen doe. The hunter had cut her legs off,
And because the doe was so small, killed out of season,
The leg wounds looked huge, like neck wounds.
I found her in summer and then I forgot about her.
But many months later, on a day of cold rain,
And then unfallen snow, when I was tired because
I had not slept, and because I was tired, anxious,
I walked back to the grotto in the oldest part of the woods.
It is a dark unsettling place and I am drawn to it.
No sun finds its way through the trees, even in winter,
And, as if the place were cursed, birds pass through
Quickly or not at all, and they will not sing. Dusk
Had come early. The steep hill rose up black
Above the cave's blue walls, and from the water
Pooled on the rocks, the mist was already rising.
I could feel it before I saw it, stirring like the clouds
Of insects that sift through the swales in summer.
And then the mist took on weight and turned silver.
And then it grew heavier still and turned white.
I was having trouble seeing. I heard the call of a night bird,
Far off, perishable, and from the branches, high
And low, water dripped, a dull repeating sound,
Like the sound of many mute people flicking one
Finger slow and hard against their palms. And then
The sound fell off, and the cold mist turned warm,
As if it were coming not from the pools of water
But from deep within the ground, and in the mist
I smelled flowers. And I was confused. I thought
For a moment it must be summer and not winter,
And that I would see, if the mist suddenly thinned,
Not a stripped thorn, clinging to the grotto's rim,
But a blooming honeysuckle bush. I could taste
The honeysuckle on my tongue, a taste that was faint
At first, slightly rancid. But as the mist grew thicker

And thicker, golden now, softly vibrating, the taste
Grew stronger, and more sweet, like the taste of ether,
Until it seemed as if I were standing in a cloud,
Or a hive. I looked up: whiteness, milky, lit from within,
Like mother-of-pearl, and in it, *something*, not clear,
The shape of an owl, say, or a snowy hawk, hanging
Perfectly still, the way a hawk will hang for hours
In a stiff wind, but there was no wind. And the shape
Was not an owl, nor a hawk, but a shape my mind
At first resisted, the way my mind sometimes refuses
To make sense of words that are perfectly clear,
Simple words, spoken slowly and with great care,
Because the words are so improbable, or will tell me,
Good or bad, the thing I most wish not to hear,
"He is dead," say, or, "Take up your bed and walk."
Below that shape I stood, a pointed shape, golden,
Not a hawk, nor a boot, nor a silk hat made of mist
Yet still somehow distinguishable from the mist,
But something else, until my mind gave in to my eyes,
And the thing I had not wanted to see, or thought
I could not see, hung suspended above me, a face,
The head on its long neck of the doe I had found
Beneath the honeysuckle—such a frail creature,
Too small to have been killed, so small the hunter
Could have carried her home on his back had he so desired,
But he had not so desired. And I knew it was *that* doe,
Though I cannot say how I knew, her narrow face small
And dark and shining, until the mist closed over it,
And it was gone. And then, almost at once, the face
Appeared in another place, and again the mist closed,
And again the face came back, as in a game,
Until I saw that the face was not one but two,
Not two faces, but four, a flock of small deer, but no,
Not a flock, and again my mind refused the shape
Taking on weight above me, four heads on four long necks,
Attached to one legless body, one golden swollen body
That smelled of fallen fruit splitting in the sun and shone
The way an image from a dream will darkly shine,

Floating up from childhood, a hand holding out
A piece of torn bread that turns for no reason
Into a block of honeycomb filled not with honey
But with a marbled black and red substance,
Dense and sweet as charred flesh. She shone
The doe, her four heads, held high and perfectly still,
Facing in four different directions. And then I saw
Something else, darker, protruding from her breast.
It was a fifth neck and head, hanging upside down
In front, like the useless third leg of Siamese twins
Joined at the torso that hangs out of the spine,
And is amputated at birth, or like the water-darkened
Rudder of a ship. I heard the hot air sucking in and out
Of the doe's many nostrils, in and out. The mist
Grew darker, and I felt afraid, for I knew even before
My eyes confirmed it, that the fifth head was not
The doe's head at all, as I had thought, but the head
Of a grown child that the doe was trying to deliver
From her breast, and I knew that the child would never
Be born, but must ride always with her, his body
Embedded in hers, his head up to the sky. I wanted
To reach up and touch that head. But I did not do so.
I kept thinking that the doe would disappear, or that
She would say something, that her four mouths, five,
Would open and she would speak, but she did not disappear,
And she did not speak. A doe will never speak.
She will bark or cry out like a child if alarmed, but she
Will not speak. The mist smelled of warm milk,
And the doe's muteness grew loud, and louder still,
Until it was as dizzying as the sound of many trumpets
Blowing a single everlasting note. And I thought
Of the tongue, of how it is a wound, a pool of blood,
And of how you should bind a wound. And I thought
Of the earth covered with poor forked creatures
Walking around with broken faces, their substance
Pouring out in the form of words. And I thought of how
The mist would thicken further until it thinned,
All at once, to nothing, in the night air that smelled

Of sewage and poor man's roses, and of how the sound
Of the water dripping from the trees would return,
Tinnier, less insistent, as the water grew colder.
And I knew that soon on the high hill above the grotto
The fine dry snow would start to fall, and the field
Would draw silence to itself, and then as the air
Grew soft, the dry snow would turn to wet snow,
And the wet snow would lie heavy against the earth,
And the silence would multiply, a dark mass of pulp
And wings stirring above a darker bed, until nothing
Was recognizable to itself, and things were as if dead,
Wrapped in sheets and soaked in spices and oil, and death
A great mercy. And the snow seemed to hiss softly,
Or the falling mist hissed softly, or the water sliding
Down the stones, and the doe's form became more ghostly—
Pale rider, lost in the woods where I was lost. And I stood
In the dark until I closed my eyes. And then I stood no more.

Masque

My foot bleeds on the rocks
Of the shallow stream. The crows
Thick above me and at their backs
The larger gravebirds. This
Is a mean task, this business
Of burying oneself before one
Is dead. The shovel always
Breaks, the weather worsens,
The spot chosen proves to be
The wrong spot, and the words,
The words of mercy one must
Mutter, possess no mercy
For the flesh: *Not with peace,*
Not with peace but with a sword
Is the flesh stripped back,
Its many masks flayed off,
Each mask more extravagant
Than the last, like Bartholomew's
Beautiful and deadly hats,
No end in sight, no fair sight
Of the bared head, the bare stage
Upon whose wooden boards
We must play with passion
Our two parts: Lazarus undone
And that goodfellow Christ.
Hardfellow Christ. *Oh do not lose*
Faith. Work it out. Work it out.
The chief crow performs with panache
His task as smart backdrop
For the naked body dishing dirt
With a broken spade. Brokered wings
And a beaten heart. Dear God! to be
More than a light-hearted jest,
Or a hard-hearted jest. My crow,
My lark, my winsome wren,

My chough, oh sweet-lipped one
Who keeps me to a task
I do not want, let me be more
Than a dove-witted fool. The light
Strikes down between the trees.
The shovel strikes dirt. If the seam
Is good. If the seam is good. Then
The heart will put on for a moment
Its royal robes and become a grave man
Standing before an open crypt
With an air of such command
The stained burial wrappings
Of one much loved, and maligned,
And many days dead, will drop
Away. The self step blind
From its watery grave. And there
Will be: No time. Nor crow.
Nor Lazarus. Nor Christ.
Nor the hand that writes this.

III

The Dragon

The bees came out of the junipers, two small swarms
The size of melons; and golden, too, like melons,
They hung next to each other, at the height of a deer's breast,
Above the wet black compost. And because
The light was very bright it was hard to see them,
And harder still to see what hung between them.
A snake hung between them. The bees held up a snake,
Lifting each side of his narrow neck, just below
The pointed head, and in this way, very slowly
They carried the snake through the garden,
The snake's long body hanging down, its tail dragging
The ground, as if the creature were a criminal
Being escorted to execution or a child king
To the throne. I kept thinking the snake
Might be a hose, held by two ghostly hands,
But the snake was a snake, his body green as the grass
His tail divided, his skin oiled, the way the male member
Is oiled by the female's juices, the greenness overbright,
The bees gold, the winged serpent moving silently
Through the air. There was something deadly in it,
Or already dead. Something beyond the report
Of beauty. I laid my face against my arm, and there
It stayed for the length of time it takes two swarms
Of bees to carry a snake through a wide garden,
Past a sleeping swan, past the dead roses nailed
To the wall, past the small pond. And when
I looked up the bees and the snake were gone,
But the garden smelled of broken fruit, and across
The grass a shadow lay for which there was no source,
A narrow plinth dividing the garden, and the air
Was like the air after a fire, or the air before a storm,
Ungodly still, but full of dark shapes turning.

The Foreskin

I planted the little curl of skin under the magnolia. For a long time I could not remember the name for it, because though I had heard the word and its definition many times, when confronted with the tiny curl of flesh, the word did not seem to resemble the thing I held in hand, as words so often do not resemble the things they represent, or what we imagine them to represent; words can even destroy in their saying the very thing for which they stand. The little curl was pinkish, like an overbred white rabbit's eyes, and yellowing white, like the petals of the magnolia blooms, and a soft blue; and it had a crust of red, for no one had washed it, those who might have done so unprepared for the request for it, so they handed it over in its sullied form, which made it, I thought, more beautiful. And then I did not know what to do with it, for it seemed of great value to me, the purest portion of the man-child's pleasure returned to god, so that the small rain of god might overshadow the rest of his pleasure, make a fertile field of it; and it seemed that the pain, too, the boy had felt when the knife peeled the portion away, and the pain of the one watching, who was afraid to follow the ancient covenants and afraid not to, were folded into this piece of flesh. So I planted it in the black dirt at the crest of the field, and then I planted the magnolia over it. That was the order, first the little petal, now dried, and then the new bush, and in one year or two the bush made blossoms that began as furred buds, like the budding horns of young deer, and turned into large flowers that seemed to have been pieced together with curls of flesh, but magnified, as if under glass, magnified and made dazzling by the sun.

~

The Orchard

I saw the dog in a dream. Huge white
Boney creature. Big as a horse. At first
I thought it was a horse. It was feeding
On apples. As a horse might. Though not
With a horse's patience. For it was starving.
Its hipbones were empty bowls. The horse
Wolfed down the apples. Without breathing.
Without looking up. The way a dog wolfs
Down meat. And then it growled. And I saw
That the horse *was* a dog. But the apples
Were still apples. Windfall from the orchard
Above the lake. Pitiful place. The few trees
There grow black and yellow. And the thin grasses
Stagger down to the abandoned north field,
Which floods in winter and then freezes—
Blue ground, marbled with red and white,
Like a slab of meat—and when the far deer
Cross over it, and the birds cross over it,
It is as if the memories held within
The meat were rising from it. Or it is like
Flies crawling....I saw the dog in a dream.
And then, days later, just before dawn,
I climbed to the orchard. And there he was.
The same dog. Chewing on a dead doe.
And it was troubling. I thought I might
Still be dreaming—as was the case
When for many months I could not sleep
And I lost the power to tell the figures
In my dreams from those we call real.
I thought the scene might have been staged
For me. By my mind. Or by someone
Who could read my mind. Someone
Who was having a good laugh
At my expense. Or testing me
In some way I could not understand.

Beneath the black and yellow trees,
The dog's skin seemed abnormally white.
And the blood on his broad muzzle shone
Like wet paint. I closed my eyes. Not because
The ghostly creature was now biting
At the neck of the doe, the way
Those dark creatures who drink blood
And live forever do—since the river
Of blood flows forever, the streams
Of an eternal city, forever running,
Forever carrying their musky loads
Of blooming and expiring words
And figures, a thousand thousand
Yellow lights forever flickering off
And on in the black liquid, gold,
Sweet liquid, fallen—I closed my eyes.
Not out of distaste. But to see if the dog
Would disappear, the way the mist
Had thinned and vanished as I climbed
The hill. But the dog was still there
When I opened them. Staring straight at me.
He lifted his large paw. Placed it
On the doe's chest, and started to rip
At her belly. There was the sound
Of cloth tearing. And what did I do?
I picked up an apple. I wanted to see
If the dog—when the apple struck his side
And he fell—would rise in a second form,
And then a third. As dream figures do.
Dog. To horse. To man. Or I wanted to see
If the apple would pass through the dog
As through a ghost. And if the dog
Like the best of ghosts would turn
And instruct me in my confusion.
Or I wanted to bring the scene down
To size. The way the bright lights
That clank on at the end of the play
Show the mad king to be nothing

But a skinny man holding a costume
Of cloth and paste. I wanted the dog
To be just a stray, gnawing on a bone.
Or maybe I wanted none of these things.
Maybe I wanted what the hunter
Wanted when he struck the doe. Maybe
I wanted a piece of the dog's feasting,
The way the hunter wanted a piece
Of the doe's improbable swiftness.
The gun fires. The smell of burnt powder
Sprays up. A knotted string of birds
Unspools across the white sky. And deep
In running blood the hunter thrusts his hands.
I wanted something. But I did not throw
The apple. It was a small fruit. The size
Of a child's hand. Black and yellow. Riddled
With worms and misshapen. I put my teeth
To it. I took a bite. Chill flesh. Rank.
The dog kept feeding. I was not bothered
By the blood. The last of the red leaves
Scudded about me. And a few drops fell
From the dark sky. There is blood
Everywhere. The trees shed it. The sky.
There is no end. And isn't it pretty?
We say. Isn't it pretty? Amn't I?
Isn't the starving dog? Isn't the doe,
Even half-eaten? She gave her body
To the dog. The fallen body looked
So heavy. It looked as if it weighed
Ten thousand pounds. More than the lake
Or the frozen field. The doe dreamed
Of her death and it came to pass.
She courted the hunter and he shot her.
And she fell. And then the man stood
Over her. A white shadow. Laughing.
And then the dog stood over her. A black
Shadow. Laughing. And the dog came close.
The way a lover might. Had the doe

Been human. And he put his mouth to her.
As a lover might. Had he been human.
And her chastened flesh was a chalice.
And she was peaceful. And there was bliss
In this. And some horror. Around her
The thorns shone black and yellow.
And the fallen fruit lay black and yellow.
And black and yellow are the colors
Of the orchard's hive when it masses
And the queen in a fiery constellation
Is carried to new quarters. The wind
Stirred in the orchard. The dog bit
Into the doe's chest. And the apple
In my hand, against my lips, small,
Misshapen, the size of a child's fist,
Full of worms, turned suddenly warm
And soft. And it was as if, on that hill,
While the dog fed and the lake lay
Frozen, I was holding in my hand,
Against my lips, not a piece of fruit,
Not a piece of bitter, half-eaten fruit,
But the still warm and almost beating
Heart of some holy being—just lifted
From the dead body. And the heart
Was heavy. And wet. And it smelled
As it would smell forever. Of myrrh.
And burning blood. And gold.

Plants Fed On by Fawns

All the flowers: the pleated leaves of the hellebore;
And the false blossom of the calla, a leaf like a petal—
The white flesh of a woman bathing—a leaf over-
Shadowing the small flowers hidden in the spadix;
And fly poison, tender little flower, whose cursed root
Pounded into a fine white powder will destroy flies.
But why kill flies? They do not trouble me. They
Are like the fruit the birds feed on. They are like
The wind in the trees, or the sap that threads all things,
The blue blood moving through branch and vine,
Through the wings of dead things and living things....
If I lift my hand? If I write to you? The letters
Can be stored in a box. Can they constitute the shape
Of a love? Can the paper be ground? Can the box
Be altar and garden plot and bed? Can there rise
From the bed the form of a two-headed creature,
A figure that looks both forward and back, keeping
Watch always, one head sleeping while the other wakes,
The bird head sleeping while the lion head wakes,
And then the changing of the guard?....No,
The flies do not trouble me. They are like the stars
At night. Common and beautiful. They are like
My thoughts. I stood at midnight in the orchard.
There were so many stars, and yet the stars,
The very blackness of the night, though perfectly
Cold and clear, seemed to me to be insubstantial,
The whole veil of things seemed less substantial
Than the thing that moved in the dark behind me,
An unseen bird or beast, something shifting in its sleep,
Half-singing and then forgetting it was singing:
Be thou always ravished by love, starlight running
Down and pulling back the veil of the heart,
And then the water that does not exist opening up
Before one, dark as wine, and the unveiled figure
Of the self stepping unclothed, sweetly stripped

Of its leaf, into starlight and the shadow of night,
The cold water warm around the narrow ankles,
The body at its most weightless, a thing so durable
It will—like the carved stone figures holding up
The temple roof—stand and remember its gods
Long after those gods have been forsaken.

Lion

It is a hollow affair. You understand. And it has four heads. But this is misleading. Because it has four chests as well and four torsos, and four front legs, which must be hard to understand, since it seems there should be eight, but it has four, and the four front legs are twice the size of a normal leg, and so are the paws, twice the size of normal paws, and the only thing the heads and legs and torsos and chests have in common is the small of the back, one small back held up by a steel post and shared by the four lions, who by this portion of metal, shaped like an inverted bowl, are made into one lion. You see how difficult this is, so forgive my clumsiness. The lion has four heads and he is made of hollowed steel, and I'm sure I could make a song of this if I wanted to, but at the moment I do not feel that cheerful. Hollow, like armor, the lion, like a thing to be worn, not a thing in its own right, except in a museum, of course, where things which are part of a bigger picture are pulled away from that picture and made to stand outside of time, all alone, apart from their given function and the things to which they were born: they stand and stand so that we can stare at them until the mind goes blank, if it were not blank before, which well it might have been. Of hollow steel the lion is made, and his handsome heads, his four rusted heads—the old gold paint now flaking as if the lion had mange or leprosy—oh poor creature—are both hollow and flat on top, as if the crowns of the heads had been cut clean off in an experiment, or a massacre; but they were not, the heads were crownless from birth, fashioned to hold high the slate table top stolen from the mansion that burned. This is true. And they do. The mansion burned, the slate was stolen, and the lion's four heads holding up the heavy stone table are flat and hollow. But how handsome the faces, bearded like pharaohs, and how beautiful the forelocks, like Elvis curls, and how high-boned and fine the cheeks, and how proud and furious the pulling of these lions below the table top, and above the cement cracked by weeds, and beside the overgrown garden, this pulling and pulling in four different directions, as if the lions were the four winds of the world yoked together, or the four guardians of the four regions—so that if you look at them long enough, look at the lions, pulling so hard, trying to get somewhere, they seem to spin in a wheel, and it is a fiery wheel they spin in, as if the sun itself that spins through the heavens had been cut loose and were doing a wild dance here in this little yard, a mad dance, a sweet disfigured dance that cannot be deciphered, but still delights, as such things on some days delight.

The Dance

She was so sick, a pathetic dog, ugly as sin, and wild, a blond bitch,
Who seemed to be old, her fur going white, though that was
    probably
Part of the sickness. And she looked as if she had just given birth,
Because her dugs were swollen, but they were also disfigured,
So maybe they were full of rot and not milk, and her gait was
    uneven,
Her head down and swinging, causing her to list in half circles
From which she had to turn back. And it was painful to watch
Her work her way up the stone path, in and out of the black
    shadows
Cast by the imported cypresses. In she walked. Out she walked.
That is how things go. But that is not how this went. For when
The dog came to the circle of stone surrounding the stone pillar
The beautiful man stood on, bent over and sideways across one
    knee,
His huge genitals pushed forward, she stopped. And at his feet,
She struggled down to her knees, the way a newborn calf struggles
Up to his feet, her hindquarters in the air, and then she opened
Her mouth wide, and turning her head to the side, as if her ear
    hurt,
She began to bring something up. I thought it might be
The sickness itself, a dark swollen mass with hair on it, but it
Kept coming, the way a child comes, a raised fist, and soon a head,
Not a child's but a man's, lay smashed against the dirt and stones,
And the dog's poor mouth seemed broken, and then broken
Further as a blunt shoulder shoved free, and then an arm,
The wretched body of the dog, if it could be called that, body or
    dog,
A shaking thing, a ghostly thing, like a trembling lilac bush,
Or a snake's lit rattle. I do not know how to describe this. The
    insects
Had gone dumb. And the newborn man began to wrestle his way
Out of the creature only half his size, unless he were half a man,
But he was not, for after a time, long or short, a full man lay

On his back on the stones, and the dog lay like a castaway coat
To the side, just a shadowy rag of cloth and bone. And then
The stone man bent over, bent to see. As if he had been standing
All these years in the same difficult position, waiting for the waters
Far below to deliver this naked creature, that looked like him,
But smaller, onto these white stones, circling his high pillar,
Circled again by a wall of trimmed privet, the imported cypresses
And their shadows stretching away in four different directions,
Through the gardens of live forever, and the gardens of marigolds,
And the beds of now-dead irises, and the dark domain of the roses,
From which, one day, the gentle marble woman vanished, never
To return, the heat high and stifling, the crow high up in the quiet,
The silence of night awake inside the silence of day—and oh, yes,
It is carried, night a little creature carried by the day, day's child,
A disfigured creature, and then night grown full, and day carried,
A beautiful creature, night's child, a white mewling thing
Like a rose—and then the pale man on the rocks climbed to his feet
And stood for a moment, the way the man above him stood,
And he did something like a little dance, assuming one still
Pose after another, his muscles tight as stones, and the light
Around him laughing ha ha ha ha ha ha, not in amusement
But in deep pleasure, the crow laughing ha ha ha ha ha ha,
And the handsome cypresses spinning like dreidels....Things
Will be fed on. The rose is fed on by blight, a white ghost,
And by beetles, tiny green stones, and the calf dead for a week
Behind the far wall is fed on by vultures, and the bending stone
Statue is fed on by the rain and the wind—they vie for his eyes,
His fruit—and the man dances for this, for the devouring.
Does a cat walk by? Yes, a black cat walks by, delicate, precise,
And the crow laughs ha ha ha ha ha ha. And now the man's time
Is up. The figure on the pillar breathes in and draws back
To his stone state, and the man below sits down and struggles
To pull on the suit of rag and bone, the man growing smaller
As the suit grows larger, the dog's mouth at last closing over
The crown of the man's head, and the poor dog laboring
To her feet, and beginning again her slow walk, up and on,
In and out of the shadows, her head swinging from side to side,
As if she were divining for water. She will walk all the way

Around the world, until she comes back to the circle of stone,
And the dance is repeated. Again and again, she will do this,
Until the game is over, and on some days, when the heat
Is a ghastly flower, someone may, for a moment, see her.

The Rain's Consort

So, the lion, so his stiff wings, so the black moss that stains
Both his mouth and his wings, moss the color of fruit blood,
Or of pity, pity for the self that labors and labors
And spins only the wind, bride of the wind, oh foolish one.
So, the lion on the post, half-buried in lilacs, and below him
The small retaining pond filled with black water so thick
And still it cannot reflect the lion submerged in lilacs,
Nor the three stone cupids who poke him with their horns
And their harps, mean as vexing sparrows, bright
As low born sparrows, lilacs the color of figs or sparrows,
Or of the rain itself, laughing, and coming, and going.
The cupids' bellies are swollen like the bellies of pregnant
Women or small overbred dogs fed on delicacies. What
Offspring will they bear?—these boys, who torment a lion
In a cloud of lilacs, his single wing struck off near the tip,
And the day now at its center, uncertain of its purpose,
And the pond at its blackest, no bigger than a skirt
Fanned out on the grass, and the small grave caged
Near the pond all pock-marked and shining. Lilacs the color
Of rain, and rain the color of plucked flowers scattering,
Or coins falling on the dirt, and at the base of the lion
A dead sparrow lying open and held in silence as if in a palm,
The bird's feathers easing the skin, the stone lion marking
For a moment the small bird's grave, though the lion
Is no gravestone but the graveyard's guardian, and the rain
Is the sparrow's consort. And now the dead sparrow's
Brother sticks its head in the mouth of the lion, a test
Of courage, beating the boys at their own game, and the name
On the caged grave comes clear, James Herod. King,
Was he, tetrarch, a sparrow like the rest....To the north,
Red sumac shoots rise up like herds of antlered deer,
Or like fences of iron spikes, and near the entrance
A rope, swinging in the wind, hangs from an oak, as a child
Once swung in the wind, grieving for her father, a grief
So pure it still holds the day on its course....Shadowy applause

For the lion. The child singing in the wind. The child
Unclothed. The tarnished silver vines looking dead
Though they are not. Always they break into blossom
And grief....Shadowy applause for the sparrow and the lion.

IV

The Sparrow's Gate

And the bird shot through, who, had the stone arms been intact,
  would have dashed his small brains out and fallen like a
  bloody cloth to the grass—

the bird shot through—

and the absence, the missing arms beneath the beautiful slope of
  the woman's shoulders, her perpetual *at ease*, the woman
  not requiring as the man might the order to relax—

the absence, beneath the beautiful birthright of the woman's
  shoulders, the domes of mosques, or snowy hills, cold
  abundant hills,

    though now all is hot, the air is hot, the grass is hot, the
    sweet stench of stewed greens rising like the savor god
    feeds on, such a lot of flesh to make a pleasing smell, bull
    flesh, and lamb flesh, and dove flesh, all the steaming pools
    of blood and flies,

    but that was long ago, as the heavy-breasted body, mulled
    in sweat and patience that gave birth beneath the scuptor's
    hands to her giant twin above, stood long ago, a thousand
    plus a thousand years or more;

beneath the beautiful slouch of the woman's shoulder, one
  shoulder to be exact, just where the shoulder and the upper
  arm meet, beside the brimming breast

the bird shot through—

and the absence we had forgotten
    came back;

and it was not, as one might expect, an insult, nor a
    disfigurement, nor a lack;

not the deflowered sun-stricken bush swamping the broken
    fountain, a stone flower thrusting out a long-dead pipe
    below the woman's feet;

not the sparrow's foolhardy bravura that blasted him safely past
    the woman's breast and into the trees, only to impale him
    soon after on the hound's blunt tooth;

not the newborn rabbit outside the gate, ghastly pink, born
    too late and bushwacked by the sudden uprising of the
    gardener's sprinklers that just as quickly dropped back and
    left the slick creature trembling like the mayflies that live for
    one day only, or like a young deer before a storm;

not an incapacity, nor a short-sightedness,
nor a tunneling of vision, the world narrowing down to this alley
    between two rows of rotting trees that leads to a fetid pond,
    screened by narrow grasses and blackened by sludge and a
    half-day's dream;

not the small girl years ago when her arm went numb after she
    had been swung and swung in a circle saying, when her
    mother pressed the mute flesh, It is hiding, it is hiding,
    Mother,

    (and what, had the arm been taken altogether, would the
    girl have said, *To a far country it has gone, Mother, it is lost and
    cannot find its way back?*);

not the terrible draining at the center of the day when the spirit
    topples like a statue to the grass, or like a woman who has
    given blood and risen too quickly to her narrow feet;

not a shame,

not a word pronounced slowly and then spelled with great care
letter by letter all wrong into the dark beyond the stage, and
the following silence that flies back and attaches itself like a
dark bird to the brain;

not the hound with no sense of smell blundering blindly through
the woods or lying in the sun with his mouth slung open to
catch flies and stray birds;

not the flushed bloom of the ripe marigolds pulled up by the
hundreds and cast onto the gardener's fire so that new
flowers can be put in and death beaten to the punch, the
perfumed smoke rising acrid as rotting fur;

not the wind butting its head against the garden wall like the boy
who long ago killed the bird or tore the cloth,

nor the remorse of the mother years later when she
remembers locking the door against him and realizes too
late that the fabric of the world—the sky itself, the trees,
the garden and its terrifying colors, the dusky texture of
the boy's hair—is woven from rebuttals and embraces,
takes on its hue, retains its shape as surely as the patterns
on the loom, to which the woman had given too much
importance, mistaking cloth for flesh;

not the murderous fanfare of the mosquitoes, a visible
derangement, multiplying over the pond's shallow water;

not the harp dropped into the pond and retrieved years later,
unstrung and warped beyond recognition, good only for the
fire, and not much good for that;

not that;

not a single sheet of paper, a letter whose words no matter how
rearranged are a dark glass held up before the world upon
which one can rap and rap and get no answer;

not that rapping;

none of it, no:

if you lie on the grass in the dead of summer, and sleep, your
     body heavier than stone, and wake to the sound of
     something tapping and tapping like a sculptor's tool on
     stone, and look up from your dream to see a sparrow
     hurtling like a missile past the stone woman's left breast,
     right where the arm would have been,

     so that it seems for a moment as if the sparrow has
     destroyed the arm or been carried off by it,

     but it is hard to tell, everything is so bright, the woman's
     body blinding against the trees, shining like snow just before
     dusk, or soiled magnolias, or buttermilk, or aged opals, or
     darkened ice, or the full moon, or arms submerged almost
     to the shoulders in a tub of water dark as tea or in the
     steeping pond;

if you wake on the grass to see a sparrow part the waters of the
     flesh you had forgotten, the milky flesh that pours back for
     a moment after the bird passes—

then the absent arms are heavy;

the arms are so heavy;

not with the dropping down of living arms, falling loosely to
     the side, a rest that contains within it the upward motion
     that will follow, the fingers moving together to grasp and
     climb an unseen rope in the deliberate haphazard way a
     vine might, blossoming here and there, fingers and flowers
     making brief bright points,

but with the heaviness of something at anchor:

the giant carp, say, grim gold, far gone, who has circled the
    pond's floor for years, lying at last taken on the grass,
    a creature so pompous and ornate it looks more like a
    painted figurehead than a fish, and so huge it seems to drag
    the foul pond it will soon be returned to behind it like some
    ancient and beautiful ship;

or heavy as a tapestry carried up from some dark crypt into the
    light that will reveal—when the bristling cloth that smells
    of fox fur and lilies is unrolled— the still golden image of a
    swooning dove, its breast impaled by a silver cross;

or heavy as the bodies of twin deer, frozen in midflight, creatures
    small and narrow as overbred dogs, and white as lamb's
    wool, the dreamy fetish of some man rich beyond measure
    or purpose raised to such elegant tomfoolery it fills us with
    delight, the way the museum's one prize possession, a life-
    sized mechanical silver swan, fills us with delight each time
    the key is turned and the bird arches his stiff and handsome
    neck over and claps from the mirror that makes his pretty
    bed a silver fish, and swallows it, as if he were swallowing a
    sword, or fire—making us laugh each time without fail, as if
    we, too, were fed on silver fish, or the gardener's sprinklers
    had just shot on, or some fool rabbit were rocketing away
    from an imaginery hound for the sheer deranged pleasure
    of it;

heavy as twin deer, the arms held out as an offering for the stone
    woman, who may, for all we know, be a goddess, for all we
    know, so old she is, so high above;

or heavy as coffers carved in the shape of deer, full of pearls
    and coins, and inlaid with cobalt and ivory patterns, like
    the patterns inside the dome of the mosque, mosaics in
    dark blue, and lighter blue, and white, or the dome of
    heaven, dead heavy with the jewels of heaven, or the Sea
    of Marmara, the moving patterns of the waves, the vast
    mosaic of scent and sound, fish oil and salt, blood and

honey tangled with voices calling people to prayer and the
brutal gulls' cries and the endless sighs of shadows slipping
across the grass;

heavy the arms, and heavy the arms' white gleam—

the gleam of snowberries, or eyes veiled over and gifted with
   second sight, or smoke from burning roses, or the scrolls of
   the altar wrapped in snowy wool, or the fairest flesh of the
   fairest child, born to be king, and carried into the dark trees
   by one brave and foolish woman who will later be punished
   as thieves are punished, but always her smile will hover in
   the air, as it hovered over the child, the way we hover over
   the past, bring it to life, or find, to our surprise, that it has a
   life of its own, turning and turning in space;

all the imaginings, sweet god, the many arms of the mind, the
   many-mindedness of the spirit descending upon itself,
   making a fullness that seeks entrance and when entrance is
   found unable—like water driven up from below—to resist
   the opening, and so it shoots out, a blossoming of sparrows
   gone mad, making a blessing, the soft spatter of the
   fountain's water upon water in the dead of the afternoon,
   and one sleeps, and then wakes, damp, as if bathed in the
   sweat of the lover, after dreaming of this or that, a darkness
   through which something white floats, a drowned boy, or
   lilies, or the languid notes of an ivory harp, or clouds of
   perfumed incense, or twin fawns breaking from cover, or
   the mime dance of arms cut loose from the body;

one wakes bathed in scented oil to see a sparrow part the waters,
   or move a mountain, or open a gate, yes, open twin gates,
   narrow walls of stone that lead into this city or that, gates
   called *Eyes of the World*, or *Blood Fully Borne*, or *Morning
   Waking Unto Morning*, or *Garden of Unearthly Delights*,

and the mind clears—mayflies, the last fruits of the season,
   trembling in the air above, like the air itself made visible—

and something comes through the gates....what?....what is it?....
   Oh, yes, it is a woman,

no, it is two women,

and they are laughing and laughing, and carrying on.

⁓

Acknowledgments

Grateful acknowledgment is made to the editors of the following publications in which these poems appeared: *The American Voice, Another Chicago Magazine, The Antioch Review, The Carolina Quarterly, The Cream City Review, The Georgia Review, The Gettysburg Review, The Journal, Journal of New Jersey Poets, The Kenyon Review, The Massachusetts Review, Michigan Quarterly Review, New England Review, The North American Review, The Northwest Review, River Styx, The Recorder: The Journal of the American Irish Historical Society, Salt Hill, The Southern Review, The Sycamore Review, Tamaqua, Third Coast, 32 Poems, TriQuarterly, West Branch,* and *The Yale Review.*

"The White Pilgrim: Old Christian Cemetery" appeared in *The Best American Poetry 1993,* edited by Louise Glück and David Lehman, published by Charles Scribner's Sons. "Courting the Famous Figures at the Grotto of Improbable Thought" appeared in *The Best American Poetry 1994,* edited by A.R. Ammons and David Lehman. "The Orchard" appeared in *The Best American Poetry 1997,* edited by John Hollander and David Lehman. "The Dragon" appeared in *The Best American Poetry 2003,* edited by Yusef Komunyakaa and David Lehman.

"Song" appeared in *The Pushcart Prize XIX: Best of the Small Presses.* "Blacklegs" appeared in *The Pushcart Prize XXII.* "The Dragon" appeared in *The Pushcart Prize XXVIII.*

"Silver Lake" and "Wild Turkeys: The Dignity of the Damned" appeared in *New Poets of the 90's,* edited by Jack Myers and Roger Weingarten, published by David R. Godine. "Blacklegs," "Elegy," The Satyr's Heart," "Sheet Music," and "The South Gate," appeared in *Hammer and Blaze,* edited by Ellen Bryant Voigt and Heather McHugh. "Elegy" received a Literary Award from the Illinois Arts Council. "The Orchard" and "Black Swan" appeared in *The New Bread Loaf Anthology of Contemporary Poetry,* edited by Stanley Plumly and Michael Collier. "Black Swan," "Elegy," and "Two Boys" appeared in *Poets of the New Century,* edited by Rick Higgerson and Roger Weingarten.

Words of Life

THE BIBLE DAY BY DAY

PENTECOST EDITION MAY-AUGUST 2006

Hodder & Stoughton
LONDON SYDNEY AUCKLAND
AND THE SALVATION ARMY

British Library Cataloguing in Publication Data
A record for this book is available from the British Library

ISBN 0 340 90896 3

Typeset in NorfretBQ–Regular by AvonDataSet Ltd,
Bidford on Avon, Warwickshire

Printed and bound in Great Britain by
Bookmarque Ltd, Croydon, Surrey

The paper and board used in this paperback are natural
recyclable products made from wood grown in sustainable forests.
The manufacturing processes conform to the environmental
regulations of the country of origin.

Hodder & Stoughton
A Division of Hodder Headline Ltd
338 Euston Road
London NW1 3BH
www.madaboutbooks.com
www.hodderbibles.com

IN THE SILENCE

In the silence listen for
   a breath
   a heartbeat
   the sound of a glance

In the silence look for
   things unseen
   details long forgotten
   the dance of a lilting melody

In the silence catch
   another's essence
   the echo of a memory
   the gentle brush of angel wings

Beyond the surface
in the deep cool clear blueness
is the place of welcome
belonging
homecoming

In this sacred place
there is no going back
no return

Barbara Sampson
New Zealand

CONTENTS

MAJOR BARBARA SAMPSON WRITES...

What are the colours of revival? Fiery colours of grace and mercy – red and yellow and orange. Crimson colours of conflict and chaos as rotten tomatoes, mud, stones, a dead cat or two are thrown at the hallelujah band. Deep fervent colours of the worst sinners in town being prayed for, spoken to, pleaded with, brought in, knelt alongside, surrounded and embraced. Bright joyous colours of testimony and victory. These were the colours of revival in the early Salvation Army.

I want a revival in my soul
I want a revival in my soul
I must apply through the blood of Jesus
To have a revival in my soul.

So I sang as a teenager new to the Army at my first Youth Councils. I had no idea what a revival in my soul was, but the vibrant colours, the rhythm of the music, the sheer joy of being part of a wholesome group of young people all wanting to get close to God was intoxicating.

My corps officer lived, dreamed and taught revival. It was his one theme. He was a fervent, sincere man who, in his nineties, still remembered the day I gave my heart to Jesus. Did he see me as one of the worst sinners in town? There is no doubt he prayed for me.

I thank God for the young blood that keeps the Army marching in these days with fervour and joy and new songs of revival. For me the colours are quieter now, deeper, more intense – lavender, paua–blue, cerise. In the deep place I find, to my delight and gratitude, that God is still doing a new work, still redeeming the unredeemed places, still doing a heart transplant from stone to flesh. I marvel at his patience, his tender persistence, his mercies offered new every morning.

'See, I am doing a new thing! Now it springs up; do you not perceive it? I am making a way in the desert and streams in the wasteland' (Isaiah 43:19).

ABBREVIATIONS USED

The Message	Eugene Peterson, *The Bible in Contemporary Language*, NavPress, 2002. Scripture taken from *The Message*. Copyright © by Eugene H. Peterson, 1993, 1994, 1995. Used by permission of NavPress Publishing Group.
NIV	New International Version
NRSV	New Revised Standard Version
SASB	*The Song Book of The Salvation Army*, 1986
SACB	*Salvation Army Chorus Book*

HAGGAI – FIRST THINGS FIRST

Introduction

In the year 536 BC the Persian Emperor Cyrus issued a decree permitting the Jewish exiles in Babylon to return to Jerusalem to rebuild the temple (see *Ezra 1:2–4*). Under the leadership of Zerubbabel, the newly appointed governor of Judah, and Joshua, the high priest, about 50,000 people returned to Jerusalem and began the task of restoration. They cleared the temple court of rubble and replaced the altar on its base, thus making it possible for the daily sacrifices to begin again. Within a few months they had laid the foundations for the temple.

Then trouble began – hostility from neighbouring tribes, and the death of Cyrus the emperor. The work on the temple ground to a halt. The people turned to their own private lives and gradually became used to worshipping among the ruins of the once-great temple. The desire to rebuild died and the years slipped by.

Then, in the year 520 BC, the prophet Haggai stepped onto the scene, bringing with him a word from God. It was a word about priorities, about putting first things first, about seeking God's kingdom before everything else. With such a theme, Haggai's message is surely a word from God for us today as well.

MONDAY 1 MAY
A Matter of Priorities

Haggai 1:1–4

'Is it a time for you yourselves to be living in your panelled houses, while this house remains a ruin?' (v. 4, NIV).

The book of Haggai is only two chapters long, thirty-eight verses in all. His story is told in five brief episodes or sermons, each with a specific date, covering a time span of less than four months.

Haggai's name comes from the Hebrew word for 'festival', which suggests that he may have been born on a feast day. His father's name is not mentioned, nor are any details of his family background given. All we know about this man is that he is a prophet with authority. In the midst of a ruined city in a country devastated by drought 'the word of the LORD came through the prophet Haggai' (v. 1).

Haggai speaks his message to Zerubbabel, the governor, and to Joshua, the high priest. He refers to 'these people' (literally 'this people') who deny that the time has come to rebuild the temple. The identity of 'these people' is unclear. He could be referring to those who have returned from exile, or maybe to those who did not go to Babylon but remained in Judah.

Zerubbabel and Joshua are responsible for the whole population of Judah, however, so 'these people' probably includes the whole community. Everyone together stands guilty of failing to rebuild the temple, a project begun years earlier, then abandoned and still uncompleted.

The prophet puts his finger on the heart of the issue. The description of the people's houses as 'panelled' (*NIV, NRSV*) does not necessarily refer to high-quality furnishings but rather to their state of completion. The people live in 'finished' houses while the Lord's house is not just 'unfinished', but desolate and in ruins.

Anyone who focuses on our failures, points out our misplaced priorities or magnifies our mistakes is an uncomfortable person to have around. But Haggai speaks not judgment but rather encouragement to the people. With the far-seeing eye of a prophet, he not only perceives the problem but also offers a clear solution.

Keep the assurance of Romans 8:1 in mind today as you consider a misplaced priority in your life that God may be bringing to your attention.

TUESDAY 2 MAY
'Give Careful Thought'

Haggai 1:5–11

'You have planted much, but have harvested little. You eat, but never have enough. You drink, but never have your fill. You put on clothes, but are not warm. You earn wages, only to put them in a purse with holes in it' (v. 6, NIV).

The proof of the pudding, as the saying goes, is in the eating. The proof of the people's neglect, the prophet says, is in what is happening to them. 'Open your eyes and look around you,' he says. 'You work hard, you plant a big crop, but you harvest nothing much at all. You eat but your food does not satisfy. You drink but you are still thirsty. Your clothing covers you but fails to keep you warm. You earn money but it disappears in no time at all.'

Haggai paints a picture of futility and frustration. No matter how much the people do, no matter how hard they work, no matter how much energy they put into life, nothing lasts, nothing satisfies. Drought covers the land. The crops of grain, new wine and oil, all symbols of fertility and lushness and signs of God's blessing, have failed.

The prophet points out that all this is the inevitable result of Judah's misplaced priorities. While working on building and beautifying their own homes, they have neglected God and his claim on their lives.

As surely as one plus one equals two, so God's formula, set down from the very beginning of his covenant relationship with his people, is that honouring him and obeying him will result in his blessing (see *Deut 28*). Failure to honour and obey will result in the very opposite, the kind of emptiness and barrenness that the people and the land itself are now experiencing.

'Give careful thought . . . Give careful thought' (*vv. 5,7*), says the prophet. With grace he sets a solution before the people. They are to go up into the mountains, gather the needed materials, and resume and complete the long–abandoned task of restoring the temple. By honouring God in this way, they will once more open the floodgates of blessing.

The application of this portion of Scripture hardly needs to be spelt out. What individual or corporate leanness might God be pointing out to you and me today?

'Take a good, hard look at your life. Think it over' (Haggai 1:5,7, . The Message).

3

WEDNESDAY 3 MAY
'I Am With You'

Haggai 1:12–15

'Haggai, the LORD's messenger, gave this message of the LORD to the people: "I am with you," declares the LORD' (v. 13, NIV).

Haggai must be one of few Old Testament prophets to witness an almost immediate response to his God–given message. He spoke out on the first day of the sixth month (v. 1) and on the twenty–fourth day of that same month the people began work on restoring the temple (v. 15).

The narrator records that the initial response of the leaders and of the 'whole remnant of the people' was twofold. They obeyed (literally 'heard') and they feared the Lord. In hearing the prophet speak, they heard the voice of God himself. In fearing the Lord they recognised and acknowledged his awesome power and his amazing faithfulness.

Even though their ancestors had not lived up to God's clearly spelt–out commands (see *Deut 4:25–31*) they knew that God was now giving them another chance, calling them back to himself, giving them a new opportunity to honour him by their obedience.

Just what happened in the twenty–three days between the prophet's word being spoken and the work being started is unclear. Maybe a building committee was set up. Timber had to be fetched from the mountains (v. 8). Other tools and equipment no doubt needed to be gathered. But when the moment was right, God 'stirred up the spirit' of the leaders and of all the people. This same expression is used in Ezra 1:5 to describe how God 'moved the heart' of the people to rebuild the temple.

As a sign of his blessing on their preparation for rebuilding and as a sure indication of success, God said, 'I am with you.' With that assurance ringing in their hearts, the people responded and began working on the temple (v. 14).

'I am with you' is the same state-ment that you and I need to hear in every new beginning we make, in every new resolve, in every new longing after God. No matter what your situation is at present, may this be the assurance that God speaks to you today as he stirs up your heart and gives you courage to face the unique task he has given you to do.

THURSDAY 4 MAY
'Work, for I Am With You'

Haggai 2:1–9

'"Be strong, all you people of the land," declares the LORD,
"and work. For I am with you," declares the LORD Almighty'
(v. 4, NIV).

As the people began work on the temple they found themselves standing in the midst of history. Some of them were old enough to remember Solomon's magnificent temple, destroyed by the Babylonians sixty–six years earlier. They may have felt that what they were now building could never compare to the glory of that structure.

While the people looked back and remembered the past, God drew their attention to the future. Speaking courage and strength to their efforts, he told them: 'Get to work! For I am with you . . . Don't be timid. Don't hold back' (vv. 4,5, The Message). God could see an even greater glory coming to this temple than Solomon had ever known.

This is the God–of–the–so–much–more, the God who can feed a great multitude with just a few bread rolls and pieces of fish, the God who is able to do 'immeasurably more' than all we could ever imagine or guess or request in our wildest dreams (Eph 3:20).

God did not wait until the job was finished before commending the people. Even as they began to work, he spoke blessing and encouragement to their resolve. He lifted their eyes from a mere building site to see something full of beauty and splendour coming to this very place: 'The glory of this present house will be greater than the glory of the former house . . . in this place I will grant peace' (v. 9). His words told them they were standing in the presence of something and Someone far greater than themselves.

Look around you today. Do you realise that you have been given a sacred task to do? If your work is with hammer and nails, are you merely making a structure or building a temple for God? If your work is with youngsters, are you just 'caring for kids' or are you raising men and women for God? In the divine economy there is no such thing as an unimportant task or an insignificant worker.

Let God's words, 'Work, for I am with you' encourage you to bring your greatest and best to your task today.

FRIDAY 5 MAY

'From This Day on I Will Bless You'

Haggai 2:10–19

'Is there yet any seed left in the barn? Until now, the vine and the fig-tree, the pomegranate and the olive tree have not borne fruit. From this day on I will bless you' (v. 19, NIV).

Two months later the word of the Lord was again given to the people through the prophet Haggai. There was nothing significant about the date, no appointed festival, no particular moment in Israel's history to remember. But on this day something very special happened – a new period of divine blessing began.

Haggai uses an inductive preaching method to make his point. He poses two questions, hears the answers, then draws his conclusion. His questions have to do with holiness and defilement.

His first question is: 'If someone carries a piece of consecrated meat in his garment and the garment touches some other food, will that food become holy?' The answer is clearly 'No'. His second question is: 'If someone who is defiled from having touched a corpse then touches food, will that food be contaminated?' The answer is clearly 'Yes'.

Haggai's point is that while holiness does not rub off on others, contamination does. Being back in their homeland, working on rebuilding the temple – God's holy place – does not of itself make the people holy. If they come to the task with wrong attitudes, sinful lifestyles, ungodly ways, they in fact contaminate the holy place in which they are working, rather than being made holy by the holiness of their surroundings. The only way to clear up their sin is by repentance and obedience.

Three times repeating the phrase 'Give careful thought' (see 1:5,7), Haggai calls the people to remember how life was for them before they began work on the temple. He reminds them of how poor harvests and leanness dogged their best efforts, how blight, mildew and hail damaged their vineyards and fig trees, how pomegranates and olive trees failed to bear fruit. But with their turning to God and their resumption of the work on the temple, a new day had begun – a day of God's blessing.

What new resolve might God be waiting for you to make today? What turning or returning might he be calling you to? Hear his words to you: 'From now on you can count on a blessing' (v. 19, The Message).

SATURDAY 6 MAY
'I Have Chosen You'

Haggai 2:20–23

'"On that day," declares the Lord Almighty, "I will take you,
my servant Zerubbabel son of Shealtiel," declares the Lord,
"and I will make you like my signet ring, for I have chosen you,"
declares the Lord Almighty' (v. 23, NIV).

On the surface the message of Haggai is a simple call for the people of Jerusalem to get their priorities straight and to resume the task of rebuilding the temple. By honouring God in this way, he tells them, they will be blessed. Haggai's words are compelling. He is a faithful spokesman for the living God. He draws no attention to himself, seeks no glory of his own. He steps on stage, speaks clearly the message he has been given, then withdraws.

The last portion of his prophecy, however, makes it clear that God has more than a rebuilding project on his mind. Conjuring up images from the past, God points to the future: 'I will shake . . . I will overturn . . . I will overthrow.'

We see Sodom and Gomorrah falling under God's wrath, Pharaoh's chariots and horses being submerged in the sea, the armies of Midian being overthrown, the people of God victorious. This is God's way of declaring that, just as he proved himself faithful in the past, so he will surely lead his people into the future.

God's chosen agent at this time is Zerubbabel, the governor. This man was the grandson of Jehoiachin, the last king in the line of David to sit on the throne in Jerusalem. God says to Zerubbabel, 'I will take you . . . I will make you like my signet ring . . . I have chosen you.' This man, covered with God's authority, will carry forward God's promise that the Messiah will one day come from the line of David.

With this magnificent word that sweeps our gaze from the present to the future, Haggai concludes his message.

'I am with you' (1:13); 'Work. For I am with you' (2:4); 'From this day on I will bless you' (2:19); 'I will make you like my signet ring, for I have chosen you' (2:23). These words of Haggai's prophecy are words from God for a certain people at a certain time in history. But as we too bring our priorities into line, may they also be words of grace that God speaks to us today.

SUNDAY 7 MAY
God's Love Song

Isaiah 54:1–10

'"Though the mountains be shaken and the hills be removed, yet my unfailing love for you will not be shaken nor my covenant of peace be removed," says the LORD, who has compassion on you' (v. 10, NIV).

These verses are a group portrait of the fellowship of the bereaved. Standing on one side is a woman who wears stigma like a shawl. Her shame is that she has never had children. Her punishment for not bearing babies when she was young is that she will have no strong sons or daughters to bear her up when she is old.

Next to her stands a widow whose husband died far too early, leaving her a non-person with no income, no insurance policy, no identity of her own. Alongside her stands a woman who married in the flush of youth when life was eternal summer and hopes grew like blossom on jacaranda trees. But summer leapt over autumn and cooled quickly to winter when her husband turned his back on her and cast her off like used goods.

Together these three sing a song of sadness. Reproach, shame and desolation are the chords of their lament.

Then suddenly another voice breaks through. The prophet, speaking on behalf of God, tells them to burst into song and sing, not for sorrow but for joy, not in sadness but in celebration. Three strong imperatives shape his message: 'Do not hold back . . . Do not be afraid . . . Do not fear disgrace.'

The reason for this new song is that the Lord Almighty, their Maker, the Holy One of Israel, the God of all the earth, is redeeming them, calling them back to wholeness, to fullness, to *shalom* blessing. God is longing to show his compassion once more, to renew his covenant promises, to be more to them than a human husband could ever be. Their days of shame and punishment are over. Sorrow is turning to joy, emptiness to fullness, barrenness to fruitfulness.

These verses are a balm to the spirit whenever sorrow or shame of any kind threaten to overwhelm us. In whatever barrenness of spirit you may find yourself today, hear God singing his song of love and blessing over you.

Look around and be distressed
Look within and be depressed
Look to God and be at rest.

8

TIMES OF REFRESHING

Introduction

Revive, renew, restore – these words are peppered throughout Scripture, from Genesis to Revelation, from psalmist to prophet. Again and again the Scriptures declare that God is at work doing 'a new thing', giving 'a new song', transplanting 'a new heart' into his people. The images are startling, fresh and compelling – dry bones coming to life, water flowing from the temple, times of refreshment coming after repentance and returning.

Such days of renewal do not belong simply to a forgotten past. Contemporary Christian literature has picked up the theme of renewal and is putting it under the microscope. What makes renewal happen? What are the elements of revival? Is there a formula that, if followed, can make it happen again?

This series will look at some of the aspects of revival and renewal. May the times of refreshing that God's word speaks of continue to happen in our day.

'Repent, then, and turn to God, so that your sins may be wiped out, that times of refreshing may come from the Lord' (Acts 3:19).

MONDAY 8 MAY

Like a Tree

Jeremiah 17:1–10

'Blessed is the man who trusts in the LORD, whose confidence is in him. He will be like a tree planted by the water that sends out its roots by the stream. It does not fear when heat comes; its leaves are always green. It has no worries in a year of drought and never fails to bear fruit' (vv. 7,8, NIV).

Once upon a time there was a tree. It lived in the heart of the forest where it grew strong and tall. If you stood beneath it and listened carefully you could hear music – rich cadences of worship to its Creator.

The tree gave welcome shade and protection to everyone. The cold and the travel–worn would come and find shelter beneath its canopy, then go on their way refreshed. Birds built nests in its branches, singing their songs of praise.

The sun shone blessing every day. Every night the rain skipped across its leaves and down into the soft earth below. In the autumn a rich, fragrant, nourishing compost gathered around its base. In spring-time parents would bring their children to see its glorious blossom. Families had their photographs taken in front of it. It was truly a magnificent tree, loved and admired by all.

Then one year a terrible drought hit the land. The earth dried up. In the forest the trees ached for rain but there was only blazing, searing sun day after day, week after week. Slowly the tree in the heart of the forest began to feel the effects of the drought. Its leaves turned a sad pale brown, not an autumn brown, but a wilted brown. Its limbs began to hang heavily. Birds no longer came to nest in its branches. If you stood close to the trunk the music was harder to hear.

'What do I do?' thought the tree. There was only one way to survive. The tree sent its roots down until they tapped into the deep streams that lie hidden in the heart of the earth. From those deep streams the roots drew up life–giving moisture that fed the trunk and strengthened the branches and gave vibrancy to the leaves. And even though the drought continued for a long time, the tree in the heart of the forest stood strong and tall, giving shade to weary travellers and shelter to all who came.

Do you have ears to hear? Then listen to what the tree says.

TUESDAY 9 MAY
Going Deep

Psalm 42

'Deep calls to deep in the roar of your waterfalls' (v. 7, NIV).

Author Richard Foster writes, 'Super-ficiality is the curse of our age... The desperate need today is not for a greater number of intelligent people, or gifted people, but for deep people.'[1]

I know how easy it is to skim along on the surface of life. Multiple roles, tasks and deadlines make me feel at times like a juggler keeping a multitude of balls up in the air. But the casualties of such a per-formance are the relationships with friends, family and with God him-self.

I can make a plan to have lunch with a friend 'one day soon when things settle down' but the family is not so easily dismissed. I can rush out of church with a mere nod to my fellow worshippers but a nod to God will not do. I catch a glimpse of a hurried, harried woman in a shop window, in my bathroom mirror, in my daughter's eyes, and I know I need to slow down and give attention to the things that really matter.

A routine of retreat helps – an hour each day, a day each month, a week each year. But such a gift does not just fall into the lap. It needs to be planned, prepared for, maybe even negotiated. If I take some extra time in the mornings or make a regular space each week, then how can I deal with the other tasks that normally need to be done during those times?

Wisdom's word in the book of Proverbs is 'Blessed the man, blessed the woman, who listens to me, awake and ready for me each morning, alert and responsive as I start my day's work. When you find me, you find life, real life, to say nothing of God's good pleasure' (*Prov 8:34,35, The Message*).

Such a blessing is not to be found on the surface of life. It is discovered in waiting and in loving attentiveness and in silence. When the outer voices are stilled the voice of God can more easily be heard.

'O thou lord of life, send my roots rain'
Gerard Manley Hopkins

WEDNESDAY 10 MAY
Giving God First Place

Mark 12:28–34

'Hear, O Israel, the Lord our God, the Lord is one. Love the Lord your God with all your heart and with all your soul and with all your mind and with all your strength' (vv. 29,30, NIV).

A university professor gave his students a large jar, then some rocks, stones and sand and asked them to fit as much as they could into the jar. The students found that if they put the sand and stones in first, there was no room for the rocks. But if they put the rocks in first, then the stones fitted around them and the sand filled all the gaps.

The professor's point was 'Priorities'. If you fill your time with less important things (sand), you will have no time for more important things (stones). But if you put the most important things (rocks) in place first, then everything else will fit around them.

This is a modern version of pivotal words spoken in both the Old and New Testaments. The first of the Ten Commandments declared, 'You shall have no other gods before me' (Exod 20:3). God was saying, 'I am to be Number One, your first Rock, making the first claim, calling for your first allegiance.'

The people found that when they kept to this commandment, everything else fitted around it. But when they put sand in place of the Rock, everything fell apart.

Jesus repeated the same call. When asked to name the most important commandment he said it was to love God 'with all your passion and prayer and intelligence and energy' (The Message). Seek first the kingdom of God, he said. Put God's claims first and everything you need will be taken care of (see Matt 6:33).

In practical terms, what does it mean to give first place to God? Such a call needs to be worked out by each individual. Authors Ray and Anne Ortlund speak of 'living from the inside out', that is, consciously, continually living in the presence of God, speaking with him, enjoying him, loving him, rejoicing, praising, crying, complaining – doing everything with an awareness of God being present.

Giving God the first place, our prior attention, is a key step to renewal.

To reflect on
'Is God really Number One in your life? Show me your chequebook and your calendar.'

Ray Ortlund

12

THURSDAY 11 MAY
A Call to Repent

2 Chronicles 7:11–16

'If my people, who are called by my name, will humble themselves
and pray and seek my face and turn from their wicked ways,
then will I hear from heaven and will forgive their sin and
will heal their land' (v. 14, NIV).

A key word in the vocabulary of renewal is the word 'repentance', in Greek *metanoia*. The word means to understand something differently after thinking it over, then making that change of mind lead to a change of action.

John the Baptist and Jesus both began their ministry with a call to repentance (*Matt 3:2; 4:17*). Peter, Paul and the other apostles also proclaimed a gospel of repentance (*Mark 6:12*). Their call was to turn, turn, turn away from sin and to turn, turn, turn towards the living God.

At a significant time in Israel's history King Solomon, famous for his wisdom, built the temple in Jerusalem as a symbol of God's presence among his people. In dedicating the temple, Solomon also dedicated the people and asked God to take care of them.

God responded, saying that if the people would humble themselves, pray, seek his face and turn from their wicked ways, then he would hear their cry, forgive their sin and heal their land. This was God's promise, his absolute guarantee that if the people did their part, God would do his.

Tragically, we know from reading the end of Solomon's story that neither he nor the people kept to this high calling. Solomon eventually turned away from God and, as a result, his son and heir lost most of the kingdom. The people themselves fell into the sorrowful cycle of sin, punishment and repentance, over and over again.

In this day of formulas for success, this formula for renewal, as given by God to Solomon, still stands and cannot be improved on. Humble yourselves, pray, seek God's face, turn from your wicked ways. While prayer has preceded every great revival in history, prayer alone is not the key. Humility alone is not sufficient. Seeking God's face is not enough. Repentance is the ultimate requirement. Without repentance no revival or renewal will take place.

Turn, turn, turn to God and he will turn, turn, turn to you.

To reflect on
What repentance, what turning, what change of mind and action might God be calling you to today?

13

FRIDAY 12 MAY
The Centrality of Scripture

Psalm 1

'Your word is a lamp to my feet and a light for my path'
(Ps 119:105, NIV).

Blessed is the man ... the woman ... the child who thrills to God's word, who chews on Scripture day and night (see *Ps 1, The Message*). In the search for renewal the Scriptures take a central place. The opening psalm of the psalter uses a rich, evocative image of fresh lushness and vitality – 'like a tree planted by streams of water'. The one meditating is the tree. The Scriptures are the streams of water that nourish the roots and feed the tree so that it can do no other but burst forth in blossom and fruit.

In Israel's history, when God brought the exiles back from their seventy years of exile in Babylon, a significant revival took place under Ezra the priest and Nehemiah the governor. The revival began with the reading of God's word. For six hours – 'from daybreak till noon' – the people stood and listened. They heard how God had called them out as a nation. They heard about the mighty acts God had performed for them. They worshipped and then they wept in repentance for their failures and sin. Through the public reading of his word God called the people back to himself (see *Neh 8,9*).

Such a national revival can also happen on a personal scale when we read the Scriptures and hear God speak to us. George Mueller, the legendary man of faith in nineteenth-century England, wrote: 'The first thing to be concerned about was not how much I might serve the Lord, but how I might get my soul into a happy state, and how my inner man might be nourished. I began therefore to meditate on the New Testament from the beginning, early in the morning.'

On the road to Damascus when Saul had his life-transforming encounter with God, he asked, 'Who are you, Lord?' and 'What shall I do, Lord?' (*Acts 22:8,10*). These are questions of identity ('Who?') and instruction ('What?'). Invite these questions to accompany you in your Scripture reading for the next few days. As God reveals more of himself, let your response be one of obedience.

SATURDAY 13 MAY
Abandoned No Longer

Mark 5:25–34

'When she heard about Jesus, she came up behind him in the crowd and touched his cloak' (v. 27, NIV).

I went, pushed on by a word. A haunting word that has held me in its grip for more than a decade. A terrible, crippling word that has labelled and choked me like a noose around my neck. A word I dread to say. Abandoned – that's the word.

I felt its first icy touch the day the bleeding should have stopped but did not. When it continued week after week I tried to hide my embarrassment but my family guessed. Rather than helping me they turned their backs. 'We cannot have you here, unclean, contaminating everything you touch,' they said. 'You'll have to go.'

I went to every doctor, every spell-caster I could find. They tinkered with me but when my money ran out they too turned their backs. 'There's nothing more we can do. You'll have to go.' So I lived an invisible life, taking up no space, voicing no need. Fear and shame and that awful word became my only companions.

Then this morning, for the first time, something gave me courage to face it, to return its chilling stare. For once I refused to cower beneath its ugliness. 'Look,' I said, 'I have heard of One who can heal. I have nothing to lose and everything to gain. If I can simply touch his cloak as he passes by, that will be enough.'

I did not mean for him to see me. I had no plan to take up his time or drain his energy. But as I reached out and touched the rough edge of his cloak, he stopped, turned round, held me in a long gaze, then whispered a word. To my amazement, he named my dreaded companion.

'You are abandoned no longer, my daughter,' he said. 'You may go now in peace. Your faith has healed you. Abandon yourself now into the hands of the God who heals you. Live abandoned to the mystery of the God who loves you.'

Down at thy feet all my fears I let go,
Back on thy strength all my weakness I throw.

Ruth Tracy, SASB 507

15

SUNDAY 14 MAY
Beauty Beyond Description

Isaiah 54:11–17

'I will make your battlements of rubies, your gates of sparkling jewels, and all your walls of precious stones' (v. 12, NIV).

If you were invited to think of the most precious things earth could offer, your mind might well take you to a jeweller's shop. There you would see diamonds, sapphires, emeralds, rubies and countless other priceless gems on display, indescribable in beauty and unbelievable in value.

The prophet Isaiah uses this image of great beauty and great value to describe 'the heritage of the servants of the LORD' (v. 17), that is, what is passed on – like a heritage – to those who follow in God's way.

Isaiah addresses Jerusalem as an afflicted city, lashed by storms, beaten and left comfortless. Tyranny and terror, havoc and destruction have taken their deadly toll. But, declares the prophet, days of judgment are over. A new day is coming. In place of broken-down walls, battlements of rubies will glitter in the sun. Smashed-down gates will again stand tall and strong, studded with jewels. The once-ruined city will rise from the ashes and be rebuilt with rare and precious stones. Sturdiness around will be matched by safety within. Security, *shalom* peace and righteousness will grow and flourish within the city as people – and their children – learn God's truth and walk in his ways.

This same image is picked up again in the last book of the Bible where the writer, the aged apostle John, describes the beauty of the new Jerusalem: 'It shone with the glory of God, and its brilliance was like that of a very precious jewel, like a jasper, clear as crystal' (*Rev 21:11*).

This language is as rich as the jewels themselves. It is the writer's attempt – in both Isaiah and Revelation – to describe the indescribable glory of the future. These large, expansive words are offered to all who name themselves 'the servants of the LORD' and give a glimpse into the future. 'No eye has seen, no ear has heard, no mind has conceived what God has prepared for those who love him' (*1 Cor 2:9*).

Hold something precious in your hand today. Hear God telling you that your value in his sight is far, far greater than this.

MONDAY 15 MAY
Dry Bones Coming to Life

Ezekiel 37:1–14

'This is what the Sovereign LORD says to these bones: I will make breath enter you, and you will come to life' (v. 5, NIV).

Writing to the Jewish people in captivity in Babylon, the prophet Ezekiel spoke words of doom, gloom and judgment. But he also spoke words of hope and restoration. A day will come, he told them, when God will bring new life to the nation. Ruined cities will be rebuilt. The land that is now laid waste will once more become lush and fruitful like the Garden of Eden.

Ezekiel illustrated his message of hope by telling them of a vision God gave him. He found himself standing in a valley surrounded by bones that were 'very dry', brittle and bleached by the sun. God asked him if he thought the bones could ever live again. Surely not! But when the prophet spoke the words God gave him, the bones rattled together, took shape and covered themselves with skin. At God's command Ezekiel spoke to the four winds and breath entered the bones. They came to life and stood up on their feet – a vast army.

This powerful image was a promise of renewal for the nation of Israel in exile. God was declaring that a day would come when his covenant people would be released from their graves of captivity and brought home again.

I think of those dry bones when I hear my corps officer (minister) preaching. He was serving behind a bar when God called him and breathed new life into him. I hear those bones rattling together when I think of a friend who was a victim of an abusive father, and is now a listening ear to other women who have suffered similar trauma. I feel the rush of life–giving wind when I see a former alcoholic now ministering hope and healing to other men walking the lonely road of addictions.

Can you see dry bones lying in the sun? Can you hear bones rattling together, taking shape? Can you feel the rush of a mighty wind giving breath to that which was once dead? Can you see a vast army standing up full of life, ready to march?

Do it again, Lord, do it again!

TUESDAY 16 MAY
A Heart Transplant

Ezekiel 36:24–30

'I will give you a new heart and put a new spirit in you; I will remove from you your heart of stone and give you a heart of flesh' (v. 26, NIV).

In *The Wizard of Oz* Dorothy and her dog Toto and her friend Scarecrow are on their way to the Emerald City to see the Great Oz when they meet a Tin Woodman.

'Why do you wish to see Oz?' the Tin Woodman asked.

'I want him to send me back to Kansas, and the Scarecrow wants him to put a few brains into his head,' Dorothy replied.

The Tin Woodman appeared to think deeply for a moment. Then he said: 'Do you suppose Oz could give me a heart?'

'Why, I guess so,' Dorothy answered. 'It would be as easy as to give the Scarecrow brains.'

The Tin Woodman expresses a universal longing. Everyone wants a heart to feel both joy and sorrow. There are times, of course, when having a heart that feels nothing would be an advantage. We could watch the movie *Shadowlands* without needing tissues. We could read of the discovery of a newborn baby abandoned and left to die, and not feel a thing. But God knows that a heart immune to pain, free from feeling, a stranger to sorrow, is a heart not worth having.

The prophet Ezekiel had a long story of doom and gloom to tell about Israel. Suddenly a word of hope and restoration breaks through his account, like a rainbow after a thunderstorm. The people will come home from exile. Their towns and cities will be rebuilt. Their vineyards will once again become fruitful. In place of devastation and ruin, prosperity will once more cover the land.

Even greater than the restoration of the land, however, will be the restoration of the relationship between God and his people Israel. Listen to God's amazing promises: 'I will gather you ... I will sprinkle clean water on you ... I will cleanse you ... I will give you a new heart ... I will remove your heart of stone and give you a heart of flesh ... I will put my Spirit in you ... I will save you.'

Is anyone needing a heart transplant today? God, the Master Surgeon, is ready.

WEDNESDAY 17 MAY
A Need for Each Other

James 5:13–20

'Confess your sins to each other and pray for each other
so that you may be healed' (v. 16, NIV).

For all the times I have gone on a diet over the years there was only once that I had any real success. It was when I was a student and went every week to Student Health Services to be weighed. Tough as it was, that regular accountability kept me disciplined.

I need that same accountability in my Christian walk to keep me disciplined as a disciple (note, the same word) of Jesus. Left to myself I get flabby and careless. Knowing that I am going to meet regularly with someone else to share the deep things of our faith keeps me on my toes – or rather, on my knees!

It was this very need for accountability that led author Richard Foster and his friend Jim Smith to begin meeting together regularly. Their first meetings were 'high, holy, hilarious times' as they laughed at their foibles, rejoiced in their successes, prayed, made confession, challenged and encouraged each other. Out of those first meetings came Renovaré (from Latin 'to renew'), a spiritual formation programme in which people get together and grow together in discipleship through mutual encouragement and accountability.

'Let us not give up meeting together . . . but let us encourage one another,' says the writer to the Hebrews (*Heb 10:25*). We need to gather together as a congregation to sing the songs of the faith, to worship together as the body of Christ, to give public expression of testimony.

But it is all too easy in the crowd to hide behind a uniform, a role, a mask. We also need the small, intimate exchanges that happen when two people or a small group of people get together to share the things of God.

A friend told me about a group of ten intellectually or emotionally challenged people who came together for an Alpha course. Long after the course had finished they continued to meet, simply because they had formed such a bond together and wanted to continue the sharing.

To reflect on
Who helps to hold you accountable in your Christian walk? To whom do you offer this same support?

THURSDAY 18 MAY

Life-Giving Water

Ezekiel 47:1–12

'Fruit trees of all kinds will grow on both banks of the river. Their leaves will not wither, nor will their fruit fail. Every month they will bear, because the water from the sanctuary flows to them. Their fruit will serve for food and their leaves for healing' (v. 12, NIV).

You do not have to be a horticultural expert to know that without water, nothing grows. Water – that most basic of commodities with no taste, no colour, no smell – is essential for life.

Throughout Scripture, water is used as a symbol of renewal and eternal life. Jesus stirred the interest and created a thirst in the woman at the well when he spoke about 'living water' (*John 4:10*). He made the amazing claim that believers who put their trust in him will have streams of living water flowing from their lives (*John 7:38*).

The deeper the water, it seems, the greater the renewal. The prophet Ezekiel is given an amazing vision when he is brought to the temple and sees a river flowing out from beneath it. The river is a symbol of life from God and the blessings that flow from his presence. It is a gentle, safe, deep river that expands as it flows.

When Ezekiel first steps into the river the water is ankle-deep. Then it becomes knee-deep, then up to his waist and finally so deep that it is over his head and he has to swim.

The water flows to change the salty water of the Dead Sea into fresh water teeming with fish. Along the banks of the river are fruit-bearing trees whose roots go down deep and draw up nourishment from the water. 'Where the river flows everything will live' (*Ezek 47:9*).

Many centuries later the apostle John, writing from Patmos, picked up this same image and declared Jesus saying, 'To him who is thirsty I will give to drink without cost from the spring of the water of life' (*Rev 21:6*).

This image of the river of life presents us with a choice. Do we plunge into the life-giving water or do we prefer to walk up and down the banks of the river, dipping our toes into the water now and again, observing the things of God from a safe distance? How do you choose today?

I plunge 'neath the waters, they roll over me.

William Booth, SASB 298

FRIDAY 19 MAY
'O Lord, Bend Me'

Matthew 4:12–17

'From that time on Jesus began to preach, "Repent,
for the kingdom of heaven is near"' (v. 17, NIV).

In the autumn of 1904 a revival broke out in Wales. It was a sovereign work of God that captured the attention of the entire world. Until that time Wales had not had a revival for more than forty years. Church membership was in decline and people had become indifferent to religious matters.

God, however, was at work. He chose a young man named Evan Roberts, a coal-miner with a burden for revival. Early in 1904 Evan sensed God calling him to preach. In a Sunday service when someone prayed, 'Lord, bend us,' the Holy Spirit touched Evan's heart. On his way home he kept praying, 'O Lord, bend me.'

He led meetings for a week at his home church. One evening he spoke of the urgency of putting away unconfessed sin and doubtful habits, and the importance of obeying the Holy Spirit and confessing Christ publicly. All seventeen young people in his congregation that evening responded to Evan's appeal. They decided to continue meeting and their numbers increased daily. In the next six months following that October meeting more than 100,000 people were converted.

Bars and taverns emptied out. Dance halls, theatres and football matches all saw a dramatic decline in attendance. Courts and jails were deserted and the police found themselves with no work to do. Some policemen closed their station and formed a choir to sing at the revival meetings. Miners stopped swearing. Long-standing debts were repaid, family feuds were healed and a new unity of purpose was felt across all the churches.

The grandfather of world-famous author Selwyn Hughes came to faith during this great revival. Selwyn himself was converted in a dramatic way and earned the name of 'Revival Boy' for his passionate preaching on the theme of revival. Millions of people around the world today read Selwyn Hughes's *Every Day With Jesus* Bible reading notes. So the ripples from that 1904 revival continue to be felt more than a hundred years later. What God can do with a life yielded to him!

Let this be your bold prayer today:
'O Lord, bend me!'

SATURDAY 20 MAY

Pentecost's Pattern

Acts 2:1–4,14–21,42–47

'And the Lord added to their number daily those who were being saved' (v. 47, NIV).

The second chapter of Acts is a remarkable portion of Scripture giving a wide panoramic view of the Early Church. The day of Pentecost begins with a dozen or so believers gathered together and ends with about 3,000 new converts added to their number (v. 41).

The Pentecost event shows in a most dramatic way the core elements of revival. Read the whole chapter and take particular note of the verbs. At the beginning of the chapter the narrator reports that 'a sound like the blowing of a violent wind came from heaven and filled the whole house' (v. 2). From then to the end of the chapter the verbs belong to the apostles, to Peter and to the people. The apostles 'saw ... were filled ... began to speak ... heard ... asked'. Peter 'stood up ... raised his voice ... addressed'. The people 'heard ... were cut to the heart ... said'. The believers 'devoted themselves ... gave ... continued to meet ... broke bread ... ate together'.

Then to sum it all up comes the glorious conclusion to the chapter: 'The Lord added to their number daily those who were being saved.'

God had watched over every event of those ten days. He saw his people gathered together and waiting just as they had been told to do. He heard their fervent prayers and sent the Holy Spirit with full technicolour and surround sound – fire and wind and a glorious fluency of language.

God inspired Peter – once a blatant denier but now a bold declarer – to stand and address the assembled crowd, to speak of Joel and Jesus, of David and deliverance, of resurrection and repentance.

God delighted to see the believers living together in harmony and fellowship, sharing what they had with others, meeting daily for worship and prayer. No wonder God was blessed! No wonder he blessed the people! No wonder the Church grew!

Do you need to look at your church fellowship in the light of this great chapter and see if any of the core elements of revival are missing?

SUNDAY 21 MAY
A Compelling Invitation

Isaiah 55:1–5

'Give ear and come to me; hear me, that your soul may live'
(v. 3, NIV).

The word 'come' is one of the most compelling invitation words of Scripture. Jesus used it often. 'Come to me, all you who are weary and burdened, and I will give you rest,' he said (*Matt 11:28*). 'If anyone is thirsty, let him come to me and drink' (*John 7:37*).

In the final chapter of the Bible, the Spirit and the bride say, ' "Come!" Whoever is thirsty, let him come; and whoever wishes, let him take the free gift of the water of life' (*Rev 22:17*).

An invitation to refreshment at no charge sounds unbelievable. We have grown up being told that there is no such thing as a free lunch. We have learned to be wary of free offers. Our rational mind tells us that if something sounds too good to be true, it probably is. But God's invitations weave their insistent way right through the Scriptures, repeating themselves over and over until we simply have to take notice.

Why does God call to the hungry and thirsty with such a compelling offer? Is it because he knows that there is a hunger and thirst deeper and more intense than can be satisfied with a hamburger and Coke? When we look at the routine of our lives it is all too easy to conclude that our days are futile and final. We get up and go to work so we can earn some money to buy food to give us energy to get up and go to work . . .

When we put God's offer of free wine, free milk, free bread – all symbols of abundance and blessing – alongside our day-in-day-out routines, our heart leaps. 'Tell me where it is to be found,' says the hungry soul. 'Take me to the table,' begs the thirsty one.

The prophet explains that this free nourishment is to be found in coming to God (*v. 1*), in listening (*vv. 2,3*) and in seeking (*v. 6*). Do these things, God promises, and our soul will delight and live.

Everything has been done. All is ready. The table is set (Ps 23:5). Please come!

MONDAY 22 MAY
A Heart for the Lost

<u>Mark 6:30—44</u>

'When Jesus landed and saw a large crowd, he had compassion on them, because they were like sheep without a shepherd' (v. 34, NIV).

'I want the whole Christ for my Saviour, the whole Bible for my book, the whole Church for my fellowship, and the whole world for my mission field.' So wrote John Wesley, a man who prayed in a large way because he had a large vision of a large God.

Revival praying is stretching praying. It takes its eyes off petty concerns and puts them on a God who has the whole world on his heart. Jesus and his disciples had gone off for some rest and recreation when they were suddenly invaded by a vast crowd numbering thousands. The disciples saw the people as intruders but Jesus saw them as sheep without a shepherd.

Revival praying is dangerous praying. When my eyes are opened to see others as God sees them, my heart may well be broken. I will learn to look at beauty and love and innocence and value them for the precious treasures they are. I will look at compromise and half-truths for what they are – simply a thin covering for evil.

Revival praying is costly praying. A calling to repent is a challenge to make changes, to admit need, to

give up arrogance, to grow in sensitivity to the Spirit, to live openly and vulnerably before God and others. Am I willing to pay such a high cost? Are you? I echo the psalmist's prayer: 'Investigate my life, O God, find out everything about me; Cross-examine and test me, get a clear picture of what I'm about' (*Ps 139:23, The Message*).

The story is told of F.B. Meyer, the famous British preacher, who once spent a night in the home of A.B. Simpson, the founder of the Christian and Missionary Alliance. Early the next morning Mr Meyer crept downstairs, thinking he was the first one up. But through the open door into the study he saw Mr Simpson hugging a world globe, crying and praying.

Have I the zeal I had
When thou didst me ordain
To preach thy word and seek the lost,
Or do I feel it pain?
                    Herbert Booth, SASB 409

TUESDAY 23 MAY
Streams of Living Water

John 7:37–39

'Whoever believes in me, as the Scripture has said, streams of living water will flow from within him' (v. 38, NIV).

At its source near the Canadian border, the Mississippi River is not a huge river. But as it flows down through the United States of America it grows in width and volume as the Ohio and the Missouri and many other rivers flow into it. Author Richard Foster sees this river as a picture of what is happening in our day as God brings together a mighty 'Mississippi of the Spirit'.

Throughout church history, different streams or traditions of faith have flowed in their separate courses. The contemplative tradition began among the Desert Fathers and Mothers of the fourth century when people fled from the busyness of the cities to seek quietness and closeness to God in the barrenness of the desert.

The holiness stream flowed when John Wesley and others in the eighteenth century wrote of purity, perfection and personal accountability. The charismatic stream, begun with seventeenth-century Quakers and revived in the Pentecostal movement of the twentieth century, emphasised the presence and gifts of the Holy Spirit in the life of the believer.

The social justice stream dates from the twelfth century when Francis of Assisi reached out with compassion to both people and animals. The evangelical stream had its roots in the Protestant Reformation of the sixteenth century when the Bible was given prime place in Christian life and conduct.

The incarnational stream which came into focus in the seventeenth and eighteenth centuries is the sacramental stream of life that sees, seeks and serves God in the ordinary moments of everyday life.

All six streams are displayed in perfect balance in the life of Jesus. He lived a pure, sinless life in intimacy with the Father, responsive to the Spirit, reaching out with compassion to all. He not only spoke the word, he was the Word of God in the flesh.

These separate streams can come together in us as well, widening our experience and walk with God. As they do, rivers of living water will flow from our lives, just as Jesus promised.

To reflect on
What stream do you need to plunge more deeply into today?

25

WEDNESDAY 24 MAY
A Capacity for God

Ephesians 4:17–32

'You were taught, with regard to your former way of life, to put off your old self . . . and to put on the new self, created to be like God in true righteousness and holiness' (vv. 22,24, NIV).

In his writings Augustine frequently referred to *capax dei*, a capacity for God, explaining that God so longs to fill us with himself that at times he gouges out of our lives the things that cannot coexist with him.

This concept became a living picture for author Joyce Huggett as she watched the creation of Rutland Reservoir, the largest man-made lake in Western Europe. Tonnes of soil and rubble were scooped out in order to make a crater that would eventually be filled with water.

The image is rugged but realistic. There are times when God does what feels like a gouging, grinding, grievous work in our lives, using heavy, heart-moving equipment of loss and sorrow, pain and suffering. We feel empty, raw and vulnerable and long for his tender healing touch on our woundedness.

Paul uses a more gentle image. He speaks of putting off and putting on, getting rid of the old garments of sin, falsehood and bitterness, and putting on the beautiful new clothing of righteousness and holiness.

Whichever image works best for you, the fact is that in the task of creating a capacity for God we have an intentional, pro-active part to play. The exercise of spiritual disciplines – which Richard Foster lists as meditation, prayer, fasting, study, simplicity, solitude, submission, service, confession, worship, guidance and celebration – is key.

Prayer and intercession open us up to dialogue with God. Confession and repentance clear away the rubble of sin. Solitude and silence enable us to hear God's voice more clearly.

Thomas à Kempis wrote, 'Let it be the most important thing we do . . . to reflect on the life of Jesus Christ and to imitate his life.' As we open ourselves up and create a space, a capacity for God, may we know the joy of his infilling.

Spirit of the living God,
Fall afresh on me.
Spirit of the living God,
Fall afresh on me.
Break me, melt me, mould me, fill me,
Spirit of the living God,
Fall afresh on me.

SACB 53

THURSDAY 25 MAY
Growing Tall

Ephesians 4:1–16

'So that the body of Christ may be built up until we all reach unity in the faith and in the knowledge of the Son of God and become mature, attaining to the whole measure of the fulness of Christ' (vv. 12,13, NIV).

What is the aim of renewal? Back to the tree image of Psalm 1 – 'like a tree planted by streams of water'. A tree displays health and vitality by its fruitfulness. A Christian believer displays health and vitality in exactly the same way.

'The fruit of the Spirit is love, joy, peace, patience, kindness, goodness, faithfulness, gentleness and self-control,' wrote Paul to the Galatians (5:22). No one can argue against such evidence of God at work. When these qualities are displayed they cannot be ignored or explained away. It is like a talented young man who wins a pop idol contest and, in accepting his prize, declares himself to be a Christian and speaks words of testimony and thanks to God. The fans have to hear it!

Or it is like an elderly friend who recalled the day of his conversion at the age of ten. 'I came home,' he said, 'knowing that this had to make a difference. From that day on I no longer threw my shirt on the floor – I hung it on a hook!' No one can argue against that!

A family rejoices when its sons grow tall.

A community of God's people displays fruitfulness in exactly the same way – by the expression of love, joy, peace, patience, kindness, goodness, faithfulness, gentleness and self-control. Paul and the other apostles regularly called believers to such fruitfulness: 'Live a life of love' (*Eph 5:2*); 'Love one another deeply' (*1 Pet 1:22*); 'Believe in the name of ... Jesus ... and ... love one another' (*1 John 3:23*).

There can be no argument against such love when it is offered to the world, especially against a backdrop of family difficulties or racial tension. When believers stand together in unity and love, the world has no choice but to listen.

The whole forest will be green when all the trees grow tall.

Let the beauty of Jesus be seen in me,
All his wonderful passion and purity,
O thou Spirit divine, all my nature
*   refine,*
Till the beauty of Jesus be seen in me.
                                        SACB 77

FRIDAY 26 MAY
Partners in Reconciliation

2 Corinthians 5:16–21

'All this is from God, who reconciled us to himself through
Christ and gave us the ministry of reconciliation' (v. 18, NIV).

That God can do anything is a certainty. That he chooses to work through frail, fallible, fallen creatures like you and me is a mystery. In fact, God not only chooses, but actually delights in such a partnership. Paul captured the essence of this divine teamwork when he wrote, 'I planted the seed, Apollos watered it, but God made it grow' (1 Cor 3:6).

Speaking both practical theology and personal testimony, Paul tells the Corinthian believers what God has done: 'He made the Sinless One carry our sin so that sinners like you and me might become sinless.' Paul himself never got over the wonder of that graced exchange. He probably never tired of telling of the day when a bolt of lightning threw him to the ground and God spoke directly to him.

For three days he was blind but when his eyes regained their sight he saw everything in a completely new light. He himself was a 'new creation' (2 Cor 5:17), with a new relationship (v. 19), charged with a new task (v. 20). What a turn-around! The one who had breathed out threats and violence against believers is now begging non-believers to come to faith.

It is tempting to put Paul in the lofty, unattainable category of 'super saint', a man whose dramatic conversion and divine calling set him apart from ordinary believers like you and me. But Paul would not agree with such thinking. His words to the Corinthians are all-inclusive: 'If *anyone* is in Christ . . .' He writes not 'I' nor 'me' but 'we' and 'us'.

This is the wonder of the ministry of reconciliation. The mission is God's, the means are God's, but he does his work through us. In fact, Jesus made the startling claim that 'the person who trusts me will not only do what I'm doing but even greater things' (*John 14:12, The Message*). So when God says, 'See, I am doing a new thing!' (*Isa 43:19*), we can be certain that he has partners, ambassadors, fellow-workers like you and me in mind.

Be reconciled . . . become a reconciler!

SATURDAY 27 MAY
New Heavens . . . New Earth

Isaiah 65:17–25; Revelation 21:1–7

'He who was seated on the throne said, "I am making everything new!"' (Rev 21:5, NIV).

Now and again we catch a glimpse of something far greater than what we can actually see with our eyes. We notice a look on a child's face. We overhear a passing comment. We watch a sunset that defies description. We hear a piece of music that stirs something deep within us. We experience a coincidence that we know could not possibly be a coincidence. We come out of a dark and desperate place only to find our way bathed in glorious light.

Such moments pass all too quickly but somehow they stand out as God-moments, to be held as treasure and remembered with gratitude. We may not understand what is going on. We see 'but a poor reflection as in a mirror', as Paul puts it (*1 Cor 13:12*), but we sense that we are caught up in a purpose far greater than ourselves.

The Scriptures give words to these images that are not easily contained in human language. In both the Old and New Testaments, God speaks of the new heavens and new earth that, even now, he is in the process of creating.

Although separated by an immeasurable time-span, the prophecy of Isaiah and the climax of Revelation speak a similar language as they tell of this new heaven and new earth where there will be no more death or mourning or pain, no more harm or destruction or sorrow. God, who is both the Alpha and the Omega, the Beginning and the End, declares, 'I am making everything new!' (*Rev 21:5*).

Do you hear dead bones rattling together and coming to life? Do you feel the pull of a stream of life calling you to plunge in deeper? Do you sense the birth pangs of a new heaven and new earth being created? God is at work, renewing his world, renewing his people, calling for our cooperation, our prayer, our willingness to walk the way of renewal with him. As we do our part, so he will do his. And the purpose of it all is:

That the King of glory may come in! (*Ps 24:7*)

SUNDAY 28 MAY

Verbs of Faith

Isaiah 55:6–7

'Seek the LORD while he may be found; call on him while
he is near' (v. 6, NIV).

These two verses contain four wonderful verbs of faith that sum up the way to salvation – seek, call, forsake, turn.

The word 'seek' has an intention about it. It is far more than 'glance at' or 'look for a moment'. It has the strength of a search that a person might make through dusty family records in the hunt for a clue to unlock the past. The mystery of seeking God is that when we set our hearts to seek him, we discover that he has already found us. Such seeking then becomes not so much a frantic search as a joyful home-coming.

The word 'call' is not the casual 'Give me a call sometime' that we might say to a friend. It is more the desperate cry from the heart that calls for light in the midst of darkness, for comfort in the midst of sorrow, for help in the midst of perplexity.

This kind of desperate calling is what the blind beggar did when he heard Jesus approaching. 'He called out, "Jesus, Son of David, have mercy on me!"' (Luke 18:38). The more the people around him told him to shush, the more loudly he called.

The words 'forsake' and 'turn' are twin sisters. One is incomplete without the other. Paul uses the different image of 'putting off' the old self and 'putting on' the new self (Eph 4:22–24), like swapping an old coat for a new one. To forsake and turn means letting go of the old way with its writhing sins and restless habits, and taking hold of the new way – God's way.

These four words – seek, call, forsake, turn – are all verbs of the faith journey. I met a young woman recently who is just at the seeking stage. She has not yet called, forsaken or turned, but she is on the way, an honest seeker after truth. Praise God!

Stretch a line between these four words – from seek to call to forsake to turn. Where do you stand along this line of faith at the moment? What is God's invitation to you today?

GOD . . . WITH US?

Introduction

The guest contributor for this Pentecost series is Major Barbara Robinson from Canada. Barbara writes:

A whimsical quilted banner hangs in the front foyer of our home. The carefully crafted design includes a modest but cheery little house and underneath is quilted the inscription, *Home is where . . . the Army sends you!* I received the quilt as a goodbye gift when we were farewelled from one appointment. Being both a Salvation Army officer and the daughter of Salvation Army officers I immediately resonated with the quilter's tongue-in-cheek observation.

Currently I am stationed in Toronto, Ontario, where my husband and I are the divisional leaders. It is the 'town' where I grew up and the largest city in Canada. In many ways, coming back to Toronto felt like coming home, although it is a very different city from the one I left two decades ago.

I have lived in a lot of houses over the years, but I have learned that there is a profound difference between a house and a home. Unlike a house, a home is something organic – created by the warmth of the relationships within the walls.

Is it possible that God would really condescend to make his home in the world of men and women? This was the question haunting Solomon as the work on the temple drew to a close. God seemed to be saying that in a unique way he was prepared to inhabit this structure, to live among the people of God. How could such a thing be possible?

The early Christians who gathered in Jerusalem in the days after Jesus' death asked a similar question. Jesus had told them that his work on earth was finished and that he would soon be with them in a new way. He instructed them to wait and pray for a sign of his permanent presence. For the next couple of weeks we are going to consider the nature of this astonishing intimacy promised at Pentecost.

MONDAY 29 MAY
Standing in the Mystery

2 Chronicles 6:1–17; Psalm 8:1–4

'But will God really dwell on earth with men? The heavens,
even the highest heavens, cannot contain you' (2 Chron 6:18, NIV).

It is not hard to imagine the disill–usionment and fear that engulfed the disciples in the aftermath of Christ's vicious execution. Having lived with and loved the 'author of life', they had stood near the cross and watched him die. Jesus had cried out, 'It is finished', and that is exactly how they were feeling. It was over, finished. Their months of creative, transforming adventure with the dynamic teacher from Nazareth were ended.

It cannot have been easy for them to recognise that Jesus' cry from the cross was not an acknow–ledgment of failure but an affirm–ation of fulfilment. His life and work on earth were finished, completed, but Jesus was not abandoning his friends. The disciples had been told they were to wait for a new and remarkable breakthrough in their life with God. Jesus had promised them a Comforter – the Holy Spirit – who would stay with them forever.

And yet, they were so human. Even in their most hopeful moments the first disciples probably found themselves asking the question Solomon asked when he stood before his own completed work – the construction of the magnificent temple in Jerusalem: *Will God really dwell on earth with men?* How could such a thing be possible?

The construction of this place of worship was a project Solomon's father, David, had longed to oversee in his own reign. But God said, 'No.' The temple was not to be built by a warrior king but by his son, a man of peace. We can imagine Solomon standing on a palace parapet, look–ing out over a star–studded night sky and remembering both his father's dreams and his poems.

When I consider your heavens,
the work of your fingers,
the moon and the stars,
which you have set in place,
what is man that you are mindful of him?
  (Ps 8:3,4)

This is a mystery we can never adequately understand. The God of all power, all majesty, the God of the galaxy, is the God who wants to share the lives of ordinary men and women. Your life and mine.

TUESDAY 30 MAY
A Plea for Attention

Psalm 121

'Give attention to your servant's prayer and his plea
for mercy . . . May your eyes be open toward this temple
day and night' (2 Chron 6:19,20, NIV).

A murder trial is currently under way in my city. Two sixteen-year-old boys are accused of savagely killing their twelve-year-old brother. Much has been made in the media of the loneliness and deprivation of the home life of the accused, and of the incomprehensible lengths to which one of the young men was prepared to go in a desperate attempt to attract the attention of a girl. What a grim example of an attempt at dialogue gone wrong!

I venture to say that while the behaviour of the two young men was extreme and profoundly disturbing, there is a sense in which their action demonstrates one of the deepest needs of the human heart. Surely they were both simply wanting to be heard, to be taken seriously, to feel connected.

There were many reasons for Solomon and his people to celebrate the construction of the temple. For a nation tired of displacement the temple symbolised stability, permanence, a place of one's own. The intricate beauty of the edifice served to showcase to the world around them the talents and dedication of God's people.

Solomon's passionate prayer was that the temple would be much, much more than bricks and mortar. Above all, he longed for it to be a place where people prayed, a place where, day and night, there would be continuous, ongoing dialogue between God and his servants. So Solomon appeals for the Lord's perpetual watchfulness.

Many of us know what it is like to try to coax a toddler to sleep. Perhaps we read a story, sing a song, share a snack. Then, as we sit by the bedside we notice the way the little one keeps opening their eyes to see if we are still in the room. Can we be trusted to stay and keep them safe? When the child is finally fast asleep we quietly slip away.

The psalmist provides a reassurance that backdrops Solomon's prayer: God never slips away from the scene.

'He who watches over you will not slumber; indeed, he who watches over Israel will neither slumber nor sleep' (Ps 121:3,4).

WEDNESDAY 31 MAY

Hear... and Forgive

1 John 1:5–2:2

'Hear from heaven, your dwelling-place; and when you hear, forgive'
(2 Chron 6:21, NIV).

We have a Salvationist friend who has been a provincial court judge for twenty-five years. He is the youngest person ever to be appointed to this position in our part of Canada. I have often wanted to ask him if the things he is required to listen to, day in, day out, make him susceptible to world weariness or heaviness of heart. How does he guard against the temptation to cynicism or despair?

By the time of Solomon's dedicatory prayer for the temple, he had spent long years on the 'bench'. He is memorialised as the judicial genius of the ancient world. Is this why he clearly assumes that his people Israel – however well intentioned – will remain in perpetual need of forgiveness?

Solomon is wise enough to know that it is not a matter of 'if' the people sin, but 'when'. So he continues his prayer by cataloguing a whole range of human activities and predicaments in which there is a need for men and women to throw themselves upon divine mercy. He begs the Lord to hear and forgive.

A few years ago the editor of the journal *Theology Today* expressed his concern for the way in which contemporary culture ignores or trivialises sin. He entitled his editorial, 'God, Be Merciful to Me, a Miscalculator'. How unlike the Scripture which refuses to minimise the seriousness of sin. Solomon was well aware that 'the main human trouble is desperately difficult to fix, even for God, and sin is the longest running of human emergencies'[2]

The Pentecostal story is all about Christ's early disciples having to relinquish a kind of untested idealism and embrace a life of Spirit-assisted realism. Peter had been so cocky, so self-confident, so sure he had it right. But his self-knowledge was shallow. His failure and sin were as dramatic and brazen as his earlier boasts. His was a spectacular betrayal.

What a wonder that disciples then and now are the recipients of a spectacular mercy!

THURSDAY 1 JUNE
Hear... and Judge

Acts 5:1–10

'When a man wrongs his neighbour and is required to take an oath and he comes and swears the oath before your altar in this temple, then hear from heaven and act. Judge between your servants, repaying the guilty by bringing down on his own head what he has done' (2 Chron 6:22,23, NIV).

Trust and truth need to be present in all close relationships. If I do not believe that you are being honest with me, how can I have confidence in your words, your behaviour, your judgments?

Stories of the child-rearing practices of Susannah Wesley are legendary. Within her large and gifted family, which included John, the founder of Methodism, and Charles, the prolific poet and composer, she reinforced the importance of truth-telling through a consistent, deliberate strategy. The Wesley children knew that, no matter what the nature of a misbehaviour, if it was frankly confessed, the culprit would not be punished. What Susannah was never prepared to tolerate was duplicity or deceit.

Solomon believed that right worship required transparent relationships among the people of God. As his dedicatory prayer moved from praise, thanksgiving and confession to intercession (v. 22), his first request was that God would preserve integrity in the family of faith: 'Hear from heaven and act. Judge between your servants.' There is a definite link between a desire for an authentic encounter with God 'at the altar' and honesty and integrity with one's 'fellow servants' in the body of Christ.

This seems to have been the first painful lesson reinforced by the Spirit in the post-Pentecostal Church. The credibility of the Church was being established on the basis of its sacrificial love and unity. Onlookers were amazed by the manner in which these early Christians cared for each other and responded to one another's needs. And they did so with a joy and sincerity that attracted new converts.

What would shatter this was hypocrisy – the sin of pretending piety. Ananias and Sapphira, evidently hungry for admiration and respect, were prepared to manipulate and falsify in order to seem pious. God responded to their pretence with a swift and terrible judgment.

Hypocrisy still ruptures the body of Christ. It drives people away. It makes it so much harder for men, women and young people to respond to God's wooing love. Only transparency makes healthy church life possible. Authenticity is a litmus test for a watching world.

FRIDAY 2 JUNE
Bringing Prodigals Home

Luke 15:11–24

'Hear from heaven . . . and bring them back to the land you
gave to them and their fathers' (2 Chron 6:25, NIV).

In less than a decade the 24/7 prayer movement has circled the globe. Inspired by the example of a Moravian prayer meeting that commenced in 1727 and went on for 125 years without ceasing, Christians around the world have responded to the challenge to commit periods of time to uninterrupted prayer.

Prayer rooms have opened on high streets. Boardrooms and buses have become sanctuaries. I read of a man in a major European city who set up a prayer booth on his front lawn. He sits there all day every day, praying for discernment, listening to the problems shared with him by passers-by and responding to requests for intercessory prayer.

Perhaps most poignant are the bulletin boards in church basements plastered with crosses upon which are written the names of prodigals – loved sons and daughters who have wandered away from God.

I remember being moved as I read the crosses tacked to the wall of a crypt in an ancient English church:

'For Randy, not heard from in ten years. May he forgive us.'

'For Sandi who has left town with her boyfriend.'

'For Mark, away at uni and feeling that he has lost his faith.'

I was even more moved as I tacked up my own: 'For Jonathan – that he may return to God.'

Solomon envisioned the temple as a place saturated with prayer for prodigals, a place where people would pour out their hearts in love and longing. In these verses the chronicler asks God in a direct way for the homecoming of the nation's people from exile in Babylon – their collective 'time away'.

Do we make enough time in our congregational life for entreating the Lord to bring back those who have gone away? Perhaps more importantly, do we examine our own hearts and attitudes and ask God to make clear to us any factors that may have contributed to their leaving?

To reflect on

'The invitation is not about being rescued by Jesus over and over again, but about joining him in rounding up God's herd and recovering God's treasure.'

Barbara Brown Taylor

SATURDAY 3 JUNE
Hear . . . and Include

Acts 2:5–21

'Hear from heaven, your dwelling-place, and do whatever
the foreigner asks of you, so that all the peoples of the earth
may know your name and fear you, as do your own people Israel'
(2 Chron 6:33, NIV).

I live in Toronto, a city claiming to be the most multicultural in the world. More than half of the 4.5 million people living here are not Canadian-born. We are home to the largest Sri Lankan population outside of Sri Lanka, home to 600,000 immigrant Chinese. We are told that Toronto's 'Little India' contains the largest Indian bazaar outside India. Greeks, Koreans, Sudanese and Jamaicans, to name but a sampling, have made this nation their home.

Canadians will boast of the 'national mosaic', a cultural life that resembles the rich diversity of colourful ceramic tiles.

One of the most startling phrases in Solomon's prayer comes in verse 33. God is entreated to listen to the prayers of 'foreigners'. The divine hearing is presumed to be inclusive and unconditional. It is not that Solomon is a religious relativist. He is not implying that he believes all religions to be equally valid. Rather, he is praying that 'all the peoples of the earth may know your name', the name of the God who revealed himself to Israel.

Few questions are as important to the way Christians understand their mission in the twenty-first century as that of how we should understand our relationship to people of other faiths. It may be helpful to remember that it was also a burning issue in the eighteenth century in the wake of a vastly expanded global awareness of non-Christian religions.

John Wesley often brought his understanding of prevenient grace to bear upon the subject. That is, 'the grace that goes before'. By this he meant the awareness that in every encounter we ever have, in every place we ever visit, grace is already at work. The action of the Spirit of God always precedes our own action. John Wesley implored for holy hearts that could recognise this gift of God's grace and burn with a love that includes and embraces all humankind.

'Let your heart burn with love to all mankind, to friends and enemies, neighbours and strangers . . . to every soul which God hath made.'
John Wesley
(from A Word to a Protestant)

37

SUNDAY 4 JUNE
Fire from Heaven

Acts 1:1–11; 2:1–4

'When Solomon finished praying, fire came down from heaven and consumed the burnt offering and the sacrifices, and the glory of the LORD filled the temple' (2 Chron 7:1, NIV).

Several years ago I was teaching modern Christian history at a secular Canadian university. I was lecturing on the roots of twentieth-century Pentecostalism and on the book *Fire from Heaven* by the American sociologist and theologian Harvey Cox.

To help the students understand something of the history of Pentecostal language, I distributed a copy of the words of William Booth's song, 'Thou Christ of burning, cleansing flame' and let them listen to a contemporary Army recording. Before long the lecture hall was rocking with a diverse assembly of 'twenty-somethings' belting out Booth's late-nineteenth-century lyrics:

God of Elijah, hear our cry:
Send the fire . . .
The revolution now begin,
Send the fire today!

But what if God had done just that? What if we had seen fire from heaven, a lectern igniting and a room filling up with mysterious smoke? We can only imagine the sense of shock and awe.

Solomon had pleaded for God's presence with his people and God responded with a very public display of his glory and power – fire from heaven! The Israelites were overwhelmed, 'kneeling on the pavement with their faces to the ground' (*2 Chron 7:3*).

Fire is a potent religious symbol because it can hold multiple meanings. It is a transformative element. Fire can purge and purify, reshape and clarify. Fire can light up a dark night and generate a heat that can comfort and heal. The supernatural fire that fell on Solomon's sacrifices indicated that the people's offerings were acceptable.

When the early Christians praying in the upper room saw what looked like 'tongues of fire' resting on each of them, all these images must have flooded their minds. They emerged from that period of preparation with lives radically open to transformation by the Holy Spirit's fire.

John Wesley is reputed to have described his own spiritual ambition with similar religious imagery. What he wanted was a heart 'lit' or warmed by the Spirit and the opportunity to call upon others to come and watch his transformed life burn.

MONDAY 5 JUNE

My Heart, His Home

Ephesians 3:14–21; 4:1–6

'Don't you know that you yourselves are God's temple and that God's Spirit lives in you?' (1 Cor 3:16, NIV).

Several years ago some friends of ours moved into a new home constructed by Habitat for Humanity. The selection process for new home–owners is rigorous and we were thrilled for them. They had immigrated to Canada some years earlier and are the kind of citizens every nation cherishes. The family watched over every phase of construction, dreaming of the day when the new house would become their home.

Solomon spent long years overseeing the construction of a house for God – the temple at Jerusalem. He authorised the building plans, selected the materials and commissioned artisans. And yet, as he paced the parameters of the building site, the biblical text suggests that he felt a certain incredulity over the whole enterprise. 'Will God really dwell on earth with men?' he wondered.

The continuing words of Solomon's prayer indicate the maturity of his religious understanding: 'The heavens, even the highest heavens, cannot contain you. How much less this temple that I have built!' (*2 Chron 6:18*).

How much more staggering, then, were Paul's words to the gifted but cantankerous church of Corinth: 'Surely you know that you are God's temple and that God's Spirit lives in you?' Does God really dwell with us? And if so, how?

This is how Samuel Logan Brengle, the Salvation Army's revered holiness teacher, attempted to describe the Spirit's mysterious tenancy:

> When the Comforter comes, he takes possession of those bodies that are freely and fully presented to Him, and He touches their lips with grace; He shines peacefully and gloriously on their faces; He flashes beams of pity and compassion and heavenly affection from their eyes; He kindles a fire of love in their hearts and lights the flame of truth in their minds. They become His temple, and their hearts are a holy of holies in which His blessed presence ever abides.[3]

How about you? Is your life characterised by this kind of ingenuous hospitality to the work of the Spirit within you? Is God really at home in your heart, in your marriage, in your workplace?

TUESDAY 6 JUNE
A Glorious Ministry

Romans 15:5–17

'Now if the ministry that brought death, which was engraved in
letters on stone, came with glory, so that the Israelites could not
look steadily at the face of Moses because of its glory, fading though
it was, will not the ministry of the Spirit be even more glorious?'
(2 Cor 3:7,8, NIV).

There are few congregations of any denomination today which do not experience some tension between tradition and innovation, between old and new ways of expressing faith and seeking to influence culture. Ways of worship, approaches to evangelism and models of leadership are all under scrutiny and open to debate. It is rather comforting to keep this in historical perspective.

I was recently reading a Salvation Army document in which the author was lamenting the demise of Salvationist tradition. He wrote, 'We are living in a period of unprecedented change.' He was writing in the late 1890s!

Paul was a wise church leader. He understood the way that tradition shapes human life. He recognised the stability it can bring to human communities. He also knew from personal experience how attachment to tradition can harden into a rigidity that becomes resistant to the Spirit.

Paul affirmed the fact that there had been grace and power in his own religious tradition. Moses had met with God. There was no deny-ing this fact. The people witnessed the light on his face when he brought them the law, received in the very presence of the Lord at Sinai.

For generations the nation of Israel tried to live by the high standard of this protective moral code. When they were faithful to God's covenant demands they were a forceful power for good, a light to the nations. But for Paul, the new in-breaking of the Spirit was 'even more glorious'.

When Jesus prayed for his friends he indicated that their fellowship would reflect the very glory of his fellowship with his Father: 'I have given them the glory that you gave me, that they may be one as we are one' (John 17:22). One commentator suggests that from the apostle's perspective it was like the contrast between the light from a candle which provides adequate illumination to make one's way around a dark room, and the flooding-in of the full light of day.

Do we have eyes to discern signs of the Spirit's glorious in-breaking in our midst? Can we pray for this?

WEDNESDAY 7 JUNE
A Liberating Spirit

Galatians 5:13–26

'Now the Lord is the Spirit, and where the Spirit of the Lord is, there is freedom' (2 Cor 3:17, NIV).

We have a daughter who works on the residential staff of a Quaker boarding-school in a historic English city. She is our middle child and has always been a 'chatterbox', so we have been amused by her reaction to Quaker worship and spirituality. Let's just say that at times she has found the periods of meditative silence a challenge!

She is quick, however, to acknowledge the helpfulness of some of the wise sayings or maxims upon which the student body has meditated in the daily morning meeting. I shared one of my own favourite quotes attributed to the Quakers with her, one that has been written on the inside cover of my Bible for many years. It states: 'If you are very firmly attached at the centre, you can dare to be free around the periphery.'

In other words, a clear sense of what genuinely matters will leave us free from the bondage of second-ary issues. But how do we deter-mine what is central? It is a question that has often been put to religious teachers and leaders. The prophet Micah both posed the question and offered an answer: 'And what does

the LORD require of you? To act justly and to love mercy and to walk humbly with your God' (*Micah 6:8*).

An expert in the law asked Jesus, 'Of all the commandments, which is the most important?' Jesus replied, 'Love the Lord your God with all your heart and with all your soul and with all your mind and with all your strength . . . Love your neighbour as yourself' (*Mark 12:28,30,31*).

Would someone looking at our family life, our work practice, our congregational involvement be able to discern that all our activities circle around these priorities?

To reflect on

Most of us seem to be more concerned with strengthening our boundaries than with developing our centre. We let our edges become brittle and hard, or we barricade them in defence against new ideas or new relation-ships, and at the same time, we leave our centres relatively unattended.

John Robinson[4]

THURSDAY 8 JUNE
A Transforming Spirit

2 Corinthians 5:11–21

'And we, who with unveiled faces all reflect the Lord's glory,
are being transformed into his likeness with ever-increasing glory,
which comes from the Lord, who is the Spirit' (2 Cor 3:18, NIV).

The Jesuit fathers were on to something with their assertion that if they were able to influence a child for the first seven years of his life, that child was 'theirs' for life. Our capacity to retain the learning of those early years is remarkable.

'Metamorphosis' is one of the words I learned in my first years of primary school. So, for that matter, is 'pneumonoultramicroscopicsilicovolcanoconiosis' – reputed to be the longest word in the English language!

Our teacher would break up the long school days with spelling bees. The class would line up in rows as teams and by turn we would be given words to spell. A mistake meant you returned to your desk in disgrace!

It must have been spring when we not only learned to spell the word *metamorphosis*, but had its meaning explained. Our teacher showed us a shaggy cocoon, hanging from a branch in a glass beaker. For days we did not see much action from the tiny, confining bundle. But she assured us that we would observe 'metamorphosis' and so we waited in hope. Within that jar transformation was taking place – real change, brand–new possibility. A caterpillar was in the process of becoming a butterfly!

At the heart of the Salvationist's understanding of holiness is a belief in real change. Through salvation and sanctification we are increasingly transformed into the likeness of Christ. It is not just a matter of God relating to us 'as if' we are different. We are, in fact, by God's grace qualitatively new – radically open to God's deep healing of every part of our life, every aspect of our personality.

The holy life is a life where all the barriers against the Spirit's transformative intent have been dismantled. It is a life that has said 'Yes' to God's creative refinement.

So we pray today in the words of John Wesley:

'O God, purify our hearts, that we may entirely love thee and rejoice in being beloved of thee; that we may confide in thee and absolutely resign ourselves to thee and be filled with constant devotion to thee.'

FRIDAY 9 JUNE
A Truthful Spirit

John 8:31-40

'We do not use deception, nor do we distort the word of God. On the contrary, by setting forth the truth plainly we commend ourselves to every man's conscience in the sight of God' (2 Cor 4:2, NIV).

'Do you genuinely believe that anyone cares about doctrine? People today are interested in spiritual experience, not religious discourse or theology.' A friend challenged me as I was preparing to leave for meetings with the Salvation Army International Doctrine Council. Her words made me pause.

For me, theology is all about the ways the historic Christian community has thought about the *really* big questions of human existence – who God is and who we are in relation to him, the nature of meaning, purpose and ultimate destiny. I replied that whether people are formally interested in doctrine or not, to be human is to ponder theological questions.

I do, however, understand the context of my friend's comment. At least in Canada, the denominational boundaries which often represent doctrinal diversity are increasingly fuzzy and fluid. People rarely leave churches over conflicting views concerning the atonement or resurrection. And they rarely join churches on the basis of particular propositional truth.

Some years ago, in a booklet entitled *Doctrine Without Tears*, General John Larsson (retired) highlighted the necessity of humility in doctrinal study. He wrote:

> Humility will save us from thinking that we, and we alone, have hold of the truth. There is no person, group, denomination or church here on earth which is the sole custodian of all truth. Final truth is beyond our comprehension and is far bigger than the insight of any man or any group will ever be.

How then could Paul, in his Corinthian letter, claim to be 'setting forth the truth plainly'? Perhaps because the New Testament so often equates truth with the Spirit of Jesus. Jesus told his disciples, 'I am the way, the truth and the life' (*John 14:6*).

It is ludicrous to think that, this side of heaven, we will have comprehensive answers to many of life's questions. Theology at best is a tentative venture. But with the apostle John we can thankfully assert that 'grace and truth came through Jesus Christ. No-one has ever seen God, but God the One and Only, who is at the Father's side, has made him known' (*John 1:17,18*).

SATURDAY 10 JUNE
An Encouraging Spirit

Luke 8:4–15

'Therefore we do not lose heart. Though outwardly we are wasting away, yet inwardly we are being renewed day by day' (2 Cor 4:16, NIV).

I believe it was the American humorist Mark Twain who claimed that he could live for months on one good compliment! There is something delightful about receiving a card of thanks, a note of affirmation, a promise of prayer. Sadly, I suspect that many Christian workers go weeks without receiving any such encouragement. This is troubling, because ministry is hard work. And it is all too easy to lose heart.

Jesus' well-known parable of the sower and the seeds suggests plenty of reasons why ministry can become discouraging. Some of the 'seed' that an individual in ministry tries to scatter falls into hard, resistant ground. Some of it lands in shallow environments. Often people are open enough to gospel perspectives but a lifestyle of obedient discipleship is 'choked' or killed by numerous secondary involvements. It can feel as if those who 'hear the word, retain it and persevere' are far too few for the mission possibilities the Spirit sets before us.

Paul's word to the Corinthians takes all these responses into account. He does not deny that ministry is hard. In fact, in both his letters to the self-absorbed, self-satisfied church at Corinth he reminds them of just how daunting spiritual leadership can be.

'Rather, as servants of God we commend ourselves in every way: in great endurance; in troubles, hardships and distresses; in beatings, imprisonments and riots; in hard work, sleepless nights and hunger,' he says (2 Cor 6:4,5).

It is very true, he states, that God's servants can find themselves hard pressed, perplexed, persecuted and struck down. But because the power is from God and not a matter of our own strength or determination, we are 'not crushed . . . not in despair . . . not abandoned . . . not destroyed' (4:8).

How wonderful it is to have friends who can remind us when the going is tough to fix our eyes not on what is seen but on what is unseen; friends who assure us that they love us and pray for our work! Can you make time today to encourage someone who regularly speaks God's word to you?

44

SUNDAY 11 JUNE
A Glimpse into the Mystery

Isaiah 55:8–9

'As the heavens are higher than the earth, so are my ways higher than your ways and my thoughts than your thoughts' (v. 9, NIV).

These verses invite us into a mystery – the mystery of God's mind and heart. In making a comparison between our thoughts and his thoughts, God is not condemning human ways but simply stating as fact the superiority of the divine way.

There are times when we need to take a firm hold on this fact and not let it go – when a baby is born and lives for just a few minutes; when a terrible accident turns life upside down for an individual, a family, or a whole community; when a violent incident leaves scars far worse than skin-deep; when a young man dies long before his potential has been realised. In such devastating moments we need to be able to bring our 'Why?' and 'What for?' and 'How?' questions to the perspective of Someone who can see far higher, wider, longer and deeper than our eyes can scan.

It was the very thought of this mystery that brought Paul to his knees (see *Eph 3:14–19*). As he prayed for the believers at Ephesus, he tried to put the mystery into words but words failed him. He prayed that they might receive God's strength. He prayed that they might have God's power. He prayed that they might know God's love. But then he checked himself, realising that such love is too high to be known, too wide to be embraced, too long to be measured, too deep to be fathomed.

All Paul could do was commit the Ephesians to the 'immeasurably more' of God. As Eugene Peterson puts it, 'Far more than you could ever imagine or guess or request in your wildest dreams!' (*Eph 3:20, The Message*).

Added to this mystery is the even greater mystery that God delights to use us, fickle, fraught and fragile as we are, to achieve his sovereign purposes. Through all that happens to us, his plans are being worked out (*Jer 29:11*).

Bow in the presence of mystery today. Bend low before the God whose love is unfailing (Ps 13:5), whose greatness is unfathomable (Ps 145:3), whose riches are unsearchable (Eph 3:8).

THE WORD BECAME FLESH

John 1 – 7

Introduction

John's Gospel is markedly different from the Gospels of Matthew, Mark and Luke. John gives no genealogy of Jesus, no account of his birth or childhood. He records no parables and tells only eight of Jesus' miracles. John is obviously coming from quite a different perspective from the other Gospel writers. He presents not narration but carefully crafted evidence that Jesus is who he says he is.

The first verse of the first chapter of John's Gospel makes the claim that Jesus is the Word of God, the very expression of God's heart and mind enfleshed in human form. John then writes twenty–one chapters to explain and expand that claim. He puts the spotlight on Jesus and presents him as the Son of God, given as a gift to the whole world (3:16). He uses recurring themes of 'light' and 'life', the wide–ranging 'I am' titles of Jesus, and a full account of Jesus' teaching to record his life, death and resurrection.

John states his purpose for writing towards the end of his Gospel: 'That you may believe that Jesus is the Christ, the Son of God, and that by believing you may have life in his name' (20:31). As you read this Gospel with both your head and your heart may John's God–given purpose be realised in your life.

> He is unparalleled and unprecedented.
> He is the centrepiece of civilisation.
> He is the superlative of all excellence.
> He is the sum of human greatness.
> He is the source of divine grace.
> His name is the only one able to save,
>   and his blood is the only power able to cleanse.
> His ear is open to the sinner's call.
> His hand is quick to lift the fallen soul.
> He's the eternal lover of us all – every one,
> And you can trust him.

From a prayer spontaneously offered by the late Dr S.M. Lockridge

MONDAY 12 JUNE
In the Beginning . . . the Word

John 1:1–5

'In the beginning was the Word, and the Word was with God,
and the Word was God' (v. 1, NIV).

'In the beginning God . . .' So begins the first chapter of the first book of the first testament. Genesis 1 describes the action of God in creating the universe. 'God said . . . it was so . . . God saw that it was good.'

Across galaxies and generations the apostle John writes of that same beginning. 'In the beginning was the Word, and the Word was with God, and the Word was God.' He uses only eight words, repeating some of them to make a sentence of seventeen words in all. Only one word has more than one syllable. It is the simplest of sentences that a five–year–old could read. It is the most profound of statements that scholars struggle to fathom.

This is John's introduction of Jesus, a human being whom he knew and loved, and, at the same time, the ultimate revelation of God, the expression of God's holiness, the One from whom all life flows.

In calling Jesus 'the Word', John speaks to both Jews and Greeks. Jews understood the Word to be the agent of creation, the God–given message of the prophets, the expression of God's law. But to their way of thinking, to call Jesus 'the Word' was pure blasphemy.

Greeks understood the Word to be both the spoken word and the unspoken word still in the mind – the reason or intention. But to the Greek way of thinking, the Word becoming flesh was pure impossibility.

For John the apostle, however, this Word is pure gospel. In the person of Jesus, God has wrapped in human flesh his purpose and intention for the whole world – for Jews, Greeks and all mankind.

John's entire Gospel needs to be read in the light of this first verse. Time and again he will introduce Jesus, explaining who he is. He is the Word, he is light, he is life, he is a great teacher, a miracle–worker and so much more.

'Who is he in yonder stall?' asks songwriter Benjamin Russell Hanby (*SASB 104*). Who is he, indeed? It may be the most important question we will ever consider.

TUESDAY 13 JUNE
The True Light

John 1:6–13

'The true light that gives light to every man was coming into the world' (v. 9, NIV).

In his opening verses John declares some of the great themes of his Gospel: 'In the beginning was the Word'; 'In him was life'; 'The light shines in the darkness'. John goes on to introduce certain key words that will weave their way like golden threads through his whole Gospel: 'witness', 'light', 'world', 'believe', 'receive', 'become', 'children . . . of God'.

In one sentence, masterful for its brevity, John writes of incarnation ('He was in the world'), creation ('the world was made through him') and rejection ('the world did not recognise him').

With just a few brushstrokes John the writer introduces John the Baptist, telling what he was and what he was not. John the Baptist was a witness, a forerunner, a signpost to someone far greater than himself. He was a flashlight shining in the darkness, drawing attention not to himself but to the source of all light – the Son of God.

Even though John the Baptist's testimony was clear, Jesus still experienced rejection. The light shining in the darkness encountered enmity and hostility. Opposition to the True Light was severe. The world that the Word entered and that God loves with a passion (see 3:16) was a place of unbelief. Those opposed to him tried by all means to silence and defeat the Word in a struggle that took him all the way to the cross.

'But the darkness has not understood it,' says John. To 'understand' in this context is both to grasp with the mind, and to grasp with the hand and thus overcome or destroy. Darkness and defeat and death will not have the last word. Jesus will overcome the darkness. The cross itself, far from being a symbol of ultimate defeat, will become a symbol of glory and of victory over death. Jesus, the True Light, will not be extinguished.

These verses are a richly textured fabric with life–giving themes. Read them out aloud today. Sense the power of the inextinguishable light that Jesus brought into the world and continues to bring to all who walk in his way (see 1 John 1:7).

WEDNESDAY 14 JUNE
The Perfect Neighbour

John 1:14–18

'The Word became flesh and made his dwelling among us.
We have seen his glory, the glory of the One and Only, who came
from the Father, full of grace and truth' (v. 14, NIV).

A recent television programme featured 'Neighbours from Hell'. They were not gruesome aliens from another planet but rude, awkward, unkempt, inconsiderate humans who let garbage overflow, children curse, animals scavenge and far, far worse.

In stark contrast, Jesus 'became flesh and blood, and moved into the neighbourhood' (*The Message*). He was literally the neighbour from heaven. When he took on human form and pitched his tent in our midst, he brought with him generous gifts of glory, grace and truth. Once again John summarises in just a few words some of the great themes of Scripture.

The Word came as the perfect expression of God in human form. Moses was given God's commandments engraved on stone tablets. The prophets were given messages to explain what was on God's heart. But in Jesus, 'the One and Only, who came from the Father', God's very nature and being were expressed in a way that could be seen, heard and touched (see *1 John 1:1*).

The Word came as the perfect teacher. If words suddenly appeared in the sky or on a wall they would be noticed but quickly forgotten as a passing phenomenon. But Jesus came and sat down among us as a rabbi, a teacher, speaking words that were compelling and life-giving. If we want to know what God thinks, we need to listen to what Jesus taught.

The Word came as the perfect example. If we want to know how God calls us to live as a Christ-follower, we need to place our feet in Jesus' footprints. The apostle Peter wrote, 'Christ suffered for you, leaving you an example, that you should follow in his steps' (*1 Pet 2:21*).

The Word came as the perfect sacrifice. Jesus came into a system of sacrifices offered 'endlessly year after year' (*Heb 10:1*) as people tried and tried to find forgiveness and peace with God. By offering himself in a once-and-for-all-time sacrifice, Jesus put an end to that futile repetition (see *Col 1:19–20*).

The Word who became flesh and made his dwelling among us is indeed the perfect neighbour from heaven!

THURSDAY 15 JUNE
Lamb of God

John 1:19–34

'The next day John saw Jesus coming toward him and said,
"Look, the Lamb of God, who takes away the sin of the world!"'
(v. 29, NIV).

Unlike the Gospel writers Matthew and Mark, John records none of the eccentricities of John the Baptist – his strange camel-hair clothing, and his way-out diet (*Matt 3:4*). But the wild man of the desert certainly causes a stir. Many people from Jerusalem and the surrounding area come out to him either to be baptised or to inquire about his work. One such delegation made up of priests and Levites is sent by the 'religious police' in Jerusalem to check him out. 'Who are you?' they ask. 'The Christ . . . Elijah . . . the Prophet?'

John the Baptist denies all three titles. He is not 'the Christ' – a Greek translation of the Hebrew word for 'Messiah'. He is not Elijah, the greatest of the Old Testament prophets, who the Jews believed would reappear at the end of time. He is not 'the Prophet', a Moses-like figure who was expected to return to Israel some time in the future (see *Deut 18:15*).

John identifies himself merely as 'a voice' and quotes Isaiah 40:3 to declare his role in Jesus' mission. He makes no claims about himself,

seeks no centre place, no glory. He is just a messenger, a signpost pointing to someone who is coming, someone so great that John considers himself unworthy even to do the most menial task that a slave would do – untying sandals.

That Someone appears almost immediately – the next day in fact. When John sees Jesus coming towards him he points and declares, 'Look, there he is, the Lamb of God, who takes away the sin of the world!' For all that John does not yet fully understand (*v. 31*), he knows from what he has seen that Jesus is the Lamb of God (*v. 29*) and the Son of God (*v. 34*). This is John's testimony, his conviction, the very reason for his own existence.

To reflect on
What would your life be like if you saw yourself in this kind of John the Baptist role? How can you be a voice or a pen or a paintbrush, drawing attention not to yourself but to Jesus?

FRIDAY 16 JUNE
Rabbi, Messiah

John 1:35–39

'Turning around, Jesus saw them following and asked, "What do you want?" They said, "Rabbi, (which means Teacher), "where are you staying?"' (v. 38, NIV).

Notice the names for Jesus that surface in this passage – Lamb of God, Rabbi, Messiah. These names and the others mentioned in John's early chapters are like the table of contents for his Gospel. They will be picked up again and again in the next twenty chapters as the identity of Jesus is revealed and confirmed through his actions.

For the second day in a row, when John the Baptist sees Jesus coming, he declares him to be the Lamb of God. Two of John's disciples hear him use this title for Jesus. One is Andrew, Simon Peter's brother, and the other is probably John, the writer of this Gospel. Note what these two do in response – 'they followed Jesus'. This is exactly what John the Baptist wanted them to do.

A spirited exchange then takes place. As Jesus sees them coming after him he asks, 'What do you want?' They reply with their own question, 'Where are you staying?' Jesus says, 'Come and you will see.' This is the vocabulary of discipleship – 'follow', 'come and see', 'stay'. Jesus invites them not only to his lodgings but also into relationship with him.

Hearing the gospel message is only ever the first step towards discipleship. There must be a 'coming and seeing' for oneself, a personal experience of meeting Jesus and the conscious choice to follow him for oneself.

Think of the villagers to whom the woman at the well told her story. They invited Jesus to 'come and stay' with them for two days then later told the woman, 'We no longer believe just because of what you said; now we have heard for ourselves, and we know that this man really is the Saviour of the world' (4:42).

Have you heard the gospel for yourself or are you living on the strength of someone else's testimony?

To reflect on
How would you respond today if Jesus asked you, 'What do you want?' and 'Where are you staying?' Consider where your spirit resides, where you are most 'at home'. Invite Jesus into this living space and show him around.

SATURDAY 17 JUNE
Son of Joseph, Son of God

John 1:40–51

'The first thing Andrew did was to find his brother Simon and tell him, "We have found the Messiah" (that is, the Christ). And he brought him to Jesus' (vv. 41,42, NIV).

There is a lot more finding and bringing, coming and seeing in these verses for today. As always, the verbs take us to the heart of the passage.

Andrew hears John the Baptist speak his testimony of Jesus. The first thing he does is go and find his brother Simon Peter. This is always Andrew's priority. He tells him about Jesus, then brings Peter to meet the Messiah for himself. The next day Jesus invites Philip to follow him and Philip immediately goes to find Nathanael and brings him to Jesus.

These verses suggest an unaffected, natural rhythm in the passing on of the gospel message. One hears, tells and brings. The next one hears, tells and brings. The next one hears, tells and brings. And so the word is spread through families and friends in ever-increasing circles.

When Simon Peter and then Nathanael are brought to meet Jesus they find that he sees them not just with a passing glance but with the far-seeing eye of One who knows their past, their present and their future. To both men Jesus speaks a word of prophecy.

'Simon, son of John . . . You will be called Cephas' (v. 42). Peter will prove, initially, to be far from rock-like. His impulsive nature and his ultimate denial of Jesus make a prediction about his solid dependability sound far-fetched. But Jesus, who sees the big picture of this man's life, knows that frailty and failure will not have the last word.

When Jesus sees Nathanael he speaks a similar word of encouragement. 'There's a real Israelite, not a false bone in his body' (v. 47, The Message). 'How do you know this?' Nathanael asks in surprise. Jesus simply replies, 'I saw you . . . before Philip called you.'

For all that these fresh-faced new recruits see of Jesus on their first day of following, they themselves have been much more deeply seen. And what they are about to see is far more than they can possibly imagine (v. 51).

To reflect on
How deeply do you think Jesus 'sees' you? Check out Psalm 139.

SUNDAY 18 JUNE
God's Powerful Word

Isaiah 55:10–11

'My word that goes out from my mouth . . . will not return to me empty, but will accomplish what I desire and achieve the purpose for which I sent it' (v. 11, NIV).

These verses are an anchor for anyone whose burden it is to preach or teach the word of God. These verses are an invitation for anyone whose privilege it is to listen to the word of God. What might God's purposes be today as his word is broken like bread and offered in the place where you worship?

God's word may come to you, as it did to the apostle John on the island of Patmos, with a voice like the sound of rushing waters. 'Out of his mouth', reported John, 'came a sharp double-edged sword' (see *Rev 1:15,16*).

God's word may confront you with teaching, as it did for Ezekiel. God may unroll a scroll before you and tell you to eat it, to let it become part of you and fill you with its sweetness (see *Ezek 3:1–3*).

God may challenge you with a task, as he did for Isaiah, calling you to go and tell and turn the hearts of men and women in your generation back to God and his ways of righteousness (see *Isa 6:8,9*).

However God's word is proclaimed and heard today, and whether you are a proclaimer or a hearer, the promise is that it will accomplish what God desires and achieve the purposes for which he sends it out. Just as rain falls and makes the earth fruitful, so God's word will flourish.

In a world where things are changing all the time or, as the prophet says, 'grass withers and . . . flowers fall' (*40:8*), the word of God stands sure and solid. Have you built your life upon it or are you still in the process of deciding? You could have no firmer foundation.

Let us not come with any casualness or carelessness to worship today. Whether your burden is to preach the word, or your privilege is to hear it preached, remember: 'The word of God is living and active. Sharper than any double-edged sword, it penetrates even to dividing soul and spirit, joints and marrow; it judges the thoughts and attitudes of the heart' (*Heb 4:12*).

MONDAY 19 JUNE
Miracle Worker

John 2:1–12

'This, the first of his miraculous signs, Jesus performed at
Cana in Galilee. He thus revealed his glory, and his disciples
put their faith in him' (v. 11, NIV).

John's Gospel features none of Jesus' teaching parables. There is no sower and soils, no treasure hidden in a field, no stories about mustard seeds, pearls or yeast. But when Jesus changes water into wine at a wedding John records it as 'the first of his miraculous signs' and gives certain clues that this is a kind of enacted parable to be read on several levels.

The timing of the event – 'On the third day' – may be John's first clue. Is he about to tell something that will have its parallel 'on the third day' of the resurrection?

Jesus and his disciples and family are at a wedding, an important celebration in ancient Israel. When the Jewish people reflected on heaven or the arrival of the Messiah they often thought of it in terms of a wedding banquet.

Following a public betrothal the family would announce the wedding date and elaborate preparations would be made for a ceremony that could last for up to a week. When the wine runs out at this particular ceremony the host is not just embarrassed but shamed.

Jesus' mother Mary, mentioned here for the first time, refers the matter to her son. She is not necessarily looking for a miracle, simply asking him to do something to redeem the situation. But he has come to redeem more than a housekeeping glitch. 'My time has not yet come,' he says. But it will (see *12:23*).

Nearby stand six stone jars used for holding water for Jewish purification washings. Jesus tells the servants to fill these stone jars with water right to the brim. When some of the liquid is drawn off and taken to the head steward, it has become wine, and not just good wine, but the best wine, real vintage wine.

The head steward and the guests have no idea where this superior wine has come from but the servants have seen and they know. This will be the pattern throughout Jesus' ministry. The servants, the poor people, the empty-handed ones will see and understand and believe. Others will be merely puzzled.

TUESDAY 20 JUNE
Temple Purger, Temple Raiser

John 2:13–25

'To those who sold doves he said, "Get these out of here!
How dare you turn my Father's house into a market!"' (v. 16, NIV).

The other Gospel writers place the cleansing of the temple after Jesus' triumphal entry into Jerusalem at the start of the week leading to his death. John, however, places the incident at the beginning of his ministry, strategically next to the miracle at Cana. Themes of replacement and fulfilment portrayed in the first incident are now played out on a larger scale.

Passover was an annual festival in spring which celebrated Israel's exodus from Egypt. Jewish families were expected to travel to Jerusalem to participate in sacrifice, share a symbolic meal and reflect on their salvation. Since pilgrims needed unblemished animals for sacrifice a considerable business had grown in the city at this time of the year. Animals were sold in the temple courts and payment for these, plus the half-shekel annual tax which Jewish men over twenty were required to pay, had to be made in special coinage – hence the need for money–changers.

Jesus' anger is not necessarily in response to greed or dishonesty on the part of the money–changers but simply that these transactions are taking place in the temple. 'Get your things out of here! Stop turning my Father's house into a shopping mall!' (v. 16, The Message). When the disciples witness his outburst they recall Psalm 69:9 (NIV): 'Zeal for your house consumes me.'

The Jews are shocked, and challenge his authority to cause such an upheaval in the temple. Jesus ignores the question and responds with a strange reference to his own destruction and resurrection. 'Tear down this Temple and in three days I'll put it back together' (v. 19, The Message). He is referring, of course, to his own body but the Jews, now confused as well as shocked, cannot understand how he could possibly rebuild in three days what has taken forty-six years to construct. Even Jesus' disciples are puzzled. It is only after Jesus' death and resurrection that they understand his cryptic saying.

John's account is still in its early stages but the scene is already set for conflict. Themes of identity, rejection and belief will wend their way right through this Gospel.

WEDNESDAY 21 JUNE

Life Giver

John 3:1–21

'Jesus declared, "I tell you the truth, no-one can see the kingdom of God unless he is born again"' (v. 3, NIV).

John's second chapter ends with his comment that Jesus 'did not need man's testimony about man, for he knew what was in a man' (*v. 25*). The next chapter opens with 'Now there was a man.' Nicodemus becomes a living illustration of the statement that has just been made.

Nicodemus is a Jewish leader who comes to Jesus at night under cover of darkness. He comes respectfully, addressing Jesus as 'Rabbi' and acknowledging that Jesus is 'a teacher... come from God'. 'We know...' he says.

His confident assurance of Jesus' identity is based on the signs Jesus has made. But Jesus has already stated that he does not entrust himself to anyone whose faith is based on signs (*2:23–24*). With Nicodemus' opening comments, therefore, John sets up a dialogue that contains certainty and confusion, knowing and not knowing – in a phrase, light and darkness.

Jesus makes a statement that goes to the heart of the matter. 'I tell you the truth, no-one can see the kingdom of God unless he is born again.'

'That's the very point,' replies Nicodemus. 'How can it happen? How can a fully grown adult like myself be born again? It's physically impossible.'

It is interesting to note that the Greek word *anothen* means both 'again' and 'from above'. To be born *anothen* speaks both of a time of birth ('again') and the place from which this new birth comes ('from above'). Jesus' words speak of a radical new birth, initiated from above, but Nicodemus' language and imagination do not stretch that far.

Using a fresh set of images to move Nicodemus out of his misunderstanding, Jesus speaks of being born of water and the Spirit. He speaks of wind but this too has a double meaning. The offer of new birth is like the wind/spirit – a mystery beyond human knowledge and control.

Nicodemus responds with incredulity: 'How can this be?' Jesus replies with irony. This man who claimed he knew certain things knows nothing much at all. He has a lot to learn before he moves out of darkness and into the light.

THURSDAY 22 JUNE
One and Only Son

John 3:11–21

'For God so loved the world that he gave his one and only
Son, that whoever believes in him shall not perish but
have eternal life' (v. 16, NIV).

In response to Nicodemus' 'How?', Jesus speaks words that gather up all the contrasting threads of the Gospel. He speaks of earthly things and heavenly things; gone into heaven, came from heaven; the snake lifted up, the Son of Man lifted up; not to condemn but to save; whoever believes, whoever does not believe; light has come, men loved darkness.

This passage is like a glorious piece of fabric woven with strong bold colours in and out, in and out, telling both the story of salvation and also your story and mine. At the heart of the passage is a verse that contains the gospel in a nutshell. For many believers this will be one of the earliest verses of Scripture ever memorised. But for all its familiarity, the depths of this verse will always be unfathomable, its broad reach far beyond our human comprehension.

To believe in Jesus is to believe that he is the Son of God and that God loved the world so much that he gave this 'one and only Son' as a gift. When John writes of 'the world' (in Greek *kosmos*) he is not referring to the natural world of trees, plants and animals, but the realm of humanity. Jesus entered this world of people in his incarnation knowing that he would face hostility and opposition, and that the sacrifice of his own life would be needed in order to redeem the world.

In the wide mercy of God, Jesus did not come to the world just to save a select few, a predetermined, privileged group. Rather he came to save the whole world; that is, the all-encompassing, all-embracing circle of men and women who inhabit this planet.

The God revealed in Jesus is a God whose love knows no limits and who asks only that we receive this gift. God loved and gave not as a judgment, but as an invitation. Whoever accepts this invitation will be forever changed by it.

How have you responded to this amazing invitation? Give thanks today for the God who has loved and given you so much.

FRIDAY 23 JUNE

Bridegroom

John 3:22–36

'The bride belongs to the bridegroom. The friend who attends
the bridegroom waits and listens for him, and is full of joy
when he hears the bridegroom's voice. That joy is mine,
and it is now complete' (v. 29, NIV).

John the Baptist and Jesus are both baptising in separate places – Jesus in Judea and John near Salim – when an argument breaks out between some of John's disciples and a certain unnamed Jew over the matter of ceremonial washing. John's disciples are disturbed because people are turning from John and following Jesus. 'Everyone is going to him,' they declare.

This complaint gives John the Baptist the opportunity to remind them of his role. 'I am not the Christ,' he says. He is merely the forerunner, the way–preparer, the signpost for the Anointed One of God. He calls himself the friend of the bridegroom who 'attends ... waits and listens' for the bridegroom and is full of joy when he hears the bridegroom's voice. Just as the arrival of the bridegroom marks the end of the friend's role, so John's work is now coming to an end as Jesus' ministry gathers momentum.

John the Baptist describes Jesus as 'the one who comes from above'. He bears God's Spirit without limit (v. 34). He has come with a revela-tion that is completely different from anything in the world, a revelation that comes directly from God the Father (v. 35).

By contrast, John is 'the one who is from the earth'. If this man ever grappled with the heady temptation to encourage a cult following ('The Camel–hair Community' or 'Locust Lovers for the Lord'!) he gives no hint of it. His whole life has been given to pointing towards the Christ. This is his high calling, the God–given vocation by which he has lived (v. 27) and for which he will die.

John continues to point to Jesus who bears the divine nature and carries God's authority. Those who believe in the Son of God are making a choice for life. Those who reject the Son of God are making a choice for darkness and judgment.

To reflect on

In these verses John the Baptist sums up his life, his calling, his role: 'He must become greater; I must become less.' How would you sum up God's calling in your life?

SATURDAY 24 JUNE
Weary One

John 4:1–26

'Jacob's well was there, and Jesus, tired as he was from the journey, sat down by the well. It was about the sixth hour' (v. 6, NIV).

This passage contains the rich portrait of Jesus meeting a Samaritan woman at a well in Sychar. Several titles for Jesus are revealed here. He is the Discerner of Human Need, Quencher of Deep Thirst, the Messiah. But an almost throwaway comment at the beginning of the account speaks yet another name. He is the Weary One.

Jesus and his team have been travelling on foot and his disciples have left him by the well of Sychar while they go off to buy food. Alone by the well with the noonday sun beating down, Jesus is 'tired . . . from the journey'. We might also add hot, dusty and thirsty.

Pause for a moment with this haunting picture of a very human Jesus. Was he merely tired by the distance he and his friends had covered that morning or is John hinting at something deeper? Having come from God, is Jesus tired of the world, tired of life, tired of time? How human is that!

Do you and I not feel a similar bone–deep weariness at times? How do you pray in that weary place? I wonder how Jesus prayed in his moments of solitude and weariness on that particular day.

With the arrival at the well of the Samaritan woman, a discussion ensues that reveals the mystery of the incarnation. As the human Son of Man, Jesus, the Weary One, asks her for a drink of water. As the divine Son of God, he offers her 'a spring of water welling up to eternal life' (v. 14).

He who needed a rest says to us today, 'Come to me, all you who are weary and burdened, and I will give you rest' (Matt 11:28).

The well is deep and I require
A draught of the water of life,
But none can quench my soul's desire
For a draught of the water of life;
Till one draws near who the cry will
* heed,*
Helper of men in their time of need,
And I, believing, find indeed
That Christ is the water of life
*   Albert Orsborn, SASB 351*

SUNDAY 25 JUNE

Go Out in Joy

Isaiah 55:12–13

'You will go out in joy and be led forth in peace; the mountains and hills will burst into song before you, and all the trees of the field will clap their hands' (v. 12, NIV).

This is a day for going out in joy! These words were originally written for the exiles returning to Jerusalem from their captivity in Babylon. God promised that all nature would join in a song of celebration at their return. Mountains and hills would burst forth in songs of praise. Trees would applaud and shout for joy. Weeds and straggly thorn bushes would give way to strong pine trees and fragrant myrtle.

Forty days after his resurrection, Jesus went out with his disciples from Jerusalem to the Mount of Olives. There he spoke his final words to them before being taken up into the sky 'before their very eyes' (*Acts 1:9*). This moment marked the end of his earthly ministry, the completion of his task.

While it must have been joy for him to return to the Father, his going left his disciples with questions: 'Why does he have to go? Why could he not stay?' All they could do was wait and pray, as he had told them to do. Within ten days they realised that Jesus' departure in fact made way for the Holy Spirit to come.

These verses from Isaiah are a promise for you and me in all the goings out that we will do this week. Our going out may take us to the ordinary routine places of work or study or shopping, or it may take us to difficult places where joy seems absent – a loved one's funeral, a hospital appointment, a court hearing. Wherever you go out to, may these strong words of Scripture accompany you.

God spoke this very promise to me almost thirty years ago on the morning my husband and children and I left Zambia. As we headed home for medical treatment and an unknown future, God said, 'You will go out in joy and be led forth in peace.' I saw no trees clapping their hands that day. I heard no mountains singing praise. But I do know that that cold wintry morning turned steadily to a new springtime in my life. Thanks be to God!

MONDAY 26 JUNE
Saviour of the World

John 4:27–42

'They said to the woman, "We no longer believe just because of what you said; now we have heard for ourselves, and we know that this man really is the Saviour of the world"' (v. 42, NIV).

In John's Gospel nothing is random. Certain words have overtones, deeper meanings, subtle references to other words. The placing of certain incidents is significant. At times John states a principle then tells a story to illustrate that principle.

The fact that John's chapter four comes after chapter three is more than a logical sequence. In the earlier chapter John wrote of God loving the world so much that 'he gave his one and only Son, that whoever believes in him shall not perish but have eternal life. For God did not send his Son into the world to condemn the world, but to save the world through him' (3:16,17). The wide embrace of these verses encompasses both the whole world and every individual ('whoever'). This is the principle stated clearly.

In chapter four John gives two examples of this principle in action. First, Jesus meets a Samaritan woman. As they speak she becomes the 'whoever' who believes. Just as the good news of the birth of baby Jesus came first to humble shepherds, so the good news of life-giving water comes to this woman who is an unlikely candidate for the grace of God because she is foreign, female and fallen.

She leaves her water jar and hurries back to town where she tells the people about this man whom she has met and who knows everything about her. 'Could this be the Christ?' she wonders out loud, longing for it to be so. The townspeople come out to the well and urge Jesus to come and stay with them. After two days of listening they are convinced that he is the Christ, the Saviour of the world. And so the principle of John 3:16,17 takes flesh, first in the woman then in the townspeople.

In between these two incidents the disciples return with food for Jesus. His earlier weariness and thirst are now forgotten. They urge him to eat but he speaks of a sustenance more satisfying than a steak sandwich. They bring 'hamburgers' but he sees the harvest all around him, ripe and ready for gathering.

TUESDAY 27 JUNE

Healer

John 4:43–54

'Jesus replied, "You may go. Your son will live." The man took Jesus at his word and departed' (v. 50, NIV).

Jesus returns to Cana in Galilee where his first miracle of changing water into wine had taken place. He knows that the Galileans are more interested in miracles than in what God is actually doing in their midst but he has no time for those who seek signs and wonders simply for their entertainment value.

In Cana he is approached by 'a certain royal official' whose son is desperately, deathly ill at Caper-naum, twenty miles away. This royal official was probably an officer in Herod's service and, as such, would have legal authority over Jesus. He comes, however, with humility of spirit and addresses Jesus as 'Sir'.

As a man used to giving orders he expresses his anguish for his son in the way he speaks to Jesus. 'Come down before my son dies,' he says. Jesus mirrors the man's abruptness by answering, 'You may go. Your son will live.'

The healing words sound so effortless. Jesus asks for no details about the child. He makes no offer to go to the man's house. He does not seem to consider the distance to be any hindrance. He simply speaks a healing, living word, then tells him to go.

As the man returns home, his servants meet him with the news that the fever has passed and the boy is recovering. The father asks when the change took place and is amazed to realise that it was at the exact moment when Jesus spoke his healing words, 'Your son will live.' The upshot is that not only the father but all his household believe and put their trust in Jesus.

Notice how faith grows out as it grows deeper. First, the official had enough faith, maybe the size of a mustard seed, to ask Jesus for help. Second, he believed Jesus' assurance that his son would live even though there was no visible evidence, and acted on it. Third, he and his whole household believed in Jesus. So the ripples reach out to encompass a family, a household, a community.

To reflect on
How far do the ripples from your faith spread?

WEDNESDAY 28 JUNE
Sabbath Breaker

'At once the man was cured; he picked up his mat and walked.
The day on which this took place was a Sabbath' (v. 9, NIV).

The large backdrop for this story is one of the three annual festivals – Passover, Pentecost and Tabernacles – which required all Jewish males to come to Jerusalem. The smaller backdrop is the Sabbath, a weekly festival observed in homes and synagogues throughout Israel as a day of rest and reverence.

The setting for the story is a pool, regarded as a sanctuary of healing, that has become a gathering place for the fellowship of the afflicted – the blind, the lame, the paralysed. Tradition had it that occasionally an angel would descend and stir the water and the first person to get into the pool would be healed.

At the centre of the story lies a man, an 'invalid' who has spent the past thirty-eight years in this place hoping that one day someone will help him to be first into the water.

Jesus sees this man and, taking the initiative, asks him a question that seems obvious to the point of bluntness: 'Do you want to get well?' Maybe there is a strange comfort in this man's state, a certain familiarity with what he can do that cushions him against what he cannot do. Perhaps his invalid state has become a valid way of life. He responds by saying he has 'no-one' to help him into the water and 'someone' always gets there ahead of him.

Jesus ignores both the superstition surrounding the water and the man's complaint. He simply tells him, 'Pick up your mat' (in Greek, a once-and-for-all, single action) and 'Get yourself up and start walking' (in Greek, both continuous actions). The man obeys. His healing is immediate. Jesus later meets him again in the temple, confirms the healing and speaks forgiveness to his sin.

Suddenly the story takes an ominous turn. A self-appointed enforcer of Sabbath law chides the man for carrying his mat on the Sabbath. The focus leaps like a bush fire from mat to miracle-worker. 'Who is this fellow?' A personal healing becomes a public furore. A miracle is overshadowed by a minor infringement. Storm clouds begin to gather around Jesus.

Son of God

John 5:16–30

'Jesus gave them this answer: "I tell you the truth, the Son can do nothing by himself; he can do only what he sees his Father doing, because whatever the Father does the Son also does"' (v. 19, NIV).

Suddenly Jesus is on trial. His healing of the paralysed man on the Sabbath has been a major offence to the religious leaders. A simple healing has thrown him into the spotlight. In their eyes he is a Sabbath-breaker. What is more, he calls God 'My Father' and thus claims to have a unique relationship with God. This makes him a blasphemer.

Boldly Jesus makes his defence against both charges. He is God's Son and, as such, if God who made the Sabbath can continue to sustain the universe every day, even on the Sabbath, and if Jesus' works are the works of God, then Jesus' works on the Sabbath are defensible.

He speaks as a rabbi: 'I tell you the truth', 'I tell you the truth', 'I tell you the truth' (vv. 19,24,25). He uses the metaphor of the relationship of a son learning a trade from his father. Just as Jesus grew up with Joseph in the carpentry shop in Nazareth, obediently learning skills and later imitating them, so in a similar manner he is now connected to the Father and is doing the works that he has seen God his Father do.

Jesus makes it clear that his activity is never independent or self-initiated, but is always dependent on the Father, always coming from the Father's will. While God as Father initiates, sends, commands, commissions, grants, so the Son responds, obeys, performs, receives. More than merely drawing inspiration from the Father, the Son imitates him.

Three things make this possible. The Father loves the Son (v. 20). The Father has given the Son sovereignty over life (v. 21). The Father has entrusted judgment to the Son (v. 22). This makes Jesus God's key agent in the world. Whoever wishes to honour the Father must also honour the Son who represents him. Whoever dishonours the Son offends the Father whose presence stands behind him (v. 23). To embrace one is to embrace the other. To reject one is to reject the other.

To reflect on

As you read these deep verses today, how do they read you?

Truth Revealer

John 5:31–47

'You diligently study the Scriptures because you think that by them you possess eternal life. These are the Scriptures that testify about me, yet you refuse to come to me to have life' (vv. 39,40, NIV).

In Old Testament law more than one witness was needed to condemn someone (*Deut 17:6*) and, in like manner, more than one person was needed to confirm someone's testimony. Jesus has just made extraordinary claims about himself – equality with God (*John 5:18*), a unique Father and Son relationship (*v. 20*), the ability to give eternal life (*v. 21*) and to judge (*vv. 22,27*). But if Jesus is the only one making these stunning claims they will carry little weight with his audience. So he proceeds to identify five witnesses in support.

The first witness is God himself (*vv. 32,37*). It is the inner presence of God that gives Jesus confidence about his mission (see *17:1–6*). Sent from the Father, Jesus carries God's word and power within him.

The second witness is John the Baptist (*vv. 33–35*). John came before Jesus, identified him, worked with him and directed his followers to become Jesus' disciples. John's whole life pointed to Jesus.

The third witness is Jesus' own works (*v. 36*). They are not simply powerful miracles but signs that will culminate in the great works of the cross and resurrection.

The fourth witness is the Scripture that testifies about him (*v. 39*).

The final witness is Moses, a prophet raised up by God (*v. 46*). As the patron saint of Judaism (*Deut 18:15*), Moses is the defender of its people and their advocate before God.

Yet in spite of all these witnesses the people of Israel have hardened their hearts and refused to see the evidence that is right before them. They love the religious life but they have forgotten how to love God. They search and study the Scriptures but they fail to see the Saviour of whom the Scriptures speak. They know the rules but they miss the revelation. They are familiar with the written word but fail to recognise the Logos, the enfleshed, incarnate Word of God standing in their midst.

To reflect on
Which of these 'witnesses' of Jesus do you find most compelling? Do you need more than these to tell you who Jesus is?

SATURDAY 1 JULY
Lord of the Leftovers

John 6:1–15

'When they had all had enough to eat, he said to his disciples, "Gather the pieces that are left over. Let nothing be wasted"' (v. 12, NIV).

This familiar story, featured in all four Gospels, shows that God is not only the Lord of the Banquet (see *Isa 25:6*) but also the Lord of the Leftovers.

It is a glorious day in early spring. Jesus' fame is spreading. Wherever he goes, people crowd around him, hungry for signs, thirsty for miracles. A private session with the disciples is suddenly swamped by people, thousands of them who come to hear what Rabbi Jesus has to teach.

Once more Jesus initiates the miracle by asking Philip where they can buy food to feed the people. Philip should have known because he himself was from Bethsaida just a few miles away. But as he looks at the crowd Philip can come up with no human solution to an overwhelming problem.

Disciple Andrew, who is always bringing people to Jesus, has spotted a boy with his lunch of five barley loaves and two salted fish. Bread made with barley wheat was the food of the poor. It is a basic lunch, enough for a growing lad, but that is all. 'How far will they go among so many?' he asks (*v. 9*).

As on other days still to come, in an upper room and later in a home in Emmaus, Jesus takes the bread, gives thanks, breaks it and offers it to the crowd. It is a divine solution to an overwhelming problem.

The people eat. They eat until they can eat no more yet still there is more. Leftovers everywhere – pieces of fish, chunks of bread. 'Gather the leftovers so nothing is wasted,' says Jesus (*The Message*). Twelve basketsful of leftovers later, the people realise they have just witnessed a miracle of provision and abundance.

On another day Jesus said, 'Steep your life in God-reality, God-initiative, God-provisions . . . You'll find all your everyday human concerns will be met' (*Matt 6:33, The Message*). It seems that when we give God what we have, small and inadequate as it may look, he is able to make it more than enough (see *Eph 3:20*). This is the lesson of the leftovers.

SUNDAY 2 JULY
A Memorial and a Name

Isaiah 56:1–8

'I will give within my temple and its walls a memorial and a name better than sons and daughters; I will give them an everlasting name that will not be cut off' (v. 5, NIV).

Isaiah 55 brings to a great climax all that can be said about the relationship between God and humankind. It is a chapter that reveals God's purpose and lays bare God's heart. God longs for people to come, to seek, to listen to him. To all who respond he promises an everlasting covenant of faithful love. What more could anyone want? What more needs to be said?

The stark difference in tone, apparent from the beginning of Isaiah 56, has made many scholars conclude that a new author takes over at this point. Yet even with a new author, the voice of God continues to be heard.

These verses have a wide reach. Justice, salvation, righteousness and blessing are promised to every person who honours the Sabbath and who does no wrong. Justice and righteousness are universal qualities. The joy of Sabbath rest is offered to all people. The temple, once the exclusive centre of worship for the Jewish people, is now open to all. God declares it will be called 'a house of prayer for all nations' (v. 7).

Anyone who comes with a heart to worship, ready to love the name of the Lord and intent on serving him, is to be welcomed. All who keep to the covenant conditions are to be included. The whole people of God will be enriched, not weakened, by this influx of new blood.

The phrase 'a memorial and a name' (in Hebrew *Yad vaShem*) has been given to the Holocaust Memorial in Jerusalem where the six million victims of Nazi persecution, not all of them Jews, are remembered. God's promise is that all who come seeking salvation will be given an everlasting name that will be recorded and remembered. As Paul said, 'There is neither Jew nor Greek ... you are all one in Christ Jesus' (*Gal 3:28*).

In a world where barriers, walls and barbed-wire fences are constantly used to include some and exclude others, these verses remind us that God sees not the colour of the skin, nor the size of the bank balance, but the condition of the heart.

MONDAY 3 JULY
Sea Calmer, Fear Calmer

John 6:16–21

'But he said to them, "It is I; don't be afraid"' (v. 20, NIV).

It is dark. The sea is rough. A strong wind is blowing. Jesus is absent. The disciples have moved from a miracle of excess to a moment of extremity. Lessons of faith learned in the sun–drenched afternoon have been swamped by the waves that now crash over the side of their boat. In spite of their best efforts and their most strenuous rowing it seems they are getting nowhere.

Pause for a moment and imagine yourself there in the boat with the disciples. Are you familiar with the feelings of fear that threaten to overwhelm your fragile vessel? If not, do you know someone who is in this place of extremity? Prayer in such moments is of the most basic sort – 'God help me'; 'Lord of wind and wave, come to my rescue'; 'Lord Jesus Christ, have mercy.'

Just when it seems that things could not possibly get worse they do get worse. Add a ghostly apparition to a fearful storm and the result is sheer terror. The disciples see a figure walking across the water towards them. But Jesus identifies himself using the divine name, 'I AM,' and tells them not to be afraid. He climbs into the boat with them and suddenly they are at their destination.

It is still dark. The sea may still be rough, the wind still blowing. But Jesus is there and they are safe. His presence makes all the difference.

The psalmist knew something of this tumultuous experience. He wrote: 'He spoke and stirred up a tempest that lifted high the waves. They mounted up to the heavens and went down to the depths; in their peril their courage melted away. They reeled and staggered like drunken men; they were at their wits' end. Then they cried out to the LORD in their trouble, and he brought them out of their distress. He stilled the storm to a whisper; the waves of the sea were hushed. They were glad when it grew calm, and he guided them to their desired haven' (Ps 107:25–30).

May God speak peace to your storm today!

68

TUESDAY 4 JULY
Bread of Life

John 6:22–59

'Then Jesus declared, "I am the bread of life. He who comes to me will never go hungry, and he who believes in me will never be thirsty"' (v. 35, NIV).

Nothing quite compares with the fragrance of bread baking. It speaks of welcome, warmth and nourishment. Such an aroma wafts right through this passage of Scripture. The people who one day witness the miraculous multiplication of bread are the next day looking for Jesus. The bread he served has stirred their taste buds and they want more.

Stored in their memory is a picture of Moses providing manna for the people of Israel during all their years of wilderness wandering. The popular belief was that when the Messiah came he would once more feed God's people with bread from heaven. But while Moses fed a whole nation for forty years, Jesus has fed only a few thousand on a single afternoon. Can he therefore really be the Messiah? They need more bread, a bigger miracle, a more compelling sign before they will believe in him.

Jesus, who knows what is in the hearts of people (2:25), points them to a deeper hunger and, in the first of his great 'I am' statements, declares himself to be the Bread of Life. What he offers is not just bread that fills for the moment but nourishment that will sustain them always.

A woman wrote of a season of her life that became overwhelmingly busy. In the space of a few weeks, while still working full-time, she moved house, kept up a speaking schedule and completed the writing of a book. On her lengthy 'to do' list, God was way down. Then, very gradually, she began to miss God. She said, 'I missed the friend who had been my constant companion and confidant for years. And maybe the Holy One missed me too, because the moment I started praying again we picked up our conversation as if we had – I had – never let it slide.'

In these days when bread features high on a dieter's no-no list, we may miss but still get by without our wholemeal or mixed grains. But we cannot do without Jesus, the Bread of Life, and the sustaining companionship, counsel and courage that he offers us.

WEDNESDAY 5 JULY
Holy One of God

John 6:60–71

'Simon Peter answered him, "Lord, to whom shall we go?
You have the words of eternal life. We believe and know that
you are the Holy One of God"' (vv. 68,69, NIV).

The Jewish religious leaders are offended by Jesus' apparent disregard for the Sabbath (5:16). The people grumble about his claim to be the Bread of Life (6:41). 'We know you as Joseph's son, Mary's boy,' they say. 'What's all this nonsense about coming down from heaven?'

When Jesus makes the even more extreme claim that those who eat his flesh and drink his blood will live forever, even his disciples become unsettled. 'This is tough teaching, too tough to swallow,' they say to each other (v. 60, The Message).

This moment marks a crossroad for the disciples. The difficult teaching sifts them like flour on a breadboard. Some fall away, offended and confused, and refuse to follow him any longer (v. 66). Another stays but struggles to understand and eventually betrays Jesus in an effort to force his hand (vv. 70,71).

Simon Peter, put on the spot by a question of allegiance, makes a courageous confession. 'Lord, to whom [else] shall we go?' He will not fully understand until after Jesus has died, been resurrected and ascended. But at this moment he drives a stake of belief and trust into the ground and declares Jesus to be the Holy One of God. In the other Gospels this title is only used by demons as they address Jesus, but throughout the Old Testament God is described as the Holy One of Israel who defends and redeems his people.

In spite of others who are turning away, in spite of all he does not yet understand, Peter chooses to believe.

What do you do when the questions become too heavy, the circumstances too complicated, the cost too great? Where do you turn for answers – to a friend, a counsellor, a doctor? Such people will all help, of course, each in their own way. But the Holy One of God, the One who has the words of eternal life, can give us answers much deeper than human skill or knowledge.

Choose to trust him today. Bring him your deepest, most anguished questions. Then wait and listen to what he speaks to you.

Lonely One

John 7:1–13

'Jesus told them, "You go to the Feast. I am not yet going up to this Feast, because for me the right time has not yet come"' (v. 8, NIV).

The picture of Jesus sitting in the midday sun by the well at Sychar (*John 4*) gave us a glimpse of the human Jesus, hot, weary and thirsty. Today's verses give us yet another very human picture – that of the lonely Jesus.

He is still a long way from Jerusalem but already is facing antagonism from the Jewish leaders, desertion by some of his disciples, and rejection and ridicule from his own brothers. The Feast of Tabernacles stands as a significant backdrop to his growing isolation.

This festival was the third of three annual pilgrimage feasts. The first, Passover, celebrated the beginning of the grain harvest in spring. Seven weeks later Pentecost celebrated the end of the grain harvest. Then came Tabernacles (also called Booths or Ingathering) which celebrated the autumn harvest of tree and vine.

Since the crops in autumn had to be protected, Israelite farmers built temporary shelters (in Hebrew *sukkoth*, hut or booth) in the fields. The booths reminded them of the temporary shelters in which their ancestors lived during their forty years of wandering in the desert. The Festival of Tabernacles lasted for seven days and was celebrated with sacrifices of bulls, rams and lambs.

Faithful to Jewish law and worship, Jesus' family probably came three times a year for these celebrations. Parallel to the theme of Jesus going up to Jerusalem for the festival is his preparation, even in these days, for going up to heaven.

His brothers urge him to stop acting in secret and to declare himself to the world. But at this stage they neither believe in him nor understand his mission. Jesus explains to them that his time has not yet come. He goes privately to the festival and in Jerusalem catches the controversy and the caution. He hears the muffled, whispered comments. Some say he is a good man while others call him a deceiver, a fraud. This is a picture of the lonely Son of God.

To reflect on

Have you ever felt lonely, isolated, misunderstood like this? Invite Jesus, the Lonely One, to walk this way with you.

Enigma

John 7:14–36

'If anyone chooses to do God's will, he will find out whether my teaching comes from God or whether I speak on my own' (v. 17, NIV).

Questions swirl around Jesus like seaweed on an incoming tide. Is he a good man or is he an imposter? How come he knows so much? Where did he get his training? Why does he accuse us of trying to kill him? Where does he come from? Where is he planning to go that we cannot find him? Who is he any–way? He surely cannot be the Messiah. Can he?

Jesus does not answer their questions. Rather he points beyond himself to the evidence. He refers frequently to the One who sent him, the source from whom he has come (vv. 16,28). He points to the great ones, like Moses, who came before him (v. 19). He points to obedience (v. 17). Anyone who wants to prove the truth of what he is teaching can do so by following that teaching. The proof of the calling is in the response and living out of that calling.

'Look at the evidence,' Jesus is saying. 'Observe what I do. Listen to what I say. What do these things tell you?' In response, some believe, some ignore, some respect, some reject.

Anyone who puts Jesus on trial puts themselves on trial. Frank Morison set out to write a book proving the impossibility of the resurrection. But as he examined the evidence, the evidence exam–ined him.

He likened himself to a man who sets out to cross a forest by a fami–liar and well–beaten track but finds himself coming out suddenly where he did not expect to come out. 'The point of entry was the same; it was the point of emergence that was different,' he wrote. The result was *Who Moved the Stone?*, a book in support of the resurrection.

Augustine wrote, 'An impure heart cannot see that which is seen only by the pure in heart.' It is all a matter of seeing. What compelling evidence do you see of God's pre–sence with you today?

Blest are the pure in heart,
For they shall see our God;
The secret of the Lord is theirs;
Their soul is Christ's abode.
John Keble, SASB 411

SATURDAY 8 JULY
Source of Living Water

John 7:37–52

'On the last and greatest day of the Feast, Jesus stood and said in a loud voice, "If anyone is thirsty, let him come to me and drink. Whoever believes in me . . . streams of living water will flow from within him"' (vv. 37,38, NIV).

In late autumn the land of Israel regularly suffered a period of drought. The heavy rains that drenched and soaked the land in spring had long since dried up. Cisterns were low, hills were barren and streambeds parched and cracked. If rain fell during the Feast of Tabernacles it was welcomed as a great blessing from God and a promise of a good season to come.

Each day of the feast a procession of priests made their way down to the Gihon Spring on the south border of the city. As a choir chanted the words of Isaiah 12:3, 'With joy you will draw water from the wells of salvation', the priest would fill a golden pitcher with water. The water was then carried back up the hill to the Water Gate.

Crowds of people followed, each carrying a *lulab* in the right hand (tree branches symbolising the desert booths) and an *ethrog* in the left hand (citrus branches symbolising the harvest). As they shook the branches the crowd would sing Psalms 113 to 118. When the procession arrived at the temple the priest would climb the altar steps and pour the water over the altar while the crowd circled around him and continued singing.

On the seventh day of the festival this procession took place seven times. In a drought-stricken land this was a spectacular vision of water, life-giving water flowing from God's life-giving temple.

On this final day of celebration as seven water processions are climbing the steps up to the temple, Jesus steps into public view and declares, 'If anyone is thirsty, let him come to me and drink.' Addressed to a people for whom the festival has held many reminders of God's gracious and abundant provision in the past, this is a statement loaded with symbolism and significance. Just as he offered himself as the Bread of Life (6:35), Jesus now offers himself as the source of the Water of Life.

Drink deep
drink often of this life-giving stream
then let it flow
through the watercourse of your heart
out to a thirsty world.

SUNDAY 9 JULY
Shepherd or Sleeping Dog?

Isaiah 56:9–12

'Israel's watchmen are blind, they all lack knowledge;
they are all mute dogs, they cannot bark; they lie around and dream,
they love to sleep' (v. 10, NIV).

The prophet launches a stinging attack on Israel's watchmen who are failing in their task. He compares them to guard dogs who cannot bark because they are asleep with full stomachs. They are shepherds 'who lack understanding' – a polite way of saying 'stupid' – interested only in taking care of themselves.

Prisoners to their own passions, they love to sleep, they love to eat, they love to drink. Above all, they want their own way. They are like King Saul whose focus never moved from himself. They are unlike King David who so gave himself to God and became 'a man after God's own heart' that he forgot himself.

Clearly the prophet is addressing the religious leaders of the nation. Far from being concerned at the desperate spiritual condition of their people, the leaders simply do not care.

Isaiah is astute enough to know that a return from captivity will not of itself guarantee holy and righteous living among the people. It is up to the leaders to be vigilant and to show a good example to the people entrusted to them. If they fail to do so, the flock will be overtaken by their spiritual enemies and devoured. The righteous will perish, he goes on to say (57:1), but their disappearance will cause no alarm at all. The passing away of an older, more faithful generation of people who have been true to their covenant promises will simply go unnoticed.

These verses are a cautionary tale for anyone who is called to be a leader of God's people. A leader must decide at the outset whose glory he is aiming for. If his goal is the glory of God then he must be willing to put his reputation, his achievements, his status, his success, his rights on the altar of God (see Rom 12:1). This is a once-and-for-all commitment that needs to be renewed every day. When problems, issues or misunderstandings arise, God can be trusted to deal with them (see Prov 3:5–6).

In the light of these stark verses, what kind of leader are you – shepherd or sleeping dog?

74

TITUS

Introduction

'How are you?' I ask my grandson Philip on the phone. 'Good,' he replies with emphasis. His firm response makes me wonder what goodness looks like to a seven-year-old. A day without squabbles with his brothers? A day when his room stays tidy and his school lessons seem easy?

What does goodness look like to a teenager or a businessman or an elderly resident in an eventide home? Does goodness look different at different stages of our lives, or does it have an enduring, unchanging quality, like a single-garment, last-forever, one-size-fits-all wardrobe?

Paul tackles this question head on in his letter to Titus as he encourages the young leader to 'teach what is good' (2:3) to older men, older women, young men, young women and slaves. He urges Titus to see that godly living and sound doctrine are wedded together. Paul gives frank advice for Christian leaders, clear directions for living out the faith, and practical guidelines for solving problems in relationships.

More than twenty centuries on from when Paul wrote this letter, his words to Titus seem remarkably pertinent for believers today. Search this letter for its unchanging truths. Study the descriptions of goodness as they apply to various groups of people. Then shine the light of goodness out into the dark corners of the world where you live.

MONDAY 10 JULY
A Smörgåsbord Greeting

Titus 1:1–4

'Paul, a servant of God and an apostle of Jesus Christ for the faith of God's elect and the knowledge of the truth that leads to godliness' (v. 1, NIV).

The opening verses of Paul's letter to Titus are a veritable feast. Reading them is like visiting a restaurant with an overwhelming number of dishes to choose from – thirty-three salads, twenty-seven meat dishes and thirty-nine flavours of ice cream all set out as a smörgåsbord. The challenge is to know where to start, where to go next, and eventually where to finish!

In one breath, it seems, Paul describes himself, his task and the God he serves. Each word has been carefully chosen. Each phrase invites our reflection.

In other places (see *Rom 1:1; Gal 1:10; Phil 1:1*) Paul declares himself to be a servant of Christ, but here he introduces himself as both a servant of God and an apostle of Jesus Christ. In Paul's day a servant was a slave with no rights whose sole purpose in life was to serve his master. An apostle was one specially commissioned to a task. Paul humbly uses these two words, 'servant' and 'apostle', to express his glorious allegiance and his high calling.

He describes the God who called and commissioned him as 'God, who does not lie'. A God who carries out his word and fulfils every promise is contrasted starkly with the immoral, untruthful, lazy Cretans among whom Titus lives (see *Titus 1:12*).

Paul defines his task using four great words that shine like beacons through this passage – faith, knowledge, godliness and hope.

Faith is trust in the faithfulness of God – that what he says, he will do. Knowledge is not just knowing facts (in French *savoir*) but being acquainted with (French *connaître*). It is the difference between knowing a mathematical formula and the comfortable stillness of a long-married couple who know each other's thoughts.

Godliness is the result that comes from building one's life on a foundation of faith and intimacy with God. More than wishful thinking, hope is the firm assurance that eternal life is both promised and guaranteed to the believer.

These luminous words are the themes of the letter Paul writes to Titus, 'my true son', to whom he extends his greeting of grace and peace.

TUESDAY 11 JULY
A Man of Sound Doctrine

Titus 1:5—9

'He must hold firmly to the trustworthy message as it has been taught, so that he can encourage others by sound doctrine and refute those who oppose it' (v. 9, NIV).

Following Paul's release from his first imprisonment in Rome, he and Titus briefly visited Crete where Paul left his young associate. The island of Crete, approximately 156 miles long and varying from eight to thirty-five miles wide, had a number of towns scattered throughout. Paul instructed Titus to appoint responsible leaders for the growing church in each of the island's towns.

In literary style, Paul's description of the elders whom Titus is to appoint reads like the description of love in 1 Corinthians 13, which looks at love from both negative and positive sides: Love 'is not rude . . . not self-seeking . . . not easily angered. Love . . . always protects, always trusts, always hopes' (1 Cor 13:5,7).

It is worth noting that the traits Paul mentions deal with personal character, not techniques or gifts or skills. Every aspect of a leader's life is to be put under scrutiny.

In his personal life an elder must be 'blameless' (literally 'cannot be accused'), a man of untarnished reputation. He must not be self-willed or quick-tempered or violent, but sober-minded, holy and self-controlled.

In his family life he must be faithful to his wife and have trustworthy, respectful children. In his social life he must be hospitable, not given to drunkenness. In his financial life he must be a good steward of God and not greedy for money.

In his professional life he must have no hidden agendas, but love goodness and justice. He must hold fast to the message of the gospel for himself, be able to exhort and encourage other believers and, at the same time, be ready to challenge and convict those who oppose it.

This impressive list describes a man of sound doctrine who expresses his faith in godly living. It reminds me of a fine Salvation Army leader who not only spoke of but also lived out his determination to be a 'good' man.

To reflect on
Who do you think of when you read this description? Could it be a reflection of you? If not, what area of your life do you need to 'straighten out' (v. 5)?

WEDNESDAY 12 JULY
A Murky Description

Titus 1:10–16

'To the pure, all things are pure, but to those who are corrupted and do not believe, nothing is pure' (v. 15, NIV).

With the word 'for' (v. 10), Paul swings from a marvellous portrait of godliness to a murky picture of godlessness. The reason Titus is to appoint upright leaders in every town on Crete is simply because there are many false teachers out there leading people astray. The increase in falsehood demands the increase in truth. The greater the darkness, the greater the need for a clear shining light. When unrighteousness stalks through the land, righteousness must outrun it.

Paul alerts Titus to the identity (v. 10), influence (v. 11), character (vv. 12–14) and errors (vv. 14–16) of these false teachers.

First of all they are rebellious, insubordinate creatures who refuse to submit to the trustworthy message of the gospel. They are mere talkers with no life-giving substance to their teaching. Worse, they are deceivers out to make money. Their teaching not only fails to build up but actually leads people astray. Not only individuals but whole households are being ruined by their influence.

They are living up to the reputation stated by one of their own poets, Epimenides of Knossos, who described Cretans as 'liars from the womb, barking dogs, lazy bellies' (v. 12, The Message).

Detestable and disobedient, corrupt and corrupting, these people claim to know God but their very actions deny him. They must be silenced, says Paul, then rescued from error and established in the truth.

This is strong, forceful language. How did these deceivers get into such a desperate state? Probably the way anyone gets into sin – one careless step, one dishonest action, one off-centre comment after another.

As an exercise in reflection today, fill a clear drinking glass with water, then add some drops of food colouring. At first the colouring stays separate but with a little agitation the stain spreads right through the water. The only way to get the water clear again is to dilute it, wash it out. Think about the stains of guilt or anger or addiction that have discoloured your life. Ask Jesus to wash you with the clear living water of the Spirit and to make you clean again.

THURSDAY 13 JULY
A Sound Doctrine

Titus 2:1–2

'You must teach what is in accord with sound doctrine' (v. 1, NIV).

As a bricklayer sets his first bricks in place he neglects to use his level to check that the row is straight. By the time he finishes it is clear that a centimetre or two off straight in his first row has resulted in a very sloping wall.

The crooked line, the careless oversight are quite the opposite of what Paul is recommending to Titus when he urges him to teach 'sound doctrine'. The word 'sound' is a medical term meaning 'healthy'. Sound doctrine is teaching that is not 'sick' but wholesome and resistant to the diseases of error. Sound doctrine is true belief in contrast to false teaching.

Sound doctrine means laying a solid, firm, straight foundation of teaching that results in careful, attentive, godly living. This is what Paul urges young Titus to pass on to the various members of the household of faith.

First in line are the older men. They need special advice and encouragement for, as an ancient writer, Chrysostom, said, 'There are some failings which age has, that youth has not . . . a slowness, a timidity, a forgetfulness, an insensibility and an irritability.'

The older men are to receive two main exhortations that may be summed up in the words 'dignity' and 'maturity'. They are to be temperate; that is, responsible and sensible, in contrast to the Cretans who were described as 'lazy gluttons' (v. 12). They are to be 'worthy of respect', not just because of their age, as is common in many societies, but because of their character.

Paul tells Titus the older men are to be self-controlled; that is, having an inner steadiness and wisdom that stands rock-like and resolute against all the trials of life. Finally, the older men are to be sound and healthy in faith, in love and in endurance.

These qualities of soundness are usually hidden and unseen but they become visible in one's reactions or when one's work is tested or put under scrutiny.

To reflect on
How straight is the wall you are building today? How healthy is the doctrine on display in your life?

FRIDAY 14 JULY
With Reverent Hands

Titus 2:3–5

'Likewise, teach the older women to be reverent in the way they live'
(v. 3, NIV).

'Likewise,' says Paul as he turns Titus' attention to the next group in the household of faith. The high moral standards encouraged in the older men must also be seen in the older women.

'Reverent in the way they live ... not ... slanderers or addicted to much wine.' Is Paul suggesting that Cretan women in general were irreverent gossips, a tad too fond of alcohol? He urges Titus to teach and encourage the Christian women on the island to live reverently.

Something within me wants to kneel when I read this instruction. To live reverently is to live with holy hands open to God's gifts and graces. To live reverently is to live as though all of life is happening in a sacred space. To live reverently is to see the opportunities all around us as invitations to meet with God – in the mess and clutter, in the demands of children, in the monotony of housework.

To live reverently is to hold an acorn and feel the oak tree within it. To live reverently is to cradle a baby and sense the rich potential of this new little person.

Paul tells Titus that by living reverently and teaching what is good, the older women will be a good example for the younger women. He uses the word 'train' which is related to the Greek word for 'self-control' (v. 5). As the older women provide an example of sober, moderate, self-controlled living, the younger women will be reminded of their commitment to their husbands and children, and will become good homemakers themselves.

With reverent hands
she holds a handful of dough
kneads the mixture
shapes the loaf
fragrant
wholesome
nourishing

With reverent hands
she holds her truth
kneads in the leaven of faith
shapes another's life
prayerful
loving
wise
a handful of dough made holy with
*   reverent hands*

SATURDAY 15 JULY
A Word to Young Men

Titus 2:6–8

'In everything set them an example in doing what is good' (v. 7, NIV).

I watch a lad who lives down the street doing his fancy twists and turns on his skateboard. Over the fence I greet a young neighbour who has an ever-growing fleet of old cars that he delights in doing up for racing.

It is to young men like these that Paul now turns his attention. He has a single instruction for Titus: 'Encourage the young men to be self-controlled' ('disciplined', *The Message*).

But Paul is wise enough to know that words by themselves will not be enough. Titus needs also to practise what he preaches, to be a model of self-controlled, clear-headed Christian living himself. He is still relatively young so his manner of conducting himself should have a positive influence on other young men.

This means that both the content of his teaching and his conduct as a teacher must be characterised by integrity, seriousness and soundness (there's that word again!) of speech. His pure motives and respectful demeanour will stand in stark contrast to the 'rebellious people . . . talkers and deceivers' whom Paul described earlier (see *1:10–16*).

The objective of such transparent Christian living is that 'those who oppose you' (literally, 'the one who is in opposition') will be put to shame when they find no valid criticisms to make regarding Titus. The passage that began as a command for the younger men thus turns out to be a challenge to Titus about his own life and ministry.

These heavy words make me think of several fine young Christian men who were like Titus to my son as he grew up. They talked and prayed and shared their lives with him. He watched them as they lived out their faith in their studies, in their relationships, in every aspect of their lives.

As I give thanks for them today, I pray for the skateboarder down the street and the boy racer over the fence. I wonder who is modelling goodness, integrity and self-control to them. With a Titus figure in their lives, what great potential might these young men reach? Without a Titus example, what will become of them?

SUNDAY 16 JULY
Hear the Heartbreak

Isaiah 57:11–21

'This is what the high and lofty One says – he who lives for ever, whose name is holy: "I live in a high and holy place, but also with him who is contrite and lowly in spirit, to revive the spirit of the lowly and to revive the heart of the contrite"' (v. 15, NIV).

The early verses of this chapter are a graphic exposé of the nation's idolatry. Using stark and shocking language, the prophet accuses the people of worshipping rocks and trees, engaging in ritual prostitution and sacrificing their children. What drives them on is their desire to use divine power for their own ends. After all, as God's chosen people, the elect, they are free to do as they like. Notice the prophet's repeated use of 'you', 'your' and 'yours'. Everything they do illustrates their failure to live righteously.

Halfway through the chapter, accusation turns to incredulity. God asks why the people are so afraid of him that they turn away and do not give him a thought (v. 11). Do they not know that God is the only One who can help them? Have they not remembered all he did for them in the past? How can they turn aside so easily to the idols of their own making?

We need to hear the divine heartbreak in these verses. Isaiah echoes the words of Jeremiah who laments that God's people have forsaken the spring of living water and have dug their own cisterns, broken ones that can hold no water (*Jer 2:13*).

Suddenly the focus moves from 'you' and 'yours' to 'I' and 'my'. The prophet declares that God will do for his people what they cannot do for themselves. Whoever turns from idols and takes refuge in God will inherit the land and find the covenant promises renewed.

The One who is far above the inhabitants of the earth in his holy place declares that his dwelling is also with the lowly and contrite. This verse recalls Paul's description of Jesus who came from the highest to the lowest place that he might lift us up (see *Phil 2:6–8*). God's intention is not to accuse and punish but to gather and restore. God's longing is to give his people a changed nature so that rebellion and pride are replaced with praise and peace.

To reflect on
Does God share his heart with you or break his heart over you?

MONDAY 17 JULY
Adorning the Gospel

Titus 2:9–10

'In every way they will make the teaching about
God our Saviour attractive' (v. 10, NIV).

Slavery was common in the Roman Empire. Slaves had no legal rights and were under the absolute control of their master. While Paul does not condemn the practice of slavery in any of his letters, he does speak forcefully here and elsewhere (see *Eph 6:5*) of how Christian slaves can make a powerful witness to the gospel by the way they live and work.

Here he gives Titus clear instructions for household slaves. In their work they must try to please ('give satisfaction to') their masters by their conscientious service. They are not to talk back to their masters – that is, no disputes, no arguments, no refusal to obey – but to be polite and respectful.

As for their characters, slaves are to be honest and not steal from their masters. The Greek word *nosphizo* is the regular term for petty filching. Paul's reference suggests that this was a common temptation for slaves who often handled their masters' business interests and were responsible for any money involved.

The genuine faith of a Christian slave should be shown in complete honesty and trustworthiness. Such faithfulness, Paul asserts, will make the teaching about God our Saviour attractive. The verb *kosmeo*, meaning 'to make attractive', was used of arranging jewels in order to display their beauty. The gospel is the jewel and a consistently godly Christian life is the setting that adorns or adds lustre to the jewel.

How are you adorning the gospel? Does the gospel–jewel shine with lustre and beauty through your sanctified, set–apart life?

But how shall we that truth declare,
Thy grace, thy love, thy beauty show?
Only as we thy nature wear
Shall men that nature truly know;
And as we walk with thee abroad
They shall perceive the mind of God.

So teach us, Lord, to use each power
As we thy doctrine shall adorn,
That truth and grace shall spring to flower
In lives renewed and souls reborn;
As we to all the world unfold
The glory of the faith we hold.
            Will Brand, SASB 656

TUESDAY 18 JULY

Two Great Appearings – Grace and Glory

Titus 2:11–15

'The grace of God . . . has appeared . . . We wait for . . . the glorious appearing' (vv. 11,13, NIV).

Paul now moves from mundane duties to sublime doctrines. He describes two great appearings, two comings of Christ, using the Greek work *epiphaneia*, from which we get our word 'epiphany'. An epiphany is a visible appearance of something or someone previously invisible, a coming into view of what has been concealed. The word was used in classical Greek to describe daybreak when the sun leaps over the horizon into view.

When Luke wrote about the storm lashing the ship on which Paul and his companions were travelling to Rome, he described the sky as so overcast that for many days the sun and stars did not appear (literally 'made no epiphany'). They were there, of course, but they were hidden from view (see *Acts 27:20*)

Paul uses this great word to describe Christ's two comings – an epiphany of grace (*v. 11*) and an epiphany of glory (*v. 13*).

God has always been 'the God of all grace' (*1 Pet 5:10*) but his saving grace appeared visibly in Jesus Christ. It was wondrously displayed in Jesus' humble birth, in his compassionate ministry and above all in his atoning death. Jesus himself was 'full of grace' (*John 1:14*), bringing salvation to all humankind. Grace the Saviour has now become Grace the Teacher, helping believers to say 'no' to ungodliness and 'yes' to godliness (*Titus 2:12*).

The One who appeared in grace will one day reappear in glory. Paul calls it 'the epiphany of the glory of our great God and Saviour, Jesus Christ'. This is the Christian's hope.

As we live in this in-between time we must do spiritually what is impossible physically; namely, look in two directions at the same time. We look back to the epiphany of grace – the purpose of which was to redeem us from all evil and to purify a people for God – and we look forward in anticipation of the epiphany of glory – the purpose of which will be perfect at Jesus' second coming the salvation begun at his first.

Celebrate these two great epiphanies today.

Christ has died!
Christ is alive!
Christ is coming again!

WEDNESDAY 19 JULY

How Then Should We Live?

Titus 3:1–2

'Remind the people to be subject to rulers and authorities,
to be obedient, to be ready to do whatever is good' (v. 1, NIV).

Paul urges Titus to 'remind' the people. The teaching he is about to give is not new, for the believers have heard it all before, but Paul knows that forgetfulness is one of the greatest dangers to faith. A bad memory was one of the main reasons for Israel's downfall. 'They soon forgot . . . they did not remember,' lamented the psalmist (Ps 106:13,7).

What Titus is to remind the people about concerns their social relationships in the world, first to the authorities in particular (v. 1), then to everybody in general (v. 2).

Paul wrote earlier to Timothy about the need to pray for those in authority (1 Tim 2:1,2). Now he writes to Titus about the need to obey them and to be public-spirited, to be ready and eager (as opposed to reluctant) to do whatever is good whenever they have opportunity.

From the Christian responsibility towards leaders of the community, Paul turns to the relationship with everybody in the community. How are believers to relate to unbelievers? He begins with a reference to 'no-one' and ends with a reference to 'all men', meaning everybody.

He names four Christian attitudes which are to be universal in their application, two negative and two positive. Negatively they are to slander no one and be peaceable (in Greek 'avoid quarrels'). Positively they are to be considerate and to show true humility (literally 'all gentleness') towards everyone.

These lovely characteristics invite our reflection today. They were seen on perfect display in Jesus' life. Paul appealed to the believers at Corinth 'by the meekness and gentleness of Christ' (2 Cor 10:1). He encouraged the believers at Philippi to have the same attitudes of humility and obedience that were seen in Jesus (Phil 2:5–8).

These verses give in a nutshell a picture of Christian behaviour in every aspect of public life. Towards those in authority, believers are to be conscientious citizens, submissive, obedient and cooperative. Towards everyone in the community, believers are to be courteous, conciliatory and humble.

To reflect on
Which quality do you most need to be 'reminded of' today?

THURSDAY 20 JULY
He Saved Us!

Titus 3:3–7

'He saved us, not because of righteous things we had done, but because of his mercy' (v. 5, NIV).

Artist Paul once more takes up his paintbrush. He uses sombre tones to paint a picture of life before Christ. These verses are not only a general description of the unregenerate life, they are also Paul's testimony. 'We too', he says ('we ourselves', *NRSV*).

'Stupid and stubborn, dupes of sin, ordered every which way by our glands, going around with a chip on our shoulder, hated and hating back' (v. 3, *The Message*). This is not a pretty picture. There is no way to beautify sin, no way to touch up foolishness and disobedience, no way to put a positive spin on malice or envy or hatred.

Then Paul says, 'But' – a glorious word that tosses out the old palette with its grubby colours and brings on a new one filled with glorious hues. 'But when God, our kind and loving Savior God, stepped in, he saved us' (vv. 4,5, *The Message*). He saved us! Savour these glorious words. Say them over and over to yourself. Speak them out to someone else today.

These three words are the hinge of this whole passage. Before them comes a picture of sin; after them comes a portrait of salvation. God rescued us from our former bondage and changed us into new people.

In a passage that is both great literature and profound theology, Paul outlines six ingredients of salvation. It is needed because of our sin, guilt and slavery. It has come at the gracious initiative of God. It rests on God's mercy. It comes to us through the regenerating and renewing work of the Holy Spirit. It leads to our full inheritance of eternal life. It shows itself in our diligent practice of good works.

All three persons of the Trinity and all tenses of time are engaged in our salvation. God the Father took the initiative, Jesus the Son died for us, the Holy Spirit brings us rebirth and renewal. The past has been forgiven. The present is the gift of a new life. The future is our inheritance of eternal life. Everything has been done. He has saved us. Hallelujah!

FRIDAY 21 JULY
Leaning Into . . . Leaning Away

Titus 3:8–11

'I want you to stress these things, so that those who have trusted in God may be careful to devote themselves to doing what is good' (v. 8, NIV).

As Paul prepares to bring his letter to Titus to a conclusion he summarises what he has told his young colleague. He is to teach and remind the believers in his care of their calling to be conscientious, obedient and peaceable citizens in the world, and in their private lives to be self-controlled, hospitable and righteous. They are to be people of sound doctrine and godly living. Again and again the phrase 'doing what is good' appears through this letter.

If Paul were asked to define goodness he would say, as he wrote to the Philippians, 'whatever is true, whatever is noble, whatever is right, whatever is pure, whatever is lovely, whatever is admirable . . . excellent [and] praiseworthy' (Phil 4:8).

While leaning into goodness and devoting themselves to things that are profitable, the believers must, at the same time, lean away from things that are unprofitable and useless. Paul cautions them against four errors – foolish controversies, genealogies, arguments and quarrels. This is not a prohibition against healthy debate but a warning against the frivolous and futile speculations of the false teachers that lead only to quibbles and squabbles (see 1 Tim 1:3–11).

Paul tells Titus to deal carefully with a divisive person. Warn him once then warn him a second time. Only then, if the offender remains unrepentant and refuses the opportunity of forgiveness and restoration, is he to be rejected. Two warnings and two refusals will show beyond any doubt that the person concerned is 'warped and sinful' and has deliberately cut himself off from grace. These firm words remind us of Jesus' step-by-step process for dealing with a fellow believer who causes offence (see Matt 18:15–17).

As in so much of his writings, Paul encourages both a turning away from and a turning towards, a putting off and a putting on (see Eph 4:22–24), a saying 'no' to sin and a saying 'yes' to godliness (Titus 2:12). We need to learn to walk as Christians with a deliberate lean – leaning away from ungodliness and leaning into goodness.

'Trust in God. Lean on your God!' (Isa 50:10, The Message).

SATURDAY 22 JULY

Just a Glimpse

Titus 3:12–15

'Everyone with me sends you greetings. Greet those who love us in the faith. Grace be with you all' (v. 15, NIV).

Paul's closing words come almost as a shock. At the end of a letter filled with duty and doctrine, practical common sense and profound theology, we suddenly catch a brief glimpse into his world. Reading these verses is like kneeling at the letter-box slot in the front door of a British house and peering through to what we can see going on inside.

With the mention of the names of his colleagues and his plans for the coming winter we are reminded that this is a man writing at a particular time in history and from a particular location.

Paul tells Titus of his plans to send Artemas or Tychicus to meet up with the young leader on Crete where they will take over the leadership of the churches. As soon as Titus is free to leave he is to come and meet Paul in Nicopolis, a city on the west coast of Greece, where Paul has decided to spend the winter.

He asks Titus to do all he can to help Zenas the lawyer and Apollos, one of Paul's well-known co-workers, on their way. Presumably these two had been entrusted with carrying Paul's letter to Titus on Crete. Once they have fulfilled their task they are to be given a good send-off with all the supplies they need for their onward journey.

Titus is to ensure that 'our people' – that is, all the believers – are dedicated to good works. He is also to arrange for an exchange of greetings. Titus must first receive the greetings sent to him by Paul and everyone with him and then he is to convey Paul's greetings to others. 'Greet those who love us in the faith,' he says; that is, in the common bond of God's love.

As he pronounces his benediction Paul looks beyond Titus to all the members of the churches on Crete, indeed to all believers who would one day read this letter. That includes you and me! A glimpse into Paul's world brings his personal greeting into our own. 'Grace be with you all,' he says to us today.

SUNDAY 23 JULY
True Seeking

Isaiah 58:1–4

'Day after day they seek me out; they seem eager to know my ways, as if they were a nation that does what is right and has not forsaken the commands of its God' (v. 2, NIV).

One of Isaiah's great imperatives was his call to 'Seek the LORD while he may be found' (55:6). The prophet's whole life was given over to the task of opening a way for his people to reach God. This meant levelling the mounds of sin, straightening out a highway of righteousness along which all Israel could make their way to God.

'Seek God and he will be found,' declared the prophet time and again. But he discovered that there is a way to seek that results in blessing, and a way to seek that results in quite the opposite.

In this chapter the prophet holds up a mirror for God's people to look at themselves. 'They're busy, busy, busy at worship, and love studying all about me,' says God (58:2, *The Message*). To all appearances they are doing everything right. They love having God on their side. They seem eager to know God's ways. They have even humbled themselves and fasted.

In spite of all their efforts, however, nothing is happening. They feel let down. Their fasting is not acknowledged (v. 3). Their prayers are not being heard (59:1). 'Why?' they ask in wide-eyed innocence. 'Why has God not come through for us?'

In a blistering attack the prophet points out their fault. They have a form of religion but it goes only skin-deep. When the surface of their piety is scratched, underneath can be seen a whole host of squirming, writhing sins like live worms in a fisherman's bait. They serve their own ends, trying to manipulate God with their pious practices. They do as they please, exploiting, quarrelling, fist-fighting.

As God had said earlier through the prophet, 'These people come near to me with their mouth and honour me with their lips, but their hearts are far from me' (29:13). What a word of caution for modern-day worshippers!

As you seek God in worship today, make sure you take your whole heart with you. Remember what Jesus promised: 'Everyone who asks receives; he who seeks finds; and to him who knocks, the door will be opened' (Matt 7:8).

ACTS 21:17 – 26
Paul on Trial

Introduction

The early chapters of the book of Acts are characterised by movement and activity. The Holy Spirit who came like a rushing wind on the Day of Pentecost sweeps right through the towns and cities of the ancient Mediterranean world as Paul travels on one missionary journey after another. As the gospel is preached people come to faith and communities of believers are established. Luke's account is dynamic, colourful and ever–moving.

The chapters of Acts featured in this series are characterised not so much by movement as by people. Luke records the details of Paul's arrest in Jerusalem and his trial in Caesarea in front of an impressive array of powerful leaders. Faced with the claims of Christ, they decide what they will do – or will not do – about the indisputable fact of a resurrected Jesus.

As you read these chapters you may well find them reading you. Who is this Jesus about whom Paul is so passionate? What claim does he make upon your life today?

MONDAY 24 JULY
Walking a Fine Line

Acts 21:17–26

'Take these men, join in their purification rites and pay their expenses, so that they can have their heads shaved. Then everybody will know there is no truth in these reports about you' (v. 24, NIV).

Paul arrives in Jerusalem and is warmly welcomed by the believers there. He meets with James and the elders of the Church and gives a report of his ministry among the Gentiles. Praise to God all round! The mood of the meeting quickly changes, however, from confirmation of Paul's mission among the Gentiles to concern over his ministry among the Jews.

The Jerusalem Council had earlier discussed how Gentile believers could best be integrated into the Church (*Acts 15*). It was agreed that Gentile converts would not be required to undergo circumcision or to keep the laws of Moses. But rumours have since spread that Paul has taken this decision further and is teaching both Jews and Gentiles that circumcision is not merely unnecessary but actually forbidden and that the laws of Moses can be ignored.

'What shall we do?' (v. 22). James and the church leaders see this matter as their problem, not just Paul's, so they voice the question then suggest a solution. They have four believers on hand who have taken a Nazirite vow (see *Num 6*) and who are about to undergo purification rites involving the sacrifice of animals and the shaving of their heads.

They want Paul to report to the priest at the start of the purification rites, inform him that he is providing the funds for the offerings of the four men, then return to the temple at regular intervals during the week for the appropriate rites. By submitting himself publicly to these rites Paul will show that he is not anti-Moses.

At the same time Paul is not being inconsistent with his declared belief that rites and rituals are not essential to salvation. What he is doing is walking a fine line between the two views – an absolute commitment to his unchanging stance that Jesus alone is necessary for salvation, but also respect for a practice that will encourage believers without offending anyone. This is a picture of Paul living with a heart of godly wisdom.

To reflect on
When does your faith require you to walk a fine line?

TUESDAY 25 JULY
Sharing the Fellowship of Christ's Sufferings

Acts 21:27–36

'When Paul reached the steps, the violence of the mob was so great he had to be carried by the soldiers. The crowd that followed kept shouting, "Away with him!"' (vv. 35,36, NIV).

Many Jewish pilgrims are in Jerusalem at this time for Pentecost (see 20:16), so it is not surprising that some Jews from the province of Asia spot Paul in the temple. They may well be from Ephesus where the synagogue's opposition towards Paul's teaching ministry was most fierce. Note the strong verbs that tell what these Jews do. They see Paul, stir up the whole crowd, then seize him and shout out their accusations.

Their first, patently untrue, accusation is that Paul is teaching 'all men everywhere against our people and our law and this place' (v. 28). This is a similar charge to what Stephen faced before his death (6:13). Their second accusation is that he has defiled the temple by bringing an unclean Gentile into the inner courts. Stone slabs inscribed in both Latin and Greek were on display throughout the temple, warning that Gentiles were not allowed beyond the Court of the Gentiles. Paul had earlier been seen walking the streets of the city with one of his Gentile companions, Trophimus the Ephesian, so his accusers assume that Paul has taken Trophimus with him into the inner courts.

The whole city is stirred up with people running in all directions. Paul's accusers drag him out of the temple and the gates are slammed shut behind him. Their clear intention to kill Paul would defile the temple if such an act were to be carried out in the inner courts. The commander of the Roman troops, Claudius Lysias, arrives on the spot in no time with hundreds of soldiers to deal with the uproar. Paul is rescued from a severe beating, arrested, bound with chains and then taken to the comparative safety of the Roman barracks where he can be interrogated away from the angry mob.

The violence of the scene, the confusion of some shouting one thing and some another, and the frenzied words, 'Away with him!' remind us of another lone figure who stood on another day in the place of accusation and misunderstanding. This is a picture of Paul sharing in the fellowship of Christ's sufferings.

WEDNESDAY 26 JULY
Permission to Speak

Acts 21:37–22:2

'Paul answered, "I am a Jew, from Tarsus in Cilicia, a citizen of no ordinary city. Please let me speak to the people"' (21:39, NIV).

Paul has been seized, dragged, beaten by an angry mob to within an inch of his life, arrested, bound, carried away, shouted at. He would have every reason to ask for a soft pillow and some healing oil. But Paul seemed to glory in such dramatic attention being given to the gospel. He quickly recovers his composure and asks permission to address the crowd.

The commander of the soldiers originally thought Paul was an Egyptian who had tried to lead some people in a revolt against Rome. The historian Josephus recorded that this Egyptian was a false prophet who led several thousand people out to the Mount of Olives, promising them God's intervention. The revolt was stopped when Governor Felix mobilised his troops, but it resulted in much loss of life and the escape of the Egyptian.

When the commander hears Paul speaking in Greek he is surprised. When he hears that Paul is a citizen from Tarsus he is impressed. When he hears later that Paul was actually born a Roman citizen (22:28) he is dumbfounded.

Given permission to speak, Paul stands in front of the crowd and gestures for them to be quiet. He addresses them respectfully as 'my dear brothers and fathers' (22:1, *The Message*) and speaks in Aramaic. When the people hear him speaking in their common language they are surprised and impressed, just as the commander was when he heard Paul speaking in Greek. Immediately they become quiet so they can hear what he has to say.

Notice Paul's skill in gaining an audience for the gospel. To the Roman commander he speaks Greek, thus proving that he is a man of culture and not just some rabble-rouser out to make trouble. To the people he speaks the language of the Jews, thus proving that he himself is a Jew and respectful of Jewish laws and customs. This is Paul at his best.

Consider your use of language for the sake of the gospel. Can people tell by hearing you speak that you are a Christian? With what 'voice' will you give your testimony today?

THURSDAY 27 JULY
Paul's Testimony

Acts 22:2–21

'Then he said, "The God of our fathers has chosen you to know his will and to see the Righteous One and to hear words from his mouth"' (v. 14, NIV).

Speaking the language of the people, Paul, so recently a captive himself, now addresses his captive audience. His eloquent defence is masterful in the points of connection he makes with his audience. He begins by identifying himself as a Jew from Tarsus and ends by claiming that God has commissioned him to go 'far away to the Gentiles' (v. 21). His Jewish identity and his Gentile commission thus provide a framework for his story.

Paul speaks first of his training in Jerusalem 'under' – that is, at the feet of – Gamaliel. This man was the most honoured rabbi of the first century, well known and respected as an expert on religious law and as a voice of moderation (see 5:34,35). To sit at the feet of such a great teacher indicates Paul's initiation from an early age, probably about five years old, into the rigorous programme of Jewish learning which would have lasted until his Bar Mitzvah at the age of thirteen.

Paul says he was 'thoroughly trained' and 'zealous' – two catchwords associated with the demands of the Pharisaic school. He adds, 'as any of you are today', thus making yet another point of connection with his audience.

His zeal for God, however, propelled him into the persecution of believers. Paul does not excuse himself for his misguided actions but tells his conversion story exactly as it happened – his trip to Damascus for the purpose of imprisoning believers there, his sudden unexpected encounter with the living Jesus, and his entry into Damascus a changed man.

There he met Ananias, whom he describes as 'a devout observer of the law and highly respected'. This description of Ananias would be yet another point of connection with the audience. The return of his sight, Ananias' words of commission, Paul's baptism and his prayer at the temple further validates the great reversal he has experienced.

Notice the flair, the drama and colour with which Paul gives his testimony. What his captive audience will do with it is up to them. Paul's part is simply to tell it as it is.

FRIDAY 28 JULY
A Citizen of Rome

Acts 22:22–29

'Those who were about to question him withdrew immediately. The commander himself was alarmed when he realised that he had put Paul, a Roman citizen, in chains' (v. 29, NIV).

As Paul tells his conversion story the crowd listens with rapt attention. But the moment he mentions God's commission to send him to the Gentiles, the G-word is like a dentist's drill touching a raw nerve. Immediately the people react with frenzied shouts – 'He's not fit to live!', and hostile gestures – 'throwing off their cloaks and flinging dust into the air'.

Just why they react so violently is not spelled out by Luke. We can only assume that, far from seeing themselves as a light to the Gentiles, these Jews are quite content to live with an 'I, me and mine' mentality. While God is opening his arms to the Gentiles through the ministry of Paul, Peter and others, many of the Jews remain unconvinced that the good news is for anyone but themselves.

The commander does not even try to restore order but quickly removes Paul from the scene, just as he had done earlier (21:34). As a pagan outsider, unfamiliar with testimony and truth, he can only conclude from the crowd's hostile reaction that Paul is guilty of something bad. In the barracks he gives orders that Paul be examined by flogging – a military routine for extracting useful information from a prisoner in an unsettled case.

As the soldiers stretch Paul out and prepare to flog him he identifies himself as a Roman citizen. The preparation ceases immediately. Under Roman law all Roman citizens were eligible for a fair public trial and were exempt from all forms of degrading punishment – beating with rods, scourging or crucifixion.

When the commander is informed of Paul's claim to citizenship he comes in person to question Paul. Having bought his own citizenship at considerable cost, the commander values the honour and prestige of being a Roman citizen. When Paul declares that he is a Roman citizen by birth, the commander's respect for Paul's rights and fear for his own public embarrassment increase greatly. From this moment Claudius Lysias is much more restrained in handling Paul's legal case.

To reflect on
What appeal to citizenship can you make? Check out Ephesians 2:19.

SATURDAY 29 JULY
A Hope in the Resurrection

Acts 22:30–23:8

'Paul, knowing that some of them were Sadducees and the others Pharisees, called out in the Sanhedrin, "My brothers, I am a Pharisee, the son of a Pharisee. I stand on trial because of my hope in the resurrection of the dead"' (23:6, NIV).

The commander still does not understand the charge against Paul so he orders the Sanhedrin, the supreme Jewish court, to look into the matter. As a Roman military commander he has no right to participate in the Sanhedrin's deliberations, but as a Roman official charged with keeping the peace he can order the Sanhedrin to investigate the cause of the riot.

Paul stands undaunted in front of the Sanhedrin and claims that he has fulfilled his duty to God 'in all good conscience'. By Jewish standards of measuring faithfulness he has lived a blameless and exemplary life.

The high priest Ananias orders that Paul be struck on the mouth for this statement, to which Paul reacts in a typically human way. He calls the high priest a whitewashed wall – that is, a hypocrite – and says that God will strike him too. It is a miscarriage of justice to strike a person before being convicted and, in Paul's case, he has not even been properly charged.

When Paul is rebuked for speaking such strong words to the high priest he apologises immediately. His failure to recognise the high priest is most likely because, as this was not a regular meeting of the Sanhedrin, the high priest was not in his regular seat or wearing his usual robes of office.

Using a skilful diversionary tactic, Paul moves from the back foot to the place of command. With sudden insight that the Sanhedrin is a mixture of Sadducees and Pharisees, and knowing that the Pharisees believed in a bodily resurrection but the Sadducees did not, Paul declares himself to be a Pharisee and the son of a Pharisee, on trial because of his hope in the resurrection of the dead.

Paul thus shifts the debate away from himself and shines a spotlight on the festering controversy between the Sadducees and Pharisees concerning the matter of the resurrection. This is manipulation of the highest order. It is also exactly what Jesus encouraged his disciples to be in the midst of wolves – 'as shrewd as snakes and as innocent as doves' (*Matt 10:16*).

SUNDAY 30 JULY
True Fasting

Isaiah 58:5–12

'Is not this the kind of fasting I have chosen: to loose the chains of injustice and untie the cords of the yoke, to set the oppressed free and break every yoke?' (v. 6, NIV).

There is a way to fast as a means of seeking after God but the people are not doing it the right way. They go through the ritual of fasting and do the performance but, instead of abandoning themselves to God and then giving themselves away to others, their focus is entirely self–serving.

They humble (literally 'afflict') themselves. They bow the head and lie on sackcloth and ashes – traditional symbols of contrition and penitence. But, says the prophet incredulously, 'You do as you please' (v. 3). They go through their formalities to show how devoted they are. But on the same day as they fast they exploit their workers, explode in quarrelling and express themselves in violence.

In stark contrast is the kind of fasting that God looks for. God calls for behaviour that is self–forgetful and outward–looking. Let acts of self–denial be done for the sake of others and not for one's own sake, he says. Work for justice, get rid of exploitation in the workplace, free the oppressed, cancel debts. We hear an echo of the prophet Micah saying, 'Act justly . . . love mercy . . . walk humbly with your God' (*Micah 6:8*).

The prophet continues. Eat less in order to have food for the hungry. Use your means to offer shelter to the homeless. Wear less–expensive clothes in order to clothe the naked. Treat all people as part of your extended family.

Then and only then will a new age dawn for the righteous. God's light of justice will shine through his people, making them a light for all nations. God will hear and answer prayer. Healing will come like new skin growing over a wound. Deep needs will be satisfied.

God's people will flourish like a well–watered garden, like an unfailing spring. Solid foundations, long since broken down, will be rebuilt. 'You will be called Repairer of Broken Walls, Restorer of Streets with Dwellings' (*Isa 58:12*). The wonderful covenant blessings of guidance, protection and strength will be assured.

These promises are a picture of restoration and renewal which all hang on the huge word 'if' (vv. 9,10).

MONDAY 31 JULY
A Promise and a Plot

Acts 23:9–22

'The following night the Lord stood near Paul and said,
"Take courage! As you have testified about me in Jerusalem,
so you must also testify in Rome"' (v. 11, NIV).

Paul's declaration of belief in the resurrection throws the whole Sanhedrin into an uproar. Some side with Paul, others against him. Some even consider that an angel has spoken to him. Yet once again the commander has to intervene and remove Paul to the safety of the barracks.

The following night God comes near and speaks courage to Paul, assuring him that the divine purposes are being worked out. One of Paul's great dreams is about to be fulfilled – he is going to Rome. His testimony, faithfully given in Jerusalem, will also be delivered in Rome.

The next scene of Paul's story is carried out with all the intrigue of a Hollywood movie. A group of Jews devise a plot to kill him. So sincere are they that they bind themselves with a vow not to eat or drink until they have carried out the deed.

In the divine economy it just so happens that a lad is listening in the wings and overhears the plot. This lad also just happens to be a nephew of Paul's. Even though he is in custody, Paul is as yet uncon-

victed and, as a Roman citizen, has the right to be treated with respect and to have visits from his family.

Paul's family has, until this point, had no mention at all and it is believed that when he became a Christian he was disowned by his father. But some streak of family affection obviously remains for his sister's son to take the risk of warning Paul about the plot against him. When he hears what the lad has to say, Paul sends him to the commander who acts decisively yet again to ensure Paul's safety.

Notice how the promise of God comes to Paul before the news of the plot against his life. God does not tell Paul all that is going to happen but simply speaks an assurance and tells him to take courage. As for us, when we know that our lives are in God's hands and his purposes are being worked out, is that not all we need to know?

TUESDAY 1 AUGUST
To Caesarea

Acts 23:23–35

'He called two of his centurions and ordered them, "Get ready a detachment of two hundred soldiers, seventy horsemen and two hundred spearmen to go to Caesarea at nine tonight"' (v. 23, NIV).

The first stage of Paul's journey towards Rome is carried out under cover of darkness and with the protection of Roman soldiers, horsemen and spearmen. Do these troops numbering at least 470 men realise that they are caught up in the great purposes of God?

Claudius Lysias, the commander who has already rescued Paul on three occasions from an angry mob, sends a letter to Governor Felix with the delegation, outlining the situation. The details about Paul are embellished a little as Claudius takes the opportunity to gain favour with Rome. He says he rescued Paul when he learned that he was a Roman citizen but in fact the commander did not learn this until he was about to scourge Paul in an attempt to gain information (22:25).

The soldiers bring Paul to the military post in Antipatris, thirty miles from Jerusalem. From there they return to their barracks in Jerusalem, leaving Paul in the care of the cavalry who take him on a further twenty-eight miles to Caesarea. There both Paul and the commander's letter are handed over to Felix, governor of Judea.

The Roman Emperor Claudius had appointed Felix as governor in AD 52. Felix came from a somewhat lowly background but rose to a high position. He successively married three women of royal birth, his current wife, Drusilla, being his third, the daughter of Herod Agrippa I. During Felix's term of office there were many insurgent uprisings which he ruthlessly put down. The Roman historian Tacitus said that Felix 'exercised the power of a king with the mind of a slave'.

After reading the letter from the commander in Jerusalem, Felix discovers that Paul is from Cilicia and so decides to hear his case. Had Paul come from a neighbouring area Felix could have sent him to that governor. Paul is kept under guard in the palace that Herod the Great built for himself, which is now the governor's headquarters.

God, it seems, can use anything – even a murderous plot, a guard of pagan soldiers and a tyrannical governor – to carry out his relentless, righteous purposes.

WEDNESDAY 2 AUGUST
The Charges Against Paul

Acts 24:1–9

'We have found this man to be a troublemaker, stirring up riots among the Jews all over the world. He is a ringleader of the Nazarene sect and even tried to desecrate the temple' (vv. 5,6, NIV).

Paul's trial before Governor Felix takes place five days later, by which time certain people have come from Jerusalem for the hearing. Ananias himself, the high priest, makes the sixty-mile journey to Caesarea to supervise the case personally. The lawyer (literally 'orator') Tertullus is most likely a Greek Jew familiar with the procedures of a Roman court.

The lawyer's task is to present the case against Paul but he begins with considerable bowing and scraping to Felix. He is lavish in his praise, speaking of the governor's good rule 'everywhere and in every way'. He expresses the 'profound gratitude' of the Jews for the peace they have enjoyed under Felix's control.

These facts are not entirely true for there were many uprisings that had been brutally stamped out by Felix. But Tertullus the lawyer is being very skilful here. His subtle reminder of the stability that Felix has won by means of severe action against troublemakers serves as an introduction to Paul whom he wants to cast as yet another rabble-rouser.

Tertullus outlines three charges against Paul. First, he is a trouble-maker stirring up riots among the Jews all over the world. Second, he is a ringleader of an unrecognised religious sect, which was against Roman law. Third, he has tried to desecrate the temple.

The Jews (v. 9) – that is, the religious leaders who have come from the Sanhedrin in Jerusalem – endorse what the lawyer says. They hope the charges against Paul will be sufficient to persuade Felix to execute Paul in order to keep the peace in Palestine.

What do you do when people say things about you that are patently untrue? Thomas à Kempis saw earthly trials and troubles as reminders of his heavenly hope. He wrote, 'When to all outward appearances others give us no credit, when they do not think well of us, then we are more inclined to seek God, who sees our hearts' (The Imitation of Christ).

Jesus said we should count ourselves blessed and rejoice and be glad (Matt 5:11,12). But making this our habitual practice is often far from easy.

THURSDAY 3 AUGUST
Paul's Glad Defence

Acts 24:10–21

'When the governor motioned for him to speak, Paul replied:
"I know that for a number of years you have been a judge over this
nation; so I gladly make my defence"' (v. 10, NIV).

While the accusations against Paul are untrue, the lawyer presents them convincingly. When the governor motions for Paul to speak, he leaps to his feet. 'I gladly make my defence,' he says. Another translation uses the word 'cheerfully' (NRSV).

There is something delightfully irrepressible about Paul. In spite of the beatings he has suffered, in spite of the long journey from Caesarea and the false charges against him, he just keeps going, bouncing back, ready to defend himself and the gospel. Long after other less-hardy souls would have given up or given in to discouragement, Paul keeps moving forward.

In beginning his defence, Paul uses none of the lavishness with which Tertullus earlier addressed the governor, but simply acknowledges the competence of Felix to judge the case. He then proceeds in an able and ordered way to refute the accusations point by point. Felix can verify when Paul arrived in Jerusalem. His accusers did not find him doing anything anywhere in Jerusalem that might suggest he was causing trouble. They have no proof for any of their charges.

Having stated, 'That is not true, nor that, nor that,' Paul swings the focus from himself to the gospel and once more boldly gives his testimony. 'I worship the God of our fathers . . . I believe everything that agrees with the Law and the Prophets . . . I have the same hope in God as these men.' He asserts his blamelessness. No one can point a finger at him regarding his personal life. He strives, just like an athlete, to keep his conscience clear before God and man.

Paul explains his reasons for coming to Jerusalem – to bring gifts for the poor and to present offerings. He was ceremonially clean when he was found in the temple, there was no crowd with him, and he was not involved in any disturbance. If the claim that he caused trouble 'all over the world' (v. 5) refers to what happened in Ephesus, then the Jews from Asia should be there to speak in person.

One by one Paul refutes all the charges against him.

101

FRIDAY 4 AUGUST
Deciding Not to Decide

Acts 24:22–27

'As Paul discoursed on righteousness, self-control and the judgment to come, Felix was afraid and said, "That's enough for now! You may leave. When I find it convenient, I will send for you"' (v. 25, NIV).

It is obvious that the charges against Paul are untrue. Governor Felix should have released him but Felix is a man with other agendas and so he does not. He merely delays making a decision about Paul until Claudius Lysias, the commander, arrives from Jerusalem. Felix orders that Paul be kept under guard but that he be given relative freedom.

Felix is an interesting character. Luke notes that he is 'well acquainted with the Way'. Having been governor for six years Felix will have had plenty of opportunity to observe the lifestyle of Christians and to know they pose no threat to peace. He treats his prisoner as some kind of exhibit, fascinating to listen to, but fearsome when he speaks the kind of truth that touches Felix personally.

Like Herod Antipas (see *Mark 6:17,18*), Felix had taken another man's wife, so when Paul speaks of righteousness, self-control and the judgment to come, Felix calls a halt to their session. 'That's enough for today,' he says. 'I'll call you back when it's convenient' (*Acts 24:25, The Message*). Paul can be sent away with the wave of a hand but the claims of Christ are not so easily dismissed.

Greater than guilt, however, Felix's problem seems to be greed. He sends for Paul regularly, listening, always listening but secretly hoping for a bribe. Perhaps he had heard that Paul brought a substantial offering to Jerusalem for the poor. Two years later, when Felix is called back to Rome, he orders that Paul be kept in prison 'because [he] wanted to grant a favour to the Jews'.

This man is well informed and has every opportunity to embrace the gospel but he chooses instead to remain an observer. He is like a man who wants to sit by the fire but when the fire gets too hot he throws a bucket of water over it. Felix's story is a cautionary tale. His motto is: Put off the day. Delay the decision. Wait for the easy, convenient moment.

Too late, Felix discovers that to decide not to decide is to decide decisively.

SATURDAY 5 AUGUST
Going Higher

Acts 25:1–12

'If I am guilty of doing anything deserving death, I do not refuse
to die. But if the charges brought against me by these Jews
are not true, no-one has the right to hand me over to them.
I appeal to Caesar!' (v. 11, NIV).

Two years on, the governor has changed but none of the Jews' antagonism towards Paul has diminished, nor their desire to get rid of him. When the new governor, Festus, arrives in the province he immediately reopens Paul's case and travels to Jerusalem to get the facts. He denies the Jewish leaders' request to have the prisoner brought to Jerusalem but tells them to come to Caesarea where he will hear the case.

As in the trial before Felix, the Jews make serious charges against Paul which they cannot prove. Yet again Paul declares himself blameless before the Jewish law, the temple and Caesar. At this stage he should have been released but Festus, bowing to Jewish pressure and wanting to grant them a favour, asks Paul whether he is willing to go to Jerusalem for trial.

For the third time Luke mentions the governor's desire to keep favour with the Jews (24:27; 25:3,9). This almost throwaway comment is like a sinister undercurrent that threatens to overwhelm and submerge Paul. He must realise that his life is in real danger and that he has no hope of a fair trial either in Jerusalem or Caesarea. The famous Roman justice system that treated him well under Gallio (18:17) is being undermined by powerful and vociferous local leaders.

Yet Paul has three reasons to be confident. He knows he is innocent of the trumped-up charges against him. He knows that as a Roman citizen he has the right and privilege of appealing to Caesar. He knows God has already promised that he will give his testimony in Rome (23:11). So he appeals to Caesar. He will go to Rome as a prisoner under Rome's full protection and, at the same time, fulfil the clear purposes of God for his life.

What more could he ask? How much higher could he go? What greater freedom could any prisoner enjoy?

To reflect on
'In all your ways acknowledge him [that is, God], and he will make your paths straight' (Prov 3:6). How is this promise being worked out in Paul's life? And in your life?

SUNDAY 6 AUGUST
A Day for Delight

Isaiah 58:13,14

'If you keep your feet from breaking the Sabbath and from doing as you please on my holy day . . . then you will find your joy in the LORD' (vv. 13,14, NIV).

I watch a young mother with her baby and see a picture of sheer delight. I read of the delight of two sisters who have been reunited after forty years of separation. I observe my grandsons delighting in a fresh pile of library books.

The word 'delight' is one that can light up a face and lift a heavy heart. To delight in something is to find joy, to take pleasure, to experience something as 'delectable' (the same word as 'delightful') as a plump juicy strawberry.

In the wisdom of God, believers are given a whole day every week in which to delight. The fourth of the Ten Commandments gives explicit instructions on how the Sabbath is to be spent (*Exod 20:8*). In celebration of the seventh day of creation on which God rested, the Sabbath was to' be set apart from the commonplace, ordinary routine of every other day.

Most Christians these days see Sunday as their Sabbath. But there are times when a Sunday filled with prayer meeting, church service, a pot-luck lunch, an afternoon outreach, visiting and hospitality can leave us feeling exhausted rather than rested.

In Isaiah's day the prophet saw how the people were breaking ('trampling', *NRSV*) the Sabbath by doing as they pleased, going their own way, treating the day carelessly. God challenged them: 'When you delight in the Sabbath, you delight in me and I delight in you.' It is clear that Sabbath obedience is a key component of true righteousness, along with issues of social justice, religious observances and human relationships.

The prophet's words are remarkably up-to-date when we consider the multiple options – from malls to mowers to marathons – that so easily crowd out our non-work spaces. Whether on a Sunday or another set-apart day of the week, it is clear that we all need a Sabbath on which we give our full attention to God. At the heart of the Sabbath stands a question: Who is this day for?

To reflect on
What would a day of Sabbath delight look like for you? Check out the promise of Psalm 37:4.

MONDAY 7 AUGUST
On Trial for the Resurrection

Acts 25:13–22

'They had some points of dispute with him about their own religion and about a dead man named Jesus who Paul claimed was alive' (v. 19, NIV).

A few days later Festus receives a visit from Herod Agrippa II and his sister Bernice. This Agrippa is the son of Agrippa I, who was the grandson of Herod the Great. Any mention of the Herod dynasty in Scripture makes us hold our breath, for every Herod was violent and brutal.

Paul seems unfazed that his case is being heard before increasingly powerful rulers. In fact he delights in every opportunity to give his testimony and speak of Jesus. Each of the rulers examining Paul is ignorant of the theological issues at stake but has an agenda of political self-interest. These two factors combined actually serve to safeguard Paul from his Jewish opponents.

As Festus is a pagan and Agrippa and his sister are secular Jews, 'well acquainted with all the Jewish customs and controversies' (26:3), Festus turns to them for help in settling his long-standing 'Paul problem'. Agrippa must already know something of the case because he was the Roman curator of the temple at Jerusalem. Even if he was not on hand the day that Paul was charged with defiling the temple (21:28), Agrippa must surely have heard about it.

Festus summarises Paul's case. He tells how he inherited the prisoner from Felix. He fills in the gaps of what took place in his meeting in Jerusalem with the leaders of the Jews (25:2). He reports that the Sanhedrin had initially wanted to bring a guilty verdict against Paul without a trial (v. 15). He states that it is not the Roman custom to hand over anyone before the accused has had an opportunity to make his own defence.

Festus makes no mention of Paul's Roman citizenship that guarantees his right to a fair trial. In fact he seems to have come to the conclusion that there is no case at all against Paul and that the dispute is over a matter of religion, at the heart of which is the prisoner's belief in the resurrection of Jesus.

To reflect on
If you were on trial for serving a risen Saviour, what compelling evidence would there be?

TUESDAY 8 AUGUST

The Prisoner and the Pomp

Acts 25:23–27

'The next day Agrippa and Bernice came with great pomp and entered the audience room with the high ranking officers and the leading men of the city. At the command of Festus, Paul was brought in' (v. 23, NIV).

The following day Agrippa and Bernice arrive at the palace 'with great pomp'. Also gathered are military officers and prominent city leaders, both Jewish and Roman. Five Roman regiments were stationed at Caesarea so their five commanders would be in attendance.

There was a time when Paul the Pharisee would have mixed and mingled easily with these well-heeled people. He had a story that put him on equal footing with the glitterati. 'You know my pedigree,' he told the believers at Philippi. 'A legitimate birth, circumcised on the eighth day; an Israelite from the elite tribe of Benjamin; a strict and devout adherence to God's law; a fiery defender of the purity of my religion, even to the point of persecuting Christians; a meticulous observer of everything set down in God's law Book' (Phil 3:5,6, The Message).

But all this renown, he realised when he met Jesus, was nothing more than rubbish. What had once been treasure became, on that great day of his conversion, nothing more than trash. He gave up his credentials for Christ, swapped the pomp for the Person, exchanged his petty self-righteousness for 'the robust kind that comes from trusting Christ – God's righteousness' (Phil 3:9, The Message).

What did Paul think as he was led in as a prisoner to face the pomp before him? Did he kneel in his heart and offer prayer, just like young David kneeling in worship as he picked up stones from the river bed while Goliath lumbered down the hill towards him (1 Sam 17:40)?

How did Paul feel as he heard Governor Festus summarise yet again the charges against him and declare him innocent? In a room filled with the high and mighty dressed in their dazzling gear, Paul is clothed in humble prison garb and the quiet dignity of a man with a message.

All I once held dear, built my life upon
All this world reveres, and wars to own,
All I once thought gain I have counted loss;
Spent and worthless now, compared to this.
Knowing You, Jesus, knowing You
There is no greater thing.

Graham Kendrick[5]

WEDNESDAY 9 AUGUST
A Powerful Testimony

Acts 26:1–11

'The Jews all know the way I have lived ever since I was a child,
from the beginning of my life in my own country,
and also in Jerusalem' (v. 4, NIV).

Paul never tired of giving his testimony, never lost the wonder of his conversion. While some details of his conversion are told in earlier chapters of Acts, this chapter brings all the threads together. Like John the Baptist pointing the way to Jesus, Paul tells his own story but steadily moves the focus away from himself to the resurrection of Jesus and the wide purposes of God.

When King Agrippa motions for Paul to speak he begins formally with a compliment, acknowledging Agrippa's familiarity with 'all the Jewish customs and controversies'. Such 'inside' knowledge makes Agrippa a suitable person to hear Paul's defence.

Paul makes an immediate connection with his audience, acknowledging 'all the accusations of the Jews' that have been made against him. He is unashamed of his Jewish roots and declares that he has lived a robust Jewish life in full public view for a long time. As a Pharisee he has been a vigorous defender of the Jewish faith and a firm adherent of the Jewish Scriptures. He knows he is on trial for two reasons – first,

his hope in what God promised to the ancestors of the Jews, and second, his own hope in the resurrection.

Referring to the pre-Jesus stage of his life, Paul speaks of his conviction that it was his religious duty to stamp out the new Messianic movement that had the resurrection of Jesus at its centre.

He tells in a form of confession some of the atrocities he committed against 'the saints'. In an inexcusable religious frenzy he locked up many believers in prison. He cast his vote against them. He tried to force them to blaspheme. He pursued them even to foreign cities – that is, far beyond Jerusalem.

Notice the progression of Paul's testimony as he moves from compliment to connection, from conviction to confession. This is Paul speaking factually of who he is and what he has done. But, praise God, the passion for punishment, pursuit and persecution that drove him on at the beginning was halted one remarkable day when he had an encounter with the risen Jesus.

THURSDAY 10 AUGUST
What a Turnaround!

Acts 26:12–23

'We all fell to the ground, and I heard a voice saying to me in Aramaic, "Saul, Saul, why do you persecute me? It is hard for you to kick against the goads"' (v. 14, NIV).

For the third time in the book of Acts, Luke records Paul telling the circumstances of his conversion and his divine call. He was on his way to Damascus, 'armed as always with papers from the high priests' (v. 12, *The Message*), his purpose being persecution. He was out to take believers captive when he himself was taken captive.

A light from heaven, blazing brighter than the sun, shone around him and his travelling companions. Falling flat on the ground with his face in the dust he heard a voice speaking to him in his own language, Aramaic. 'Saul, Saul,' said the voice, the repetition of the name adding urgency. 'Why do you persecute me? Why are you kicking against the goads?' A goad was a sharp stick used to prod cattle. To kick against the goads would cause great injury to oneself. 'Why do you do it, Paul?' asked the voice.

Pause for a moment with Paul in this place of sensory overload. He could feel the heat of the sun, hotter than high noon. He could taste the choking dust in his mouth. He could hear a voice that was insistent and strangely familiar. Did Paul know, even before he asked the question, 'Who are you, Lord?' that this was a divine encounter that would prove to be life-changing? Have you ever touched, tasted or heard the heart-invading, life-transforming presence of God in such an unmistakable way?

As soon as Jesus identified himself, Paul found himself being commissioned as a servant and witness of the living Lord. His task was threefold – to open the eyes of the Gentiles to the truth of the gospel, to turn them from darkness and ignorance to the light of the gospel, with the result that they would receive forgiveness and eternal life from God. Note the verbs – 'open', 'turn' and 'receive'.

What a turnaround! From snuffing out the light, Paul is now to be a light-bearer. From silencing believers, he is now to be their spokesman. From lining up the persecuted, he is now to live out the promises of God.

FRIDAY 11 AUGUST
Short Time or Long

Acts 26:24–29

'Paul replied, "Short time or long – I pray God that not only you but all who are listening to me today may become what I am, except for these chains"' (v. 29, NIV).

Festus and King Agrippa listen to Paul's salvation story without interruption. They can hardly question what he states as fact – his interrupted journey, the heavenly voice, his commissioning to a new cause. But Paul's claims about Christ suffering and rising from the dead are too much for Festus.

The Roman governor is a man of the mind who has no understanding at all of the things about which Paul is so passionate. Festus can only conclude that Paul's intense learning has somehow unbalanced him. 'Paul, you're crazy!' he declares. But Paul responds by insisting that what he is saying is both true and reasonable.

Once more showing his skill in playing one character against another, Paul turns to the king. He is sure that Agrippa already knows many of the facts about Christianity because none of it has been done surreptitiously. If Agrippa feels a sudden flush of pride at his superior knowledge, the moment is short-lived. Like a hot knife cutting through butter, Paul challenges him: 'You believe the prophets, don't you, King Agrippa? . . . I know you believe' (v. 27, *The Message*).

The king is immediately thrown into a dilemma. If he says, 'Yes, I believe what the prophets say,' Paul will press him to recognise Jesus as the fulfilment of the prophets' words. If he says, 'No, I don't believe the prophets,' he will offend the devout Jews. So the king brushes off the challenge with an evasive answer. He has not come to this gathering to make a decision about Christianity but simply to help Festus with his 'Paul problem'.

Paul responds by declaring his own personal mission statement. 'Short time or long,' whether now or later, his greatest desire is that everyone would come to Christ. This is the passion that has driven him since the day of his conversion. This is the substance of his teaching, the focus of his prayers. Does such a passion drive your heart?

Make a list of people you know who are not yet Christians. Pray that, whether in a short time or long, they too might become Jesus-followers.

SATURDAY 12 AUGUST
In the Midst of the Powerful

Acts 26:30–32

'The king rose, and with him the governor and Bernice
and those sitting with them' (v. 30, NIV).

As the gathering adjourns, the general feeling is that Paul has done nothing to deserve punishment. He could have been released if he had not appealed to Caesar. As a Roman citizen he has that right. The leaders are left with no choice but to take him to Rome.

This, of course, is exactly what God had earlier told Paul. After the uproar in the Sanhedrin when Paul cleverly pitted the Sadducees against the Pharisees over the question of the resurrection, God had drawn near to him during the night to reassure him: 'As you have testified about me in Jerusalem, so you must also testify in Rome' (23:11).

That the purposes of God are being worked out should not be surprising. That the purposes of God are being worked out through such unlikely people as Claudius Lysias, Felix, Festus and King Agrippa II is nothing short of remarkable.

Claudius Lysias was the commander of the Roman troops in Jerusalem. He rescued Paul at least three times from an angry mob, and made arrangements to transfer him quietly to Caesarea when the plot against Paul's life was unearthed. Claudius Lysias was a man just doing his job, trying to keep the peace.

Felix, the governor before whom Paul appeared at Caesarea, was both acquainted with the way of Christ and immune to its claims. Fascinated by Paul, he listened and observed but made no personal commitment. Festus, who succeeded Felix as governor, was of similar bent. He was a man of rational understanding and self-interest, anxious both to do the Jews a favour and to keep the peace with Rome.

King Agrippa II also heard and observed but held himself at arm's length from the kingdom of God. Although clearly challenged, he chose to remain unconvinced. Not one of these men is a man of faith, yet they are all caught up in the divine drama.

In the midst of the powerful Paul stands, not unlike Jesus himself, unashamed, unafraid, undeterred. There is a serenity about him, a wholeness, a quiet confidence, an unwavering trust in the sovereign purposes of God.

SUNDAY 13 AUGUST
A Portrait of Sin

Isaiah 59:1–8

'Your iniquities have separated you from your God; your sins have hidden his face from you, so that he will not hear' (v. 2, NIV).

If you have ever wondered what sin looks like, here is a most graphic description. When the people ask, 'What is the matter with God? Why does he not hear our prayers? Why does he not do something?' the prophet tells them that their lack of blessing is not God's fault but their own. God is not blind or deaf or helpless, but their iniquities and sins have opened up a gaping chasm between them.

To illustrate his point the prophet picks up his paintbrush. He por-trays sin with an amazing array of human characteristics. It has hands stained with blood and fingers dripping with guilt. It has lips smeared with lies and a tongue that constantly utters obscenities. It has feet that rush to do evil. Sin rubs its hands in delight over evil dreams and villainous schemes.

Using the startling metaphor of conception and birth, the prophet describes how sin conceives trouble, gives birth to evil, hatches the eggs of vipers and produces spiders' webs. These things are not simply useless but worse – deadly.

In contrast to the highway of holiness that God is preparing for his people (35:8), or the level road on which the ransomed of the Lord will return with great joy to Jerusalem (51:11), sin's roads are crooked. All who travel on these paths will meet with destruction and disintegration. Nowhere to be found on sin's roads are wholeness, peace or the blessing of *shalom* that God longs to give to his people.

In our post–modern world, where sin is an outmoded concept and people prefer to describe their failings as 'a little white lie' or 'a minor infringement' or 'a careless oversight', we need this stark re-minder of the utter crookedness and degradation of sin.

The fact is that sinners of every generation need a Saviour. Doing better, being nicer, trying harder will never conquer sin, nor bridge the gaping chasm between God and ourselves. Only Jesus can span that gap. By his death on the cross he has made a way for all humankind to be reconciled to God (see *Eph 2:14–18*).

LOVING THE QUESTIONS

Introduction

On her deathbed Gertrude Stein is said to have asked, 'What is the answer?' Then, after a long silence, 'What is the question?' Frederich Buechner says, 'Don't start looking in the Bible for the answers it gives. Start by listening for the questions it asks.'

It is all too easy to live life on the surface of things. Endless questions fill our days – 'Where is my cell phone? Where did I leave my glasses? Who's going to be home for dinner tonight?' But what about the deeper, universal life questions that we all, at some time or another, need to address?

This series looks at some of the great life questions from Scripture, such as:

- What is truth?
- How can a person be born when they are old?
- What does a person gain from all their labour at which they toil under the sun?
- Is anything too difficult for God?
- Where can I go from your Spirit?

In this series I introduce you to a host of guest contributors – Salvation Army colleagues whom I met at the International Literary and Publications Conference in Washington, USA, in April 2005. At the conclusion of a workshop on devotional writing I gave the opportunity for people to take one of the questions from Scripture and to write a piece suitable for this series.

It is my pleasure to introduce you to these friends and their fine work.

'Be patient toward all that is unsolved in your heart and try to love the questions themselves.'

Rainer Maria Rilke

MONDAY 14 AUGUST
What is that in your hand?

Exodus 4:1–5

'The LORD said to him, "What is that in your hand?" "A staff,"
he replied' (v. 2, NIV).

Immediately after his dramatic encounter with God at the burning bush Moses received his commission. The assignment was awe-inspiring – to set the Israelites free from slavery in Egypt. Moses was fearful and also sceptical that anyone would believe his story of a burning bush, clearly spoken words from the God of creation, and his incredible commission. Most of us would say his scepticism was well founded.

Moses was given more than verbal assurance that throughout his life he would have the presence of the living God with him at all times. Furthermore, sensing the apprehension and doubt that was showing through in Moses, God asked him a question – a crucial, leading question: 'What have you got in your hand?'

Moses held the one piece of equipment that was his constant companion, the shepherd's crook or staff. When God told him to throw it on the ground, Moses obeyed, then leapt back with fright as the rod immediately turned into a serpent. God reassured him and told him to grasp the serpent by the tail

and, as Moses did so, the serpent turned back into a shepherd's staff. The significant thing to note in this story is that God took the symbol of the everyday working life of Moses and touched it with a miracle.

As we seek God's will and purpose in our lives we may well hear him say the same thing to us: 'What is that in your hand?' It may be a hammer or a scalpel, a teapot or a computer keyboard. He still waits to show us, as he showed Moses, that he is able touch the everyday 'tools of our trade' with a miracle. How reassuring is that?

This is the time for us to move on past any feelings of uncertainty, anxiety or inadequacy. We can experience the Spirit of God empowering us daily. We need to be still and listen to what God is saying and then encourage one another to use what is already there in our hands. Then . . . get ready for a miracle!

Lieut–Colonel Alan Bateman
United Kingdom

TUESDAY 15 AUGUST
Who am I, O Lord God?

1 Chronicles 17:16–27

'Who am I, O LORD God, and what is my family, that you have brought me this far?' (v. 16, NIV).

David is at the pinnacle of his career – king over Israel, victor over his enemies, commander over an impressive fighting force. He is loved by the people and surrounded by loyal warriors who would risk their very lives for him. The ark of the covenant, symbol of God's presence, is back in Jerusalem, the city of God, where it belongs.

David himself lives in a brand-new palace with a bevy of new wives who are producing child after child, heirs to David's name and fortune. He is held in awe by all the nations and his fame spreads throughout every land (14:17).

Everywhere he looks David sees signs of blessing. In a great public thanksgiving he acknowledges all that God has done and calls the people to 'Sing to him . . . Look to the LORD . . . Remember the wonders he has done' (16:9–12).

Back home, blessing his family (16:43), David wonders why he is living in a palace built of cedar when the ark of God is housed in a tent. The thought prompts other questions: 'Who am I, God, and what have I done to deserve all this?' Righteous and regal on the outside,

David knows he is nothing more than human and ordinary on the inside. 'You know me just as I am,' he says to God (17:18, *The Message*).

'Just as I am' are the words songwriter Charlotte Elliott has given to the world (*SASB 293*), 'Without one plea . . . tossed about . . . poor, wretched, blind'. When someone honours or commends us, when we look around and see success or blessing, when we stand tall in the eyes of others, it is helpful to remember, like David, that our giftedness is the gift of a gracious God.

'It is our light, not our darkness, that most frightens us. We ask ourselves, who am I to be brilliant, gorgeous, talented, fabulous? Actually, who are you not to be? You are a child of God . . . We were born to make manifest the glory of God that is within us.'
Words attributed to Nelson Mandela

WEDNESDAY 16 AUGUST
Where can I go from your Spirit?

Psalm 139

'Where can I go from your Spirit? Where can I flee
from your presence?' (v. 7, NIV).

One night in an isolated village in Indonesia all was quiet and dark. Pale moonlight was the only light shining on the village street. Suddenly there was a noise. A man walked along the street, followed by a pony. 'Andreas, is that you?' my mother called out. The man and pony stopped still.

As we looked out onto the street we saw that it was indeed my brother Andreas. He had walked for three days through the jungle to find his way to a house he had never visited before. In her intuitive way, my mother knew that the stranger in the night was her son.

Is it possible for a mother, or even a father, to forget their child? asks the prophet Isaiah (*Isa 49:15*). No, it is not possible because the child is their flesh and blood. Yet even if it were possible, says God, I will not forget you. Is it possible to escape from God's Spirit, to flee from his presence, to go so far away that his love will not reach us? No, says God, it is not possible.

There are many people, of course, who live with no reference to God. They may think they are on their own, living according to their own will, separate from and independent of God. But this is a false assumption.

Wherever we are, God watches over us, not like a suspicious prison guard monitoring our every movement, but like a loving father or an alert mother. No matter how far from home we may wander like the prodigal son, there is always Someone watching, waiting, praying for our return.

---

*Afar from Heaven thy feet have
  wandered,
Afar from God thy soul has strayed;
His gifts in sin thy hand has
  squandered,
Yet still in love he calls thee home.*

*God is near thee, tell thy story;
He will hear thy tale of sorrow,
God is near thee, and in mercy
He will welcome thy return.*
        Richard Slater, SASB 225

Major Habel Laua
Indonesia

THURSDAY 17 AUGUST
What does a man gain from all his labour?

Ecclesiastes 1:1–11

'What does a man gain from all his labour at which he toils under the sun?' (v. 3, NIV).

'What am I accomplishing? Why am I working so hard?' These are questions we all ask ourselves now and again. In Ecclesiastes the Teacher, Solomon, son of King David, asks: 'What's there to show for a lifetime of work, a lifetime of working your fingers to the bone?' (*v. 3, The Message*).

Solomon was one of the wealthiest men in history. Early in his reign as King of Israel he pleased God by asking for wisdom and knowledge to rule his people. He could have asked for personal wealth or a long life but he chose instead to ask for wisdom (see *2 Chron 1:10*).

In response God gave him not only what he requested but also riches and honour beyond what any other king before him had ever experienced. Solomon's crowning life achievement was to build Jerusalem's temple. So why was he cynical about the worth of a man's labour?

Solomon knew that nothing is enjoyable unless it is first acknowledged as a gift from God (see *Eccl 2:24*). Work itself is a gift and, when done with passion and love, work also becomes its own reward.

What happened to Solomon to bring him to such pessimism? Gradually, it seems, he lost his first purpose in life: namely, his passion to love and serve God. He accumulated seven hundred wives and three hundred mistresses who were all foreign worshippers of other gods. We wonder how a man who asked for wisdom could be so senseless.

Unfortunately, Solomon's is not the only story in history of irresponsible behaviour. We hear too often of men and women whose ardour for God cools as they become friends of the world.

It seems that in the end Solomon found his way back to God. After enjoying every pleasure and pursuit the world had to offer, he concluded: 'Fear God and keep his commandments, for this is the whole duty of man' (*12:13*).

To reflect on
'It is in the ordinary duties and labours of life that the Christian can and should develop his spiritual union with God.'

Thomas Merton

Major Ruth Sundin
USA

116

FRIDAY 18 AUGUST
Who will go for me?

Isaiah 6:1–8

'Then I heard the voice of the Lord saying, "Whom shall I send?
And who will go for us?"' (v. 8, NIV).

'Who will go for me?' God asks. Even before the details of the assignment are given Isaiah raises his hand, like a child in class eager to take on a challenge. He responds, 'Send me. I'll go!'

'Who will go for *us*?' reads the *NIV*, the word 'us' representing God the Father in relationship with the Son and the Spirit. The question echoes the heart cries of people every day: 'Who will go for us? Who will be our advocate? Who will understand? Who will offer us words of healing and comfort?'

These questions are the anguished cry of the ageing couple looking into an uncertain future, the man struggling with depression, the woman who has received fearful medical news, the grieving child.

What need does God have for broken human beings to do his work? In Isaiah's vision it is heavenly seraphs who do God's bidding. Their voices thunder, the threshold and the doorposts shake. It is terrifying. In the presence of God, Isaiah sees his own brokenness and that of his people. He cries out in fear, 'I am a man of unclean lips and I dwell among a people of unclean lips.' What need would God have of him?

Have you heard the words, 'God has no hands but our hands, no feet but our feet to do his work in the world today'? Do you shrink from God's call to service? Do you allow your weaknesses to deafen you to the appeals for help from those around you?

The seraph approaches Isaiah with coals from the altar and touches his lips. The action absolves him of guilt and his sins are forgiven. It is only then that Isaiah hears the appeal and responds. Isaiah's vision of God is complete and so compelling that he need hesitate no longer.

Surely God can accomplish his work without us, yet he delights to use us. May our response today be, like Isaiah's, 'Here am I – it is written about me in the scroll – I have come to do your will, O God' (*Heb 10:7*).

Karen Young
USA

SATURDAY 19 AUGUST
Is anything too hard for God?

Jeremiah 32:16–29

'I am the LORD, the God of all mankind. Is anything too hard for me?'
(v. 27, NIV).

The simple answer to the question is 'No!', but why is God asking it?

God is speaking to Jeremiah who has been imprisoned in the house of Zedekiah, King of Judah. His imprisonment is punishment for prophesying that God is planning to hand Zedekiah and his city over to the King of Babylon and that he will be held in captivity until God chooses to deal with him.

Perhaps Zedekiah thinks that if he can silence Jeremiah, his dreadful prophecy will not come to pass. Jeremiah, however, is sure of God's message because everything has happened just as God said it would.

God then tells Jeremiah to buy his cousin's field in Anathoth. The prophet does as he has been instructed. He gives the legal documents to Baruch and tells him to put them in safe keeping. But he is puzzled about being told to buy the field when God has warned him that the country of Judah is about to be placed in captivity. He wonders what good it will be to have legal documents to a field ruled by the Babylonians. Puzzled, he expresses his confusion in prayer.

First he proclaims that God is the creator of all things and that nothing is too hard for him. He speaks of God's great deeds and how disobedient God's people have been. At this point Jeremiah begins to see the inevitable calamity unfold but he is still puzzled about the instruction to buy the field.

God replies, 'I am the LORD, the God of all mankind. Is anything too hard for me?' God assures Jeremiah that he has the situation under control then explains his plan. Yes, the people of Judah will go into captivity as punishment for their sins but in God's time they will be restored to their land.

'I am the LORD, the God of all mankind. Is anything too hard for me?' Even when we do not understand the circumstances we can rest assured that God knows what he is doing. In his time, in his way, his sovereign plans will be accomplished.

Major Joyce Gauthier
USA

SUNDAY 20 AUGUST
A Cry of Confession

Isaiah 59:9–15

'Justice is far from us, and righteousness does not reach us. We look for light, but all is darkness; for brightness, but we walk in deep shadows' (v. 9, NIV).

Sin's portrait turns to confession's cry. From speaking about 'they' in his graphic description of sin (vv. 1–8), the prophet now refers to 'we'. He knows that he too stands with his people in need of forgiveness. His intimacy with a holy God does not give him immunity against the infection of sin.

In the absence of righteousness, sin has come in like a flood, causing the whole community to suffer. Like blind men, the people grope their way along, stumbling at high noon as if it were already twilight. Like bears they growl, impatient and frustrated. Like doves they moan, filled with sorrow.

Justice and righteousness (vv. 4,14) stand at a distance, observing a veritable menagerie of sins on the loose – offences, iniquities, rebellion, treachery, oppression, revolt and lies. 'Justice is beaten back, Righteousness is banished to the sidelines, Truth staggers down the street, Honesty is nowhere to be found, Good is missing in action' (vv. 14,15, The Message).

Isaiah the prophet reminds us of the psalmist who worked out what to do when sin has us in its wretched grip. The first step is to realise that sin is primarily against the Creator. 'Against you, you only, have I sinned and done what is evil in your sight,' declared David (Ps 51:4). On the surface his sin was against Bathsheba and her husband Uriah, but in looking deep within himself, David realised his outward sinful actions came from his own evil heart.

The second step is to confess it and let it out like pus from a wound. Only then can deep healing happen. 'When I kept it all inside, my bones turned to powder, my words became daylong groans. The pressure never let up; all the juices of my life dried up. Then I let it all out; I said, "I'll make a clean breast of my failures to GOD." Suddenly the pressure was gone – my guilt dissolved, my sin disappeared' (Ps 32:3–5, The Message).

Do you need to make the psalmist's confession your own today? Praise God that guilt and helplessness do not have the last word.

MONDAY 21 AUGUST
What good will it be . . . ?

Matthew 16:24–28

'What good will it be for a man if he gains the whole world,
yet forfeits his soul? Or what can a man give in exchange for his soul?'
(v. 26, NIV).

Peter must have been feeling good about the new name Jesus gave him just after his bold declaration of Jesus as 'the Christ, the Son of the Living God' (16:16). Life for Peter, now Simon Peter, was looking promising. Jesus had a bright political future and he, Peter, a prominent part to play in the new kingdom.

That is, until Jesus began to describe the cruel and painful death he would soon face. Peter recoiled from the thought. 'Never, Lord!' he protested. Jesus' recent affirmation turned to rebuke as he addressed Peter with some harsh words.

Peter thought he was in on great glory but Jesus knew that he and his followers would find great glory only through great sacrifice, denying themselves and taking up their cross.

Sacrifice. It is a harsh word that flies in the face of our human desires and our natural inclination for comfort, fame and pleasure. Even when we manage to 'deny' ourselves, it can turn out to be selfishly motivated! 'I deny myself that pastry so I can be healthy and look terrific in those jeans.' Is that the life of sacrifice Christ is referring to?

A life of hardship, submission and trials does not sound like something anyone would sign up for. Self-denial is about recognising what Matthew Henry called 'the worth of the soul and the comparative worthlessness of the world'. Martin Luther said, 'I have held many things in my hands and I have lost them all. But whatever I have placed in God's hands, that I still possess.'

An American tourist went to visit the nineteenth-century Polish rabbi, Hofetz Chaim. Astonished to see that the rabbi's home was only a simple room with a table, a bench and some books, the tourist asked, 'Rabbi, where is your furniture?'

'Well, where is yours?' replied the rabbi.

'Mine?' asked the puzzled American. 'I'm just a visitor here. I'm only passing through.'

'So am I,' said Hofetz Chaim.

When we wrap our minds around the reality of God's eternity we can hold loosely to the things of this world.

Captain Lisa Smith
USA

TUESDAY 22 AUGUST
Who do you say I am?

Mark 8:27–30

'"But what about you?" he asked. "Who do you say I am?"
Peter answered, "You are the Christ"' (v. 29, NIV).

When we ask the average person on the street, 'Who is Jesus?' we get a variety of answers. Some people might say, 'Jesus is my Lord and Saviour. He died on the cross for my sins and has given me the gift of eternal life.' Other people may respond, 'I think he was a good teacher, an honourable man, a prophet.' Someone might say, 'Jesus? I don't know who you are talking about.'

As Jesus and his disciples were travelling around Caesarea Philippi, Jesus asked them, 'Who do the people say I am?' They replied, 'Some say John the Baptist; others say Elijah; and still others, one of the prophets.' Just as in our day, the answers were varied. A wide range of opinion was canvassed with that one question.

Jesus pressed the question by asking his disciples, 'But what about you? Who do you say I am?' Like a child in class with his hand up, Peter knew the correct answer. 'You are the Christ,' he said. In confessing Jesus as Christ – that is, the anointed one of God – Peter was showing that he understood the particular role Jesus had been given. As the only begotten Son of God, Jesus had been sent into the world to suffer and die for the sins of all humankind.

The question, 'Who do you say Jesus is?' is still a vital one for people today. Knowing the answer to this question is worth infinitely more than knowing the answers to a college entrance exam or to the million-dollar question on a game show. Knowing the answer to this question will affect the relationship one has with God in this life. Knowing the answer to this question will determine one's eternal destiny.

Remember the woman at the well who rushed back to tell her neighbours about her encounter with Jesus. Within a few days, having listened to Jesus, they came to faith themselves.

The question is put before us all today: 'Who do you say Jesus is?' Consider it prayerfully. Answer it wisely. Your life depends upon your answer.

Captain Linda Ward
USA

WEDNESDAY 23 AUGUST
Who is my neighbour?

Luke 10:29–37

'He wanted to justify himself, so he asked Jesus,
"And who is my neighbour?"' (v. 29, NIV).

The story of the good Samaritan was told by Jesus to illustrate what it means to be a neighbour. A man fell into the hands of robbers and was left for dead on the side of the road. A priest and a Levite passed him by but when a Samaritan came along he took pity on the wounded man and did all he could to help him.

When Jesus asked the expert in the law who was the man's neighbour, he answered, 'The one who had mercy on him.'

We live in a world where an attitude of selfishness reigns supreme, where few seem to care about what happens to the man or woman or child next door. The strong do not seem to care about the weak. The rich have no apparent concern for the poor. The privileged take advantage of the under-privileged.

The question asked by the expert in the law still rings out loud and clear in our day: 'Who is my neighbour?' Is my neighbour simply a member of my own family? Is my neighbour someone who attends church with me? Is my neighbour someone with whom I get along

well and who demands nothing from me?

Jesus' story about the good Samaritan shows exactly who my neighbour is. Today's good Samaritan is anyone who sees a need and does something about it to bring healing and comfort. Today's good Samaritan is anyone prepared to help those who are weak or vulnerable.

Today's good Samaritan is anyone who will sit by another person in their time of need and give support and encouragement. Today's good Samaritan is anyone who will visit and pray with those who are bereaved. Today's good Samaritan is the one who takes care of those living with HIV/AIDS. Today's good Samaritan is anyone who offers help to the elderly and those who are orphans. Today's good Samaritan is anyone who defends and seeks justice for those who have no voice.

'Now you go,' says Jesus, 'and be this kind of good Samaritan to others.'

Major Samuel Baah
Ghana

THURSDAY 24 AUGUST

What do you want me to do for you?

Luke 18:35–43

'Jesus stopped and ordered the man to be brought to him. When he came near, Jesus asked him, "What do you want me to do for you?"' (vv. 40,41, NIV).

Jesus asked this question of a blind man who was sitting by the roadside begging. The day was hot and dusty. People were walking wearily along the road. They were not in any hurry and they did not talk much, as if they were trying to preserve their strength.

Then suddenly the road came to life with people running all over the place. There was much noise, some indistinguishable phrases, laughter and crying. What was going on? It turned out that Jesus of Nazareth was approaching. Hearing this, the blind man began calling out to Jesus. When he heard the man's cry, Jesus stopped and asked him, 'What do you want me to do for you?'

'Lord, I want to see,' replied the blind beggar. 'I want to be healed. Please help me.'

How often do we hear people asking us for help, counting on us, believing we can help them? I recall a story about a married couple who were both doctors. One day the husband received a message from his elderly mother, saying she was not well. Without hesitation he jumped into his car and drove off to see his mother, promising to be back home within two days.

His mother recovered quickly, however, so he left for home earlier than planned. Arriving home late in the evening, he was just walking upstairs to his flat when he suddenly doubled up with pain. He happened to be carrying some metal objects that went flying as he fell.

Awakened by the noise, one of his neighbours opened her door slightly and saw the man lying on the landing, but did not recognise him as her neighbour. Knowing there were doctors in the apartment next door she knocked on their door. The woman doctor shouted her questions through her closed door: 'What?' 'Who?' 'Why?' When she did finally open her door it was to find her own husband lying dead outside.

Jesus is never too late. He does not hesitate. His help always comes on time. What do you need him to do for you today?

Captain Galina Drozdovsky
Russia

FRIDAY 25 AUGUST

How can a man be born when he is old?

John 3:1–15

'"How can a man be born when he is old?" Nicodemus asked. "Surely he cannot enter a second time into his mother's womb to be born!"' (v. 4, NIV).

A Pharisee, a member of the Sanhedrin and a teacher of Judaism, Nicodemus was a man of political, religious and social stature.

He had heard the teachings of Jesus and seen his miracles. It is clear that Nicodemus was a sincere seeker after truth for he came to Jesus under cover of darkness, wanting to learn from the rabbi who had 'come from God' (v. 2). When Jesus said, 'No-one can see the kingdom of God unless he is born again' (v. 3), Nicodemus asked, 'How can a man be born when he is old?'

This learned and sophisticated man was obviously not confused by the language Jesus used. In fact, it was because Nicodemus understood how physical birth happens that he asked the question. Given the inevitable process from conception to growth to ageing and death, how can a 'rebirth' possibly happen?

Nicodemus' confusion was that he thought Jesus was referring to natural birth. He had no concept of spiritual birth. When a person is born physically, it is the beginning of an earthly life. But when a person is born of the Spirit, it is the beginning of a spiritual life. A person can be born 'when he is old' (v. 4) by being born again. But, unlike the first physical birth, this 'born–again' birth is entirely the work of God. The apostle Paul wrote that the one who is born again becomes 'a new creation; the old has gone, the new has come!' (2 Cor 5:17).

A young man, Derrick, spoke about his life of hard drinking, smoking, drugs and nightclubs. 'I started stealing, dropped out of college and eventually lost my job. I quickly became a gang leader organising robberies to support my drug habit,' he says. But today, through God's grace and power, Derrick has been born again and is now a Salvation Army officer.

Physical birth is one thing; spiritual birth is another. Physical birth gives entrance into the world; spiritual birth gives entrance into the kingdom of God. The question is: Have you been born again?

Major Rose–Marie Leslie
USA

SATURDAY 26 AUGUST
Do you want to get well?

John 5:1–9

'When Jesus saw him lying there and learned that he had been in this condition for a long time, he asked him, "Do you want to get well?"' (v. 6, NIV).

An unnamed man lay in a helpless state by the Bethesda Pool near the Sheep Gate in Jerusalem. He, along with many others, was waiting for a miracle. There was a belief that from time to time an angel of the Lord would come down and stir up the waters. The first person into the pool when the water stirred would be healed. Being second or third was too late. First in, only one healed. That was the belief.

A great number of people were there, all waiting, watching, listening for the water to ripple. Some of them were blind, some lame, others paralysed. The unnamed individual at the heart of this story had been an invalid for thirty-eight years. He was both hopeless and helpless because, without assistance, he could never be the first one into the pool. But still he came every day, hoping against hope, waiting for the miracle.

When Jesus saw him lying there and was told he had been in this state for a long time, he asked, 'Do you want to get well?' It seems a strange question. The answer was surely obvious.

This question may be the very one that Jesus asks us when we find ourselves in a hopeless and help-less situation: 'Do you want to get well?' Even if the answer is obvious, maybe Jesus wants us to verbalise our response and acknowledge our need of his healing.

There may be things that keep us from seeking healing, of course. We may have given up hope of ever being any different. There may even be a strange kind of comfort in being unwell. After all, if there was nothing wrong with us, certain things, certain ways of behaving, would have to change.

Pause for a moment by the pool of Bethesda. Listen as Jesus speaks his healing words to the man who has been there for thirty-eight years. Then watch as Jesus turns to you and asks you the very same question: 'Do you want to get well?' How will you respond to that question today?

Major Keith Welch
USA

SUNDAY 27 AUGUST
There is a Redeemer

Isaiah 59:15–21

'The Redeemer will come to Zion, to those in Jacob who repent of their sins' (v. 20, NIV).

When God needed a woman to work among war-stricken people in China during the 1930s he called Gladys Aylward, an English parlourmaid with no education, no money, and no mission board to send her.

When God needed a medical missionary in French Equatorial Africa in the early years of the twentieth century, he called Albert Schweitzer, theologian, surgeon, pastor and writer.

When God needed a man with a clear mind and a ready pen to record the good news, he called a tax collector, Levi son of Alphaeus (Mark 2:14).

When God needed a Redeemer, someone to save his people, to restore justice and reinstate righteousness, there was no one to be found.

There was no other good enough
To pay the price of sin;
He only could unlock the gate
Of Heaven, and let us in.
    Cecil Frances Alexander, SASB 133

When a Redeemer was called for, God answered his own call, sending his Son into the world, not to condemn but to save all humankind (see John 3:17). God clothed him in the garb of a warrior, with righteousness as his breastplate, a helmet of salvation on his head, and zeal as his cloak. He came forth dressed for battle against sin, ready and able to defeat every opposing foe. Notice how similar this warrior garb is to the armour available to every believer (see Eph 6:10–18).

With the same 'arm' that made it possible for people to be restored to fellowship with God (Isa 53:1), the Redeemer broke sin's stranglehold and has made it possible for God's people to witness to the world that God is indeed the only Saviour. In Jesus, our Redeemer, God has done for us what we could not do for ourselves.

There is a Redeemer, Jesus, God's own Son,
Precious Lamb of God, Messiah, Holy One.
Thank you, O my Father, for giving us your Son,
And leaving your Spirit till the work on earth is done.
    Melody Green[6]

MONDAY 28 AUGUST

Has no one condemned you?

John 8:1–11

'Jesus straightened up and asked her, "Woman, where are they? Has no-one condemned you?"' (v. 10, NIV).

'Woman, where are they? Has no-one condemned you?' The words slipped gently into the stillness, penetrating the dust stirred up by men grudgingly dropping their stones and leaving the circle of accusation. Moments before, there were countless accusers, but now there are none. Only a fallen woman and the Saviour.

She could have answered 'Yes' to his question. The law–enforcers, the neighbours, her husband – all had a right to condemn her. There was no doubt as to her guilt for she had been caught in the act, and in Old Testament thinking guilt equalled condemnation. An eye for an eye and stoning for the adulteress.

But the discarded stones, scattered on the floor of the temple court, bore witness to the woman's halting response: 'No one, sir.' No one stood to condemn her for each had weighed the stone in his hand against his own sin and found it too heavy to bear. Without sin? Hardly.

In Ocean Grove, New Jersey (USA), a marvellous picture was painted of this grace. Men and women from adult rehabilitation centres across the USA Eastern Territory gathered as part of congress meetings. They stood as one body, their words sweeping in a crescendo across that great auditorium: 'Redeemed, redeemed, redeemed by the blood of the Lamb.'

These were guilty people. Some had served prison terms. All had injured others in some way through the consequences of their addictions. Yet they were no longer condemned because 'through Christ Jesus the law of the Spirit of life set [them] free from the law of sin and death' (Rom 8:2).

In the courtyard of our own disgrace we stand alone with the Saviour, guilty. Nevertheless, the stones slip from our own reproachful fingers and we hear him say, 'Neither do I condemn you. Go now and leave your life of sin.'

No condemnation now I dread;
Jesus, and all in him, is mine.
Alive in him, my living head,
And clothed in righteousness divine,
Bold I approach the eternal throne
And claim the crown, through Christ,
my own.

Charles Wesley, SASB 283

Major JoAnn Shade
USA

What is truth?

John 18:33–38

'"What is truth?" Pilate asked. With this he went out again to the Jews and said, "I find no basis for a charge against him"' (v. 38, NIV).

When I was six years old my mother sent me to the corner store to buy two ice cream cones. One was to be for me and the other for my little brother. When I returned home I walked up to my mother eating a single ice cream. When asked about the absence of a cone for my brother, I replied that I had eaten his one first by mistake and now I was eating my own.

This unusual, if original, twisting of the truth was not as well received as I had hoped. As a small boy I felt the events that followed proved my parents did not understand truth. Had my biblical knowledge been a bit deeper, I might have quoted Pilate and asked my parents, 'What is truth?'

Jesus stood in front of Pilate. The cross was barely an hour away. As part of an answer Jesus said that he had come to witness to the truth. He said, 'Everyone on the side of truth listens to me.' Pilate ended the discussion with his famous question.

Notice, however, that the question 'What is truth?' is quite different from 'What is true?' When I came home with my ice cream I told my mother many truths. I had eaten my brother's cone first. That was true. I was now eating what truthfully believed to be 'my' cone. I had faithfully followed her directions to go to the corner store and buy two cones. All true but not 'the truth'.

The truth is, I was greedy. I was trying in my six–year–old way to say what was true, but not tell the truth. I wanted my own pleasure rather than that of my brother.

When Jesus said, 'I am the way the truth, and the life' (John 14:6) he was describing himself as truth. Therefore truth must be like Jesus. Like him, it must be complete. Like Jesus, truth must not be self–serving. Like Jesus, truth must be tender, self–sacrificing, full of mercy. Truth makes sure your brother gets his ice cream cone!

Steve Garrington
USA

WEDNESDAY 30 AUGUST
What does this mean?

Acts 2:1–13

*'Amazed and perplexed, they asked one another,
"What does this mean?"' (v. 12, NIV).*

It was the Day of Pentecost, the fiftieth day after the Sabbath of Passover week. The ten days before had been given to waiting and praying. The forty days prior to that had been filled with Jesus. Resurrected he stood among them, unbelievably yet fully alive again.

He walked with them, giving final instructions, making sure they knew what to do. 'I have to go,' he told them, 'so that the Holy Spirit can come. He will be with you all, not just in one confined location but wherever you go. Until then you must wait and pray.' Which is what they did.

'Come, Holy Spirit, and abide with me,' they prayed again and again. Just how the Holy Spirit would come, they were not sure. That he would come, they had no doubt.

His coming happened in a moment. Suddenly there was a rushing, a roaring, a flaming, a firing. It was impossible to describe but they knew, deep within, that something had come upon them. No, Some One had come upon them.

Suddenly a dam broke loose of language and dialect, a torrent of words of praise and thanksgiving. There was no way to contain the joy, the exuberance, the sheer wonder of God within. The disciples poured out onto the street, telling the amazing news, drawing people in, crossing barriers of language and colour, race and gender. The people heard the good news of the Spirit's coming and, 'amazed and perplexed, they asked one another, "What does this mean?"'

Peter picks up the question. 'I'll tell you what it means,' he says. 'It is exactly what the prophet Joel said would happen. It means that "everyone who calls on the name of the Lord will be saved"' (*2:21*).

What happened in microcosm – on a small scale – on that first Day of Pentecost is happening in macrocosm – on a cosmic scale – around the world today. God's word is spreading with the speed of wind and fire. People are calling on the name of the Lord and are being saved.

Let the wind blow!
Let the fire fall!

THURSDAY 31 AUGUST
What must I do to be saved?

Acts 16:25–34

'The jailer . . . brought them out and asked, "Sirs, what must I do to be saved?"' (v. 30, NIV).

The news reports of the huge tsunami on Boxing Day 2004, caused by an earthquake in the depths of the Indian Ocean, sent shock waves throughout the world. Centuries earlier the Scriptures record another earthquake, with eternal consequences, taking place in ancient Philippi.

Paul and Silas were in prison, praying and singing hymns to God, when 'a violent earthquake' (v. 26) rocked the prison. It shook open all the doors and loosened the chains on every prisoner. Suddenly everyone was free!

The jailer woke up, saw the open doors, assumed that all his prisoners had escaped, and was on the verge of killing himself. After all, the loss of his prisoners meant not only that he would lose his job but also, according to Roman law, he would have to take the punishment of those who had escaped.

Aware of the man's distress, Paul called out, 'Don't harm yourself! We are all here!' Trembling, the jailer fell on his knees before Paul and Silas and asked, 'Sirs, what must I do to be saved?' Paul gave his response, 'Believe in the Lord Jesus, and you will be saved – you and your household' (v. 31).

That day the prison guard and his whole household found eternal life through faith in the Lord Jesus Christ. This was the third occasion when people in Philippi – Lydia, a wealthy businesswoman, an unnamed slave girl, and now a prison warden – were profoundly changed by the gospel. Three people of unequal means, understanding and faith were adopted into the family of God through faith in Christ Jesus. From their crisis came community.

Deep personal issues such as the loss of a loved one, shrinking finances, failing health, wars and rumours of wars may prompt us to cry out the same question, 'What must I do to be saved?' Paul's answer then is still our answer now: 'Believe on the Lord Jesus Christ.' God is with us and has promised that our 'earthquakes', those tsunamis of the soul that shake our personal world, will be met with his unfailing grace.

Major Randall Davis
USA

NOTES

1 Richard Foster, *Celebration of Discipline: The Path to Spiritual Growth*, Hodder & Stoughton, 1989.
2 Cornelius Plantinga Jr., *Not the Way It's Supposed to Be: A Breviary of Sin*.
3 Samuel Logan Brengle, *When the Holy Ghost is Come*.
4 John Robinson, *Truth is Two-Eyed*.
5 Graham Kendrick, 'Knowing You', Copyright © 1993 Make Way Music, PO Box 263, Croydon, Surrey, CR9 5AP, UK.
6 'There is a Redeemer', Melody Green, Copyright © 1982 Birdwing Music/Ears to Hear Music/BMG Songs Inc. Administered by CopyCare, PO Box 77, Hailsham, East Sussex, BN27 3EF, UK.

INDEX (PENTECOST 2006)

(as from Easter 2001)

Words of Life Bible reading notes
are published three times a year:

Easter
(January–April)

Pentecost
(May–August)

Advent
(September–December)

In each edition you will find:

- informative commentary
- a wide variety of Bible passages
- topics for praise and prayer
- points to ponder
- cross references for further study

Why not place a regular order for *Words of Life*?
Collect each volume and build a lasting resource
for personal or group study. If you require further
information about how you can receive copies of
Words of Life, please contact: The Mail Order Department,
Salvationist Publishing & Supplies, 1 Tiverton Street,
London SE1 6NT, UK. Telephone (020) 7367 6580 or
e–mail mail_order@sp–s.co.uk. Alternatively, contact your
territorial Trade Department

If you would like to contact Barbara Sampson,
her e–mail address is:
barbara_sampson@nzf.salvationarmy.org

READER'S NOTES

READER'S NOTES